Francis A. March

Selected Writings of the First Professor of English

Edited by Paul Schlueter and June Schlueter

Friends of Skillman Library
Lafayette College
Easton, PA
2005

Manufactured in the United States of America

Francis A. March: selected writings of the first professor of English / edited by Paul Schlueter and June Schlueter

ISBN 0-9765162-0-9

Printed in the United States of America on acid-free ∞ paper.

Cover artist: Albert K. Murray; *portrait of Francis A. March*, 1941; oil on canvas
Credit: Lafayette College Art Collection. Gift of Thomas J. Watson

Dedicated with deep appreciation of and gratitude to
Lafayette College's librarians and library support staff,
who wonderfully carry on the efforts and devotion
of the College's first librarian,
Francis A. March

Philologists, who chase
A panting syllable through time and space,
Start it at home, and hunt it in the dark
To Gaul, to Greece, and into Noah's Ark.

—William Cowper, "Retirement" [1782]

Mr. Francis A. March, professor at Lafayette College, who sends me an address to the Phi Beta Kappa Society at Amherst College,—and a good discourse it is,—at the close of it, quotes from Thomas Dekker these lines;—

"The best of men
That e'er wore earth about him, was a sufferer;
A soft, meek, patient, humble, tranquil spirit,
The first true gentleman that ever breathed."

—Ralph Waldo Emerson, *Journals and Miscellaneous Notebooks*, ed. Ronald A. Bosco and Glen M. Johnson (Cambridge: Belknap Press of Harvard University Press, 1982), p. 83.

Two admirable works—*An Anglo-Saxon Grammar* and *Anglo-Saxon Reader*, by Professor March, of Lafayette College—show that the studies of a philological character carried on at a comparatively small institution are not surpassed in thoroughness by those we are accustomed to associate with the German universities.

—*The Athenaeum* [London], January 7, 1871

Contents

On Philology

On Lexicography

On Orthography

On Literature

On Education and Philosophy

On the Civil War

Editors' Note

The texts reprinted in this collection follow accurately the numerous original sources except in a few minor respects: obvious typographical or spelling errors accidentally introduced in the handset typesetting common in the nineteenth century have been silently corrected; titles of book-length works and periodicals have been routinely italicized; and March's sometimes excessively long paragraphs have at times been divided logically to conform to a modern audience's expectations. Although readers may at times be troubled by March's punctuation, here, too, we have preserved the original despite changes in convention since the nineteenth century.

A special warning needs to be issued about spelling, for March often spells words phonetically. To illustrate the extent of his wished-for spelling reform, we have scanned one essay that makes extensive use of such spelling. Entitled "Spelling and Progress," the essay (pp. 130-32) is not so impenetrable as it would appear: just read each sentence aloud.

"The Opening Address Before the International Convention for the Amendment of English Orthography" (pp. 99-112) also needs an explanatory note. For in it, March regularly distinguishes between and among sounds by introducing variations on the familiar Roman alphabet. He uses a conventional "s," for example, in "spelling" or "chaos" but a reversed "s" when the letter is sounded like a "z" as in "his" or "used." Given the difficulties of replicating such phonetic letters in print, we have relied on March's narrative to make the point. In its current form, the essay will serve general readers well; those with a serious interest in phonology should consult the source.

All footnotes are in the original, styled by March or by the editors of the publication in which the essay appeared. The source is given at the foot of the first page of each essay.

Introduction

Though it is common for one academic generation's leaders to be eclipsed by succeeding generations, some groundbreaking researchers have been so instrumental in advancing the profession that it is imperative they be remembered. Francis Andrew March (1825-1911), distinguished American philologist, lexicographer, educator, and professor of English at Lafayette College, is such a figure. For March in his day was preeminent among both American academicians and scholars of language. Note these specifics:

- He was the first to hold the title "Professor of English Language and Literature" anywhere in the United States or Europe.
- He was the first to teach a required Shakespeare course.
- He was the first to teach Milton as well as a number of other English and American authors, including then-contemporary writers, at the college level.
- He was the first to study and write about the history of English from a historical perspective, thus establishing the ground from which most subsequent historical linguistic research sprang.
- He was among the first to embark on then-uncharted linguistic frontiers such as spelling reform and phonetic spelling.
- He formulated concepts about the teaching of English in college and about the role of liberal arts colleges that still resonate with relevance and original insights.[1]

As Frederick L. Rudolph, an historian of higher education, has noted, March, in combining literary analysis and comparative philology, "wrested English literature away from the old rhetoric tradition, with its stultifying emphasis on form and rules, and took to it some of the concern with thought, criticism, and esthetics that had characterized the uses of literature in the literary societies" (Rudolph 140). Lexicographer Clarence L. Barnhart observed that the fact that "English has been established as a serious discipline instead of an avocation is in no small part owing to March" (Barnhart

[1]Francis A. March, "Recollections of Language Teaching," *PMLA* 8 (1893): xix-xxii; rept. in part in *The Origins of Literary Study in America: A Documentary Anthology*, ed. Gerald Graff and Michael Warner (New York: Routledge, 1989), pp. 25-27 (though March's middle name is given incorrectly); rept. in *PMLA* 115 (2000): 1738-41.

iv). Stuart Berg Flexner called March "a true linguistic pioneer" and "one of the best linguistic minds America has produced" (Flexner 1193). Norman Cousins quotes an editor for whom he worked when he was young as believing March's famed *Thesaurus-Dictionary* to be the "most remarkable reference book about words to grace the English language"; the editor stated that although Peter Mark Roget "employed the basic principles of a thesaurus," it was March who "converted those principles into art" (Cousins n.p.). Kemp Malone, himself a pioneering linguistic and literary researcher, once noted that March "raised collegiate instruction in English to the dignity of a mental discipline, and gave it the place which it has since occupied alongside the study of the classics" (Malone 269).

In addition, during his long professorial career, spent wholly at Lafayette College, Easton, PA, from 1855-1906, March demonstrated unusual breadth and dexterity, even for the relatively relaxed professional standards of the era, by also teaching numerous other subjects, including constitutional, public, and Roman law (he was also an attorney), mental and moral philosophy, political science, languages (French, German, Latin, and Greek), and even botany, and he served as the college's first librarian. Were the term not so easily abused, one would be tempted to apply the label "renaissance man" to March, for it seems in retrospect that there was little that he tackled that he couldn't do well.

Nor were March's contributions to higher education limited to one distinguished private college. He was president of the Modern Language Association from 1891-93 (succeeding James Russell Lowell) and subject of an MLA tribute by James W. Bright subsequently published by the MLA in 1914 as a pamphlet. He was, moreover, president of the American Philological Association (1873-74 and 1895-96) and the Spelling Reform Association (1876-1905), vice-president of the New Shakespeare Society (London), and the first American member of the Philosophical Society (London) and L'Association Fonetique de Professeurs de Langues Vivants (Paris). March's memory is honored by an eponymous award given periodically since 1984 by the Association of Departments of English division of the MLA; as the ADE's statement of criteria indicates, nominees for this award "should be eminent scholar-teachers who serve the profession and the larger community. The prime criterion is the stature of the individual's professional contribution, not fame from publication." More recently, in 2004, Oxford University Press honored March by establishing a "Francis A. March Internship," which, appropriately, was given to a Lafayette College senior, Jessica Lasak.

Lafayette College itself honored March's memory by proposing an endowed chair in English in his name as early as 1879 and, once the needed funds were raised, establishing such a chair in 1906 and continuing it to this day.[2] Indeed, Lafayette College's English Department was routinely considered in the nineteenth century to be one of the most distinguished in the country, in no small part because of March's influence and accomplishments locally as well as nationally and internationally (Skillman I, 232).

March was a prolific, pioneering author of papers and books—some 195 in one incomplete 1895 compilation—in philology, the historical study of grammar, lexicography, spelling reform, the teaching of literature, and pedagogy. He was director of American readers for the creation of the *Oxford English Dictionary* (and is cited some 15 times in the OED as the source of various usages), he was instrumental in the creation of the *Standard Dictionary* (1893-95), and he edited four volumes of Greek and Latin classics.

March has long been recognized for these contributions; for example, he has been the subject of an entry in the *Encyclopædia Britannica* since 1910, he is the subject of a fine tribute by Kemp Malone in the *Dictionary of American Biography*, and he has been praised for his pio-

---

[2]Lafayette College faculty who have held the Francis A. March Chair are Francis A. March, Jr. (1906-28), Theodore B. Hunt (1938-47), William W. Watt (1947-72), James R. Vitelli (1978-87), James P. Lusardi (1990-2002), and Carolynn Van Dyke (2003-).

[3]March is included in these reference works, among others: *Allibone's Critical Dictionary of English Literature: A Supplement*, ed. John Foster Kirk (Philadelphia: Lippincott, 1891; rept. Detroit: Gale, 1965); *American Authors, 1600-1900: A Biographical Dictionary of American Literature*, ed. Stanley J. Kunitz and Howard Haycraft (New York: Wilson, 1938); *American Authors and Books: 1640 to the Present Day*, 3rd rev. ed., ed. W. J. Burke and Will D. Howe; rev. by Irving Weiss (New York: Crown, 1972); *American Biographies*, ed. Wheeler Preston (New York: Harper, 1940; rept. Detroit: Gale, 1974); *Appleton's Cyclopaedia of American Biography*, ed. James Grant Wilson and John Fiske (New York: Appleton, 1888-89; rept. Detroit: Gale, 1969); *Biographical Dictionary of American Educators*, ed. John F. Ohles (Westport, CT: Greenwood, 1978); *Cambridge Dictionary of American Biography*, ed. John S. Bowman (New York: Cambridge UP, 1995); *Dictionary of American Authors*, ed. Oscar Fay Adams, 5th ed. (Boston: Houghton, 1904; rept. Detroit: Gale, 1969); *Dictionary of American Biography*, ed. Dumas Malone (New York: Scribner, 1928-36); *Dictionary of North American Authors Deceased before 1950*, ed. W. Stewart Wallace (Toronto: Ryerson, 1951; rept. Detroit: Gale, 1968); *Encyclopædia Britannica* (Chicago: Encyclopædia Britannica, all eds. since 1910); *Harper's Encyclopaedia of United States History: from 458 A.D. to 1915*, ed. Benson John Lossing, rev. ed. (New York: Harper, 1915; rept. Detroit: Gale, 1974); *Lincoln Library of Language Arts*, 3rd ed. (Columbus, OH: Frontier, 1978); *National Cyclopaedia of American Biography* (New York: James T. White, 1901; rept. Ann Arbor: Univ. Microfilms, 1967-71); *Reader's Encyclopedia of American Literature*, ed. Max J. Hertzberg (New York: Crowell, 1962); *Twentieth Century Biographical Dictionary of Notable Americans: Brief Biographies of Authors, Administrators, Clergymen, Commanders, Editors, Engineers, Jurists, Merchants, Officials, Philanthropists, Scientists, Statesmen, and Others Who Are Making American History*, ed. Rossiter Johnson (Boston: Biographical Society, 1904; rept. Detroit: Gale, 1968); *Webster's American Biographies*, ed. Charles Van Doren (Springfield, MA: Merriam, 1974); *Who Was Who in America: Vol. 1: 1897-1942* (Chicago: Marquis, 1943).

neering work by other, varied voices.[3] Gerald Graff, though acknowledging the extent to which his "institutional history" of higher education "does not do justice to the small-college experience" (Graff *Professing* 2), does cite and discuss March's contributions (though he also criticizes his hesitation to depart more substantially from the kind of philological instruction used in studying the Classics). Phyllis Franklin, in noting that March, by adding texts in English literature to the curriculum and having his students write about those texts, initiated the now-conventional concept of students researching "questions that had no certain answers" and then writing about that research. He thus "influenced the way English composition evolved from Greek and Latin rhetoric" (Franklin 362). And, Franklin notes, March's emphasis on a "philological study of language assumed that the study of literature was essential" (Franklin 363), a sentiment corroborated by Bright's familiar statement that March was "conspicuously in the position of a national leader in all that pertained to the thoro study of English" (Bright cxxxiii; quoted in Franklin 363).

Even when March is not cited explicitly for these contributions, his implicit role is clear. Graff, in noting the "strict ideological and social orthodoxy" based on Christianity and the Greek and Latin languages in American colleges during the mid-nineteenth century, points out that those colleges and universities that continued to focus on instructing "gentlemen of good breeding" had no need to offer instruction in interpreting textual "hidden meanings" (Graff *Beyond* 128-29). And, Graff adds, since "academic humanists had to establish themselves as scientific investigators, bringing the same rigor to the study of languages and literatures that physicists and chemists brought to the study of nature," these "academic humanists" necessarily based their "scientific credentials" on the kind of philological approach that March pioneered (Graff *Beyond* 130-31).

Controversies regarding the teaching of college-level language and literature, of course, are always with us. And though there is no reason to attempt a resurgence of emphasis on what today may seem too rigorously narrow a pedagogical method as March's philological emphases, it remains true that these currents of opinion sometimes recur cyclically. As Graff mentions, such "controversies echo old ones as far back as the beginnings of the profession" (Graff *Professing* 2). And David Bartine, in discussing the tension between the "ancients versus the moderns" that always seems to be present in the profession, notes the ironic implications so far as "philology" is concerned since this approach to studying and teaching English was once counted among the "moderns" (Bartine *Early* 15). What Bartine says elsewhere about theories of reading applies equally well to March's emphasis on philology as a radical (for the day) method of approaching works of literature: "The damaging naiveté of starting from scratch to reinvent reading theory and pedagogy on a 'scientific' basis resulted in the fact that modern reading theory has worked ponderously to rediscover principles of contextual meaning, about which it could have learned a great deal if it had not cut itself off from its own past" (Bartine *Reading* 73). To a great extent, March anticipated such ongoing controversies by venturing into uncharted pedagogical territory; he thus remains instructive for our day.

Given these varied explicit and implicit acknowledgments of March's pioneering efforts, it is astonishing to realize that only one of his highly influential books—*A Comparative Grammar of the Anglo-Saxon Language . . .* (1870)—is currently listed in *Books in Print*, though not from a major academic or scholarly press. His most popular work, *A Thesaurus Dictionary of the English Language*, prepared with his namesake son and published in 1903, went through five editions and remained in print for more than 40 years; it was reprinted (with slight variations in title) in 1958 by Doubleday in both cloth- and paperbound editions and in 1980 by Abbeville Press. March prepared the theoretical organizational plan for this influential work in 1861, the year before English philologist Peter Mark Roget (1779-1869) issued the first edition of his more renowned—and endlessly reprinted—thesaurus; initial editions of Roget's thesaurus used a cumbersome organization that was changed in succeeding editions to the format that March initially proposed and that even today makes March's thesaurus far more usable.

March's many influential papers include the first linguistic analysis and suggested modifications of Grimm's Law. Jacob Grimm (1785-1863) had formulated principles in *Deutsche Grammatik* (1819-37) to explain consonantal change in Indo-European languages, principles that were subsequently modified in 1875 by the great Danish linguist Karl Verner (1846-96) and hence labeled "Verner's Law," but March had previously suggested such modifications in his 1873 essay.

March's work may not be widely read today; indeed, to a modern audience, removed from the century in which his groundbreaking analyses first saw print, his ideas may seem dated. Today, there is little interest in some of his concerns, or obsessions, such as spelling reform, and twenty-first century students would have great difficulties were March's philological approach to literature standard classroom fare. Nor have all of March's critical opinions worn well, a fact most easily confirmed by an 1881 review of Walt Whitman's *Leaves of Grass*. There is a dated frame around all of March's writing, identifying him securely with the mid- to late-nineteenth century. Yet much of his scholarship remains remarkably current, and there is no dispute about the major role this distinguished figure played in the establishment of English as an independent discipline.

Francis Andrew March was born 25 October 1825 in Sutton (now Millbury), Worcester County, MA, a sixth generation descendent of Hugh March, who had emigrated from England in 1638, and his wife, Judith, of Newbury, MA.[4] Hugh and Judith March's great-grandson Daniel settled near the Blackstone River in Sutton. Daniel March's grandson, Andrew Patch March (1798-1874), his wife Nancy Parker March (d. 1830), and their family moved to Worcester, in which city their son Francis Andrew March grew up. The intellectual atmosphere in Worcester public schools was such that March was in good company as a student; his classmates included Horace Davis, subsequently president of the University of California, and Thomas Chase, later president of Haverford College; Hasbrouck Davis, who would become a general in the U.S. Army; J.C.B. Davis, later a distinguished judge and ambassador to Germany; nephews of the historian George Bancroft; and several who would also become professors. He was considered precocious, even by Worcester's intellectual standards, and in addition to using the unrivalled resources of the library of the American Antiquarian Society, based in

[4]Biographical details have been assembled from a variety of sources, including (in chronological sequence) Selden J. Coffin, *Record of the Men of Lafayette: Brief Biographical Sketches of the Alumni of Lafayette College from Its Organization to the Present Time* (Easton, PA: Skinner and Finch, 1879), p. 342; *The Centenary of Leicester Academy, held September 4, 1884 . . .* (Worcester, MA: Charles Hamilton, 1884); *Addresses in Honor of Professor Francis A. March, LL.D., L.H.D., Delivered at Easton, Pennsylvania, on the 24th of October, 1895* (Easton, PA: Lafayette College, 1895) (contains Francis A. March, Jr., "Biographical Note" [pp. 11-20], William C. Cattell, "Introductory Remarks" [pp. 21-22], William B. Owen, "Professor March's Work for Lafayette" [pp. 23-36], Thomas R. Lounsbury, "The Standard of Pronunciation (Abstract)" [pp. 37-41], James W. Bright, "Professor March's Contributions to English Scholarship" [pp. 43-65], "Professor March's Response" [pp. 67-68], William Hayes, "Alma Mater (Amherst)" [pp. 69-73], John Fox, "The Teacher of Philosophy" [pp. 75-80], S. G. Barnes, "The Philologist" [pp. 87-89], James C. MacKenzie, "The Teacher" [pp. 91-101], John R. Davies, "The Beloved Professor" [pp. 103-06], and [anonymous], "Bibliography of Professor March's Writings" [pp. 107-19, including "Dedications" and "Notices" of March's Anglo-Saxon Text-Books"]); Richard N. Hart, *Francis Andrew March: A Sketch, the "Grand Old Man" of Lafayette College* (Easton, PA: [Lafayette College], 1907); *Encyclopædia Britannica*, 11th ed. (1910) and all succeeding editions; "Mrs. March Passes Away," *Easton* [PA] *Express*, February 11, 1911, n.p.; "Dr. March Dies at Home on the Campus," *Easton* [PA] *Express*, September 9, 1911, n.p.; "Prof. Francis A. March Dead," *New York Times*, September 10, 1911, Sec. 2, p. 13; "A Veteran Scholar," *Outlook* 99 (September 23, 1911), 149-50; "Addresses in Memory of Prof. Francis A. March, LL.D., L.H.D.," *Bulletin of Lafayette College* 6.1 (November 1911) (contains "Memorial Address by Prof. William B. Owen, Representing the Faculty of the College" [pp. 5-16] and "Memorial Address by Hon. Robert E. James, as a Representative of the City of Easton" [pp. 17-22]); "Addresses in Memory of Prof. Francis A. March, LL.D., L.H.D.," *Bulletin of Lafayette College* 6.4 (August 1912) (contains memorials by

Worcester, March was active in local literary societies, wrote prose and verse, and acted in local dramatic productions.

March's father had fallen on difficult times when Francis was a boy; the elder March's cutlery factory failed when his partner absconded with the inventory, and both a store in which he had an interest and the family home had gone up in flames. Hence attending college for young Francis was considered impossible until Alfred D. Foster of Worcester, an Amherst College trustee, offered to pay the $200 tuition for March to attend that college. March, who entered Amherst at age 15 in 1841, was considered a brilliant student and achieved distinction in such disparate areas as public speaking and athletics. He developed an early interest in language through attendance at lectures by Noah Webster (1758-1843), pioneering American lexicographer and a founder of Amherst College in 1821, and through instruction by Webster's son-in-law, William Chauncey Fowler (1793-1881), who taught rhetoric and oratory at Amherst from 1838-43 and who is best remembered for his *The English Language in its Elements and Forms* (1850).

March graduated from Amherst College in 1845 as valedictorian, a member of Phi Beta Kappa. He received the M.A. degree from the same

---

Basil L. Gildersleeve [pp. 5-6], Andrew C. Trippe [pp. 7-10], James McKenn Cattell [pp. 11-16], Edwin Watts Chubb [pp. 17-21], J. George Becht [pp. 22-24]); "Professor Francis A. March, LL.D., L.H.D." (pp. 86-99) and "Professor March" (pp. 100-10), both in William Baxter Owen, *The Humanities in the Education of the Future* (Boston: Sherman, French, 1912); James Wilson Bright, "An Address in Commemoration of Francis Andrew March, 1825-1911, Delivered at the Joint Session of the American Philological Association and the Modern Language Association of America, at Cambridge, Mass., 30 December 1913," *PMLA* 29 (1913), cxvii-cxxxvii; James W. Bright, *Francis Andrew March 1825-1911* (New York: Modern Language Association, 1914); Kemp Malone, "March, Francis Andrew (Oct. 25, 1825-Sept. 9, 1911)," *Dictionary of American Biography*, ed. Dumas Malone (New York: Scribner, 1928-36), vol. 12, pp. 268-70; Theodore Hunt, "Francis A. March and the Development of the English Language," unpub. ms., Lafayette College, c. 1930; David Bishop Skillman, *The Biography of a College: Being the History of the First Century of the Life of Lafayette College*, 2 vols. (Easton, PA: Lafayette College, 1932), vol. 1, *passim.*; Henry W. Simon, *The Reading of Shakespeare in American Schools and Colleges: An Historical Survey* (New York: Simon and Schuster, 1932); *Amherst College Biographical Record of the Graduates and Non-Graduates*, Centennial Ed., ed. Robert S. Fletcher and Malcolm O. Young (Amherst, MA: Trustees of Amherst College, 1939); William Gardiner Hammond, *Remembrance of Amherst: An Undergraduate's Diary 1846-1848*, ed. George F. Whicher (New York: Columbia UP, 1946); E. G. Swem, "Reminiscences of Lafayette College, 1893," unpub. ms., Williamsburg, VA, 1955; Clara M. Kirk, "Realty and Actuality in the March Family Narratives of W. D. Howells." *PMLA* 74.1 (1959): 137-52; William W. Watt, "Professor of Philology and Other Fonetic Fenomena," *Lafayette Alumni Quarterly* 58.2 (Winter 1987): 26-31; June Schlueter, "Francis A. March: First Professor of English," *Shakespeare Bulletin* 8.1 (Winter 1990): 5-6; Roger Clow, "What's Past Is Prologue," *Lafayette Magazine*, Fall 1996, pp. 20-21; Patricia Donahue and Bianca Falbo, "A Story of Reading and Writing: The Example of Francis A. March, Lafayette College," in *Local Histories*, ed. Patricia Donahue and Gretchen Moon, forthcoming.

college in 1848; his oration for the degree was entitled "Relation of the Study of Jurisprudence to the Baconian Philosophy," printed in the *New Englander* as his first published work. While studying for this second degree, he also served as tutor at Amherst from 1847-49 (one student referred to him as a "Demigod"!) and taught in Swanzey, New Hampshire (1845), and as "assistant preceptor" at Leicester Academy in Worcester (1845-47). He initially contemplated becoming an attorney and studied law in his spare time under the direction of Worcester attorney (and later judge) Francis H. Dewey, after which (in 1849) he continued his studies in the offices of a New York City law firm, Barney & Butler. He was admitted to the New York bar in 1850 and opened an office in New York City with Gordon L. Ford. A lung infection in 1852 required that he leave New York for a less severe climate, so after sojourns in Cuba and Key West, Florida, and another attempt to practice law in New York City, again aborted because of his lungs, he left the practice of law and accepted a position to teach law in a school in Fredericksburg, Virginia, where he stayed from 1852-55.

In 1855, at age 30, March was appointed tutor at Lafayette College, a school established in 1826 in Easton, PA, an appointment made by the college's newly-installed president, G. Wilson McPhail, who had been principal at the Fredericksburg academy where March had taught law. March was named "Adjunct Professor of the English Language" the year after and appointed "Professor of the English Language and Lecturer in Comparative Philology" in 1857, the first such professorship anywhere in the United States or in Europe. Writing of the appointment, David Bishop Skillman, author of a history of Lafayette College, called the establishment of this position "the greatest pioneering step ever made in the realm of scholarship by Lafayette College. It gave to Lafayette the honor and distinction of being the first college in America to establish a chair for the extended and systematic study of the English language in the English classics in the light of modern philology" (Skillman I 228). March's simple question, "Why not teach English like the Latin and Greek?", sounds almost disingenuous to modern ears, but it was a revolutionary concept at the time. Indeed, it was so sweeping a change that the weekly journal *The Independent*, in admitting that though opportunities to study English were "ample" at Harvard and Cornell, they were "the best in the country" at Lafayette; the *British Quarterly* noted that "nowhere else" was the subject treated with "equal competence and success"; and the *London Athenaeum* claimed that March's philological instructional methods "are not surpassed by those which we are accustomed to associate with the German universities" (Skillman I 232-

33). March continued as professor at Lafayette for his entire professional career, retiring in 1906 after a tenure of half a century, and declining repeated invitations to move to major universities, though he accepted honorary degrees from such institutions as Princeton University (1870 and 1896), Amherst College (1871), Columbia University (1887), Cambridge University, and Oxford University (both in 1896).

March was married August 12, 1860, to Margaret Mildred Stone Conway (January 25, 1837-February 11, 1911), daughter of Walter P. Conway, presiding justice of Falmouth, Stafford County, Virginia, and great-granddaughter of Thomas Stone, a signer of the Declaration of Independence. The Marches had nine children, several of whom also distinguished themselves: his namesake Francis Andrew March (1863-1928), also a Lafayette College professor of English with whom the elder March collaborated on several scholarly projects and himself co-author of two historical works on World War I; Peyton Conway March (1864-1955), U.S. army general and chief of staff who reorganized the War Department and consolidated various military divisions into the modern U.S. army; Thomas Stone March, superintendent of schools in Greensburg, PA; Alden March, Sunday editor of *The New York Times*; and John Lewis March, professor of modern languages at Union College, Schenectady, NY. Francis A. March died, never having recovered from a fall in which he broke his hip, on 9 September 1911, a few months after his wife died from apoplexy.

Even at the risk of retrospective hyperbole, it seems difficult to claim too much for Francis March's scholarly accomplishments, for they greatly influenced several generations of scholars in some of the United States' foremost academic institutions. For example, one of March's students at Lafayette, James Wilson Bright (1852-1926), continued groundbreaking scholarly work at Johns Hopkins University; another, Theodore Whitfield Hunt (1884-1930), did the same at Princeton; and March's exegetical system of linguistic analysis of literary works was subsequently adapted or applied by many others, including those who were not direct beneficiaries of March's instruction, notably George Lyman Kittredge (1860-1941) at Harvard University.

March specialized, in common with then-contemporary interests and tastes, in "Anglo-Saxon," i.e., Old English or early medieval English. His landmark book *A Comparative Grammar of the Anglo-Saxon Language, in Which its Forms are Illustrated by Those of the Sanscrit, Greek, Latin, Gothic, Old Saxon, Old Friesic, Old Norse, and Old High German* (1870), is not just a mouth-filling title; it also suggests the kind of work he was attempting in virgin scholarly territory, a profoundly detailed comparative analysis of the forms of the English language with other major Indo-European tongues. As Kemp Malone noted, in this book March "laid the foundation on which all future historical grammarians . . . were destined to build, and his fame will ever rest secure as . . . the founder of a science" (Malone 269). In the same year of 1870, March published his *Introduction to Anglo-Saxon: An Anglo-Saxon Reader*, a textbook intended for classroom instruction (and in continual use for graduate study for some 80 years, until 1950 or thereabouts), suggesting his dual thrust of scholarly writing for both specialists in the field and for students just beginning linguistic analysis, a practice also illustrated in his earlier *Method of Philological Study of the English Language* (1865).

Nor was March interested solely in linguistics, for, as indicated by some of the selections that follow, he was also a pioneer in teaching works of literature previously unrepresented in college classrooms. March had much to say, of course, about writings in Latin and Greek, for these were the heart of the nineteenth-century literature curriculum. But recognizing the importance of literature in English, March transferred his instructional methods to the study of the vernacular, relying on select literary passages for an analysis that the professor would "make . . . as hard as Greek." Though pioneering in his time, it is not surprising that March's exegetical approach—using the question-and-answer method about the language used in a work of literature to determine that work's meaning—is now considered as limited as the formal lectures supplanted by his method. What survived long into the twentieth century was March's esthetic sense: a lover of both language and literature, he characterized the language of literature as "an ideal language, shaped to peculiar forms by men of genius under the direction of an idea of the beautiful."

March edited several volumes of Latin and Greek literature and wrote numerous essays and reviews of literature in English. He showed a special interest in Malory, Shakespeare, and Milton, but he also had perceptive comments to offer on nineteenth-century figures, including Lamb, Tennyson, Arnold, Browning, and Morris. Generally respectful of these now-canonical writers, he bristled on his first encounter with Whitman, railing in his review of *Leaves of Grass* against the poet's "dullness" and "repulsive" diction. (It is an essay we may now say reflected more about the nineteenth century's squeamishness about sexual expression in literature than about Whitman's merits as a poet.)

March wrote about education as well: the idea of the scholar; tributes to other scholars; high school instruction as preparation for admission to and success in college. His comments about the teaching of English at Lafayette College, his sole home as a professor, are equal mixtures of dated pedantry and tributes to a college that had proven willing to concur with his innovative ideas. Even the address he gave at the 1880 re-dedication of Lafayette's Pardee Hall, which had sustained serious damage in a fire and been rebuilt, provides him an opportunity to expound on "organized structures" of instruction, an early "co-op" program, and the need for open-shelf libraries. And an after-dinner speech in 1880 provided the occasion for addressing the importance of chapel attendance and a "gentlemanly" approach to athletics.

The last essay in this volume is not about language, literature, or education but about the Civil War, which at the time had been underway for just a few months. It is a plan of "pacification," including a proposed amendment to the U. S. Constitution, which was intended to satisfy both sides in the conflict between the North and South. Since he had lived in Virginia and his wife was from that state, though from an anti-slavery family from the "southern aristocracy" (Hart 26), he had a broader perspective than many other northerners regarding the war. His plan was published in the *New York Times*, which gave the proposal editorial support, and also in *The World*, but it failed to persuade either side to shorten the conflict. The Virginia legislature endorsed the proposal, and the distinguished statesman Sen. Charles Sumner (1811-74) took it before the U.S. Congress. But it died there without action being taken. Nonetheless, the proposal stands as testimony to March's initiative: here was a man willing to advocate change, whether in pedagogy or politics.

Francis A. March's innovative ideas were evident throughout his scholarly career. Much of his pioneering work in language and literature was accomplished before the Civil War, but he was still active in his 70s, contributing important and influential writing. Although only a fraction of his work remains in print a century after his death, his essays form a body of historical literature that remains fascinating and instructive, not only to those holding a Lafayette College degree but to all who use and admire the English language.

In 1907, Richard N. Hart, in *Francis Andrew March: A Sketch, the "Grand Old Man" of Lafayette College*, noted that March had "been publishing in the periodicals of this and other countries . . . all his life. . . ." and offered the judgment that his essays "should be collected and reprinted together" (Hart 49). Nearly a century later, no such compilation has been attempted until now. Hence we are happy to bring this decades-overdue collection, even in this limited manner, into print.

Paul Schlueter and June Schlueter
Easton, PA

WORKS CITED

Barnhart, Clarence L. "Introduction" to *March's Thesaurus-Dictionary*. Garden City, NY: Hanover House, 1958, pp. iii-v.

Bartine, David. *Early English Reading Theory: Origins of Current Debates*. Columbia: U of South Carolina P, 1989.

_______. *Reading, Criticism, and Culture: Theory and Teaching in the United States and England, 1820-1950*. Columbia: U of South Carolina P, 1992.

Bright, James Wilson. "An Address in Commemoration of Francis A. March, 1825-1911. Delivered at the Joint Session of the American Philological Association and the Modern Language Association of America, at Cambridge, Mass., 30 December 1913." *PMLA* 29 (1913), cxvii-cxxxvii; rept. Baltimore: Modern Language Association of America, 1914.

Cousins, Norman. "Foreword" [expanded and updated version]. *March's Thesaurus and Dictionary of the English Language*. New York: Abbeville P, 1980, n.p.

Flexner, Stuart Berg. "Introduction to the Supplement." *March's Thesaurus and Dictionary of the English Language*. New York: Abbeville P, 1980, pp. 1193-94.

Franklin, Phyllis. "English Studies: The World of Scholarship in 1883." *PMLA* 99.3 (May 1984): 356-70.

Graff, Gerald. *Beyond the Culture Wars: How Teaching the Conflicts Can Revitalize American Education*. New York: Norton, 1992.

Graff, Gerald. *Professing Literature: An Institutional History*. Chicago: U of Chicago P, 1987.

Graff, Gerald and Michael Warner, eds. *The Origins of Literary Studies in America: A Documentary Anthology*. New York: Routledge, 1989.

Hart, Richard N. *Francis Andrew March: A Sketch, the "Grand Old Man" of Lafayette College*. Easton, PA: [Lafayette College], 1907.

Malone, Kemp. "March, Francis Andrew (Oct. 25, 1825-Sept. 9, 1911)." *Dictionary of American Biography*, ed. Dumas Malone. New York: Scribner, 1928-36, vol. 12, pp. 268-70. (Also see Malone's entry on March's son, "Francis Andrew March (Mar. 2, 1863-Feb. 28, 1928)," in the same volume of *DAB*, p. 270.)

Rudolph, Frederick L. *Curriculum: A History of the American Undergraduate Course of Study Since 1636*. San Francisco: Jossey-Bass, 1978.

Skillman, David Bishop. *The Biography of a College: Being the History of the First Century of the Life of Lafayette College*, 2 vols. Easton, PA: Lafayette College, 1932, vol.1, *passim*.

Acknowledgments

Gathering writings by Francis A. March presented an unusual array of difficulties, even granted our proximity to Lafayette College, where March spent his entire academic career. March's office and classroom were located on the second floor of West College, a two-story building constructed in 1838; it has been speculated that his papers were lost in a 1953 fire that destroyed the building and its contents, thus making it impossible to use March's own files and collections, if indeed they were stored within that building. What is certain is that no library or archive now contains any substantial holdings of manuscript materials, though Special Collections in Lafayette College's Skillman Library has most of the published and some of the unpublished items. Serendipity, however, sometimes helped in locating primary materials; for example, in consulting bound volumes of the *Transactions* or *Proceedings of the American Philological Association* from the early 1890s in Lafayette's library, we discovered (the bad news) that one article by March had been torn out but (the good news) that a marked-up galley-proof of the same article had been inserted in its place, presumably the one March himself had corrected. Evidently the volume hadn't been examined closely in more than a century, despite various moves by the college library.

Though Lafayette College had long held special collections in its library, a formal archive was first set up in 1977 under the direction of the late Albert W. Gendebien, professor emeritus of history at the college and author of *The Biography of a College III: A History of Lafayette College: 1927-78* (Easton, PA: Lafayette College, 1986), a volume updating the two-volume set by David B. Skillman (Easton, PA: Lafayette College, 1932). Gendebien, who retired from the post of archivist in 1987, spoke of the college's earlier years from the perspective of a trained historian, who himself had been on the faculty for some 30 years. He was succeeded as archivist by Diane Windham Shaw, special collections librarian at Skillman Library, who has been remarkably and continuously helpful in offering advice and in providing or searching out primary works when they were available. In several indispensable ways, Diane Shaw has been such a complete co-editor in this project that these few words cannot fully represent—or thank her for—her contributions.

Special and enthusiastic thanks go to Neil McElroy, Director of Libraries and Academic Information Resources, for his consistent encouragement of and support for this project. We are also grateful to former and present members of the interlibrary loan staff at Skillman Library at Lafayette College for their continuous assistance in this research: Betsy Moore, Richard Everett, Janemarie Berry, Karen Haduck, Doug Moore, and Therry Schwartz. Thanks, too, to former and present members of the reference staff, including Amy Abruzzi, Robert Duncan, Terese Heidenwolf, Marilyn Kann, Reid Larson, Rani Sinha, and Teresa Weisser; to former and present members of Lafayette College's English Department: Richard E. Dickson, Patricia A. Donahue, and Bianca Falbo; and to Glenn Airgood, Director of Public Information at Lafayette College, and Dale Mack, Graphic Designer, for their help in seeing this book through to publication.

In the course of our work, we consulted holdings in various other libraries to locate particularly obscure or elusive materials. One indispensable source was the Northampton County Historical and Genealogical Society in Easton, PA, whose former executive director, Paul W. Goudy, was of particular help in locating and providing copies of early documents, some of which were to be found solely in the Society's collections.

On Philology

One should note that the term "philology," used so commonly in March's day, is increasingly an obsolete term in the United States. March and his contemporaries used it to apply to the study and analysis of both language and literature, disciplines that today are normally treated separately; if the term is used at all today, it usually refers to the study of language, i.e., linguistics.

True, the term survives in the titles of a number of American and English scholarly journals that date their founding to the nineteenth century or at the latest to around the turn of the twentieth century (e.g., *Transactions* or *Proceedings of the Philological Society* [established in 1842], *Modern Philology* [1903], *Studies in Philology* [1906], *University of California Publications in Modern Philology* [1909], and *Publications of the Philological Society* [1913]); one also still finds the word in the titles of more recently-established publications of various state or regional professional societies (e.g., *Pacific Coast Philology* and publications of philological associations from Arkansas, Kentucky, Mississippi, Missouri, and Tennessee). But the term is especially common in its earlier senses among many European and other international groups, as is nicely suggested by an editorial description offered by *REAL: The Yearbook of Research in English and American Literature* in which "philology" is defined parenthetically as "poetics, rhetoric, textual criticism."

Another indication of the term's decline can be glimpsed in several recent editions of the *Encyclopædia Britannica*: in 1964 the term received an entry of c. 750 words, including numerous cross-references and a selected bibliography of other readings; a decade later the entry ran only c. 100 words, along with a shorter list of cross-references; and in the most recent editions it is a mere 70 words, with no cross-references at all. It's quite a contrast to the 25-page essay in the famed 11th edition from 1910!

March refers on several occasions to various other philologists, notably Henry Sweet (1845-1912). This distinguished English linguist, noted for his work on the history and sounds of English pronunciation, wrote several well-received books on phonetics, grammar, linguistic history, and Anglo-Saxon; he was also instrumental with March in advocating spelling reform. More about Sweet is in the preface to the section on orthography in this volume.

The English Tongue: A New Speech

An Address Delivered before the Society of the Alumni of Amherst College, at the Commencement of 1860

Fellow-Students! Brothers of the Alumni of Amherst College! We meet to-day to laud and honor our Foster Mother.

His mother tongue is the scholar's true foster mother. She takes him as soon as the light of consciousness shines in his eyes; teaches him how to analyse and name the indefinite apparitions of sense; leads him on to reason, and supplies him with instruments; moulds his passions and sentiments to sympathy with the great hearts and souls whose words of fire she loves to repeat; raises his religious feelings to supernatural elevation by her utterance of the revealed Word; and ever present to his consciousness, like the light which surrounds us, or the air we breathe, or the blood in our own proper veins, quickens us, develops us, leads us, serves us with an ever active attention which may be fitly compared to the providence of God.

We are about to speak of the English language, our most noble foster mother; and what we have to say is in the form of an illustration of the proposition that the English is a new speech. A new speech! It is not, as it used to be called, a mixture of Anglo-Saxon and Norman. It is not, as it is now pronounced by Teutonic scholars, a development of Anglo-Saxon. In opposition to the mixture doctrine, it is a living unity, an organic whole; having its final causes within itself, its laws peculiar to itself, its beauty of part, its beauty as a whole; its vitality, growth, and symmetry. In opposition to the development statement, it is a new being. It is not the Anglo-Saxon grown. It may be called a son of Saxon and Norman parents. But then it should be said that this son is a genius. Some sons are only copies of their father or mother; but this son is a Shakspeare, whose wonderful gifts come from neither father nor mother.

"The English Tongue: A New Speech. An Address Delivered before the Society of the Alumni of Amherst College, at the Commencement of 1860. *American Theological Review* 3.9 (January 1861): 18-36; also published separately as a pamphlet (New York: W. H. Bidwell, 1861).

And it should further be said that it is the founder of a new line, and not the flower of an old race. Its look is to the future, not to the past. The Greek had its genius, sovereign, unapproachable. It is the foremost and the greatest of the languages of its class. It has a peculiar quality and flavor, the mysterious vitality and charm which belong to the rarest favorites of nature. But the Greek is the flower of the Indian languages. It is many-doubled, lustrous, fragrant, but the stamens and pistils are all turned into petals. It will bear no seed, will have no successor. Such a language could never be spoken except by such a people; and such a people could not live except in such a country, beneath that clear sky, within hearing of those laughing waters. There could be no hope of daughters more beautiful than this most beautiful mother. It is a possession for all time, but only for the choice spirits of all time. It may be felt by those who love it, but its historical position can be understood only from the side of the Sanskrit, and the kindred eastern dialects. The qualities which are strangest to us are those which are common to the East—the abundance, the flexibility, the smoothness, the flow. In these qualities it is surpassed by the Sanskrit; it is identical in kind, and surpassed in degree. It is like the eastern serpent, winding, involved, many-jointed, flexible, smooth, brilliant in color; or a tropical forest, with its palms and vines and flowers interlocked and interwreathed, but shot through to its depths with the sunlight. Seen from our side, these seem miracles of nature; from the eastern side, they are the common heritage of the Arian race. The Greek is the bright consummate flower of the Eastern languages, not the tough seed whence new forests were to spring in the West.

What we have said of the Greek is true of the German, the flower of Teutonic tongues; and of the French, the flower of Romance languages; but the English looks to the future, not to the past. The Teutonic hen which hatched this eagle's egg looks with increased amazement at the gnarled muscles, the talons, the beak, the terrible eye of this proud bird, and cackles confusedly at his scream. He looks to the future, the true lord of nations.

As an element in history, then, when we compare its relations to the past and to the future, the English language stands forth as new.

This is not the place to develop a complete classification of languages, and assign its place to the English with scientific precision.

We proceed, however, to characterize it as well as we can. And we begin with the very general statement that it is the most analytic of languages. Language, like knowledge, begins with the indefinite, and proceeds by analysis to the more definite. Sound is still more indefinite than speech. Sound seems to be an original function of matter, already from its creation prophesying and prepared for the hearing ear and the human soul which were to come after so many ages. In sound, as in so many other respects, there is seen a resemblance in the progress of the world to the growth of a man. In the infancy of the earth, before ever a crust was spread over its fluid mass, it lay hushed in the murmurs of a myriad ripples and dimples, the most indefinite of possible sounds.

It used to be the habit in our college days to spend summer evenings on the chapel steps, watching the glories of the setting sun, and the coming on of twilight. As the sounds of day died away, and the college and town were whist, there used to arise in the dusk a faint, low murmur, like the rustling of the garments of night, swelling gently, falling away into silence, never loud, never distinct. Whether it was some strange vibration about the buildings, the soughing of the evening air in pine trees, or the faint murmurs of some far-off stream, we never could agree, and when we heard the President's eloquent discourse, which told us that the universe was one vast sounding-gallery,[1] we were well content to say that our music was what it surely symbolizes—the reverberation of the voice of total nature.

Lulled by this very strain, the infantile world lay dreaming through its early ages—dreaming who knows what prophetic dreams of pine trees in which wind is soughing, of the summer bees and brooks, of the far-off hum of populous cities.

Then came boyhood, which rejoices in the explosive—the banging of guns, the cracking of fire-works; and the hardening shell of the world resounded like a bomb with the bursting of volcanic bubbles, and the far-off rumble of earthquakes. The demiurgus celebrated a long independence day with a perpetual sound of fire-works. Sound was become more definite.

The animals came in time. Their cries are more definite in their expression than the sounds of lifeless things, but they still speak the whole character or the general wants of the being that utters them, apparently without analysis—the utterance of life, but of life which does not discriminate, of instinct, not of thought. We say *apparently* without analysis, because we know not how definite the cries of animals are to their own kind. To the ear of man they have the indefiniteness of a strain of music—pleasing, elevating, seeming just on the point of saying what never is heard. "Away! Away!" cried Jean Paul's immortal tenant of earth, when he heard the sound of music, "thou speakest to me of things which in all

[1]See *Religion of Geology*, by President [Edward] Hitchcock, p. 410.

my endless life I have found not, and I shall not find." The poets have been always searching for this secret relation of sound to sense, have always been striving to articulate the song of birds, and the ripple of river or wind. Some philologist perhaps, with a poet's heart, may sometimes catch the key and tell us what the nightingale sang.

> "To the sad heart of Ruth,
> When sick for home, she stood in tears amid the alien corn;"

put in fitting words the hymn which the wood-thrush caroled for the drooping Audubon, storm-drenched in the primeval forests, when "as the first glimpses of morning gleamed doubtfully among the forest trees, there came upon his ear, thrilling along the sensitive chords which connect that organ with the heart, the delightful music of this harbinger of day," inspiring feelings that were thoughts, and raising the thoughts of the fresh old man to Him who sent the bird.

Finally came man, whom all preceding ages looked for and sung for, gifted with reason and the coördinate power of speech. We shall not enter on the question of the origin of language. It is certain that the world was shapen and fitted up for a hearing and speaking tenant. It is certain that speech is as natural to man as reason. It is plain that the languages with which we are acquainted are in different stages of development. My purpose lies wholly in the open field of science; it is only to show that development proceeds from the indefinite to the more definite. Though our first parents were at once inspired to speak a language for which ages of development would have been needed in the ordinary course of things, it is yet true that a great part of the world now speaks just about such a language as we see must be the natural product of their faculties.

The language of miracle has so long ago been degraded to the level of the savage tribes, that they now speak languages which are substantially adjusted to their unripe reason. Man begins with the indefinite in thought and feeling, with a speech indefinite and unsteady in articulation, indefinite and unsteady in the functions of its words. Every confused volume of sound, in comparison with the parts of speech of refined languages, seems like one of those animals of the lower orders, who are nothing but a cell, a sack—one indefinite mass, where stomach, brain, and limbs are undistinguished, and digestion, sensation, and locomotion are all in the whole, and all in every part. So when man speaks an undeveloped speech, a succession of utterances come forth which are neither noun, verb, adjective, adverb, pronoun, nor preposition, neither notional nor relational, but indefinitely all of these.

The speech of the aborigines of America, as described by the earliest observers, may serve as an illustration. These tribes had the senses developed in their highest perfection for observation and imitation; but even abstraction, the first movement of reason, seems to have been in a rudimental state. They could speak of things only as they are found in nature with their relations and surroundings. They could not say *tree* or *house,* for example. They must put something in every word to indicate *what* tree or house. They did not even say oak-tree; their most general designation still indicates the particular species, if not the individual oak. There are no such words as adjectives and nouns distinct from each other; but the same utterance designates indefinitely things and their qualities.

A pronominal sense is also mingled in the same indefinite mass. They cannot say father, son, master separately. They must say whose father, or what father. The missionaries, therefore, cannot translate the Doxology literally, but teach them to chant: "Glory be to *our* Father and to *his* Son and to *their* Holy Ghost."

Nor is this pronomino-, adjectivo-substantive utterance the extent of indefiniteness. This agglomerate of sounds takes another modification of utterance, and expresses an assertion or activity—becomes a sort of verb, which has a sort of conjugation.

By inserted or supplementary sounds are expressed or suggested times, modes, voices of all sorts, passive, middle, animate, inanimate, negative, frequentative, causative, so that the forms of a verb are five or six thousand in number. And this assertive form is indeed a *verb,* the *word* by eminence, for it swallows up all others.

Besides all the mass which has already been mentioned, the verb expresses its *object* in the same word and the adverbial modifications.

What we mean by parts of speech remains undistinguished in these languages of nature. Speech is with them a perpetual creation of utterance to image indefinitely the total picture in their minds exactly as it is impressed by nature. "The Indian does not analyze his thoughts or separate his utterances," as Bancroft expresses it; "his thoughts rush forth in a troop. His speech is as a kindling cloud, not as radiant points of light." To take a figure from an art not then known, it is like a daguerreotype of a landscape, where every leaf is quivering in the breeze, struck off at once in a blur by the sunbeams, not like an ideal landscape drawn in distinct and imperishable colors by the successive touches of the pencil of Turner.

These general traits are given only in generals to illustrate the indefiniteness of the languages of nature. They would, of course, need qualification, and the statement of many exceptions, if a description of any particular dialect were intended. Like other products of nature, language answers only generally to a general description.

The first great step, which I shall mention in the development of language, gives us what are called the inflected languages.

In these, the noun, verb, adjective, and adverb, are analyzed and definitely separated from each other, but the syllables merely indicative of relation are still left in a state of fusion with the words indicative of notions; utterances equivalent, in an indefinite and little precise manner, to pronouns, prepositions, and auxiliary verbs, expressing or suggesting the prominent relations in space and time, and those of cause, measure, degree, mode, and the personal relations, remain fused with the roots standing for the ideas between which they express or suggest the relations. The notional and relational are two in the spontaneous consciousness, but only one in reflection and in grammar.

These are the peoples to whom our civilization dates back, the languages which have been studied as models ever since language has been studied at all—the Hebrew, the Greek, the Latin, the German, the Anglo-Saxon. If scholars had directed the world, the development of speech would have stopped here, and language would have kept its wings forever; but true hands, with all the fingers and thumbs, were to come. Prepositions accumulated. The general indefinite designation of relations by case-endings became useless and embarrassing. The analysis of mode and time became more and more refined. Separate words were adopted to express these refinements, and the comparatively indefinite designation of tense, mode, and person by inflection-endings became useless and embarrassing. Languages were becoming more analytic all over Europe and Arian Asia.

Just at the most favorable moment there were thrown together on the island of Great Britain picked men of two great peoples, speaking representative languages of two great stocks, the Romanic and Teutonic. They had already been prepared for mutual interaction. The Anglo-Saxon had newly combined the dialects of many tribes, and had not yet grown into literary consciousness. The Normans still felt their Scandinavian blood, and had northern tongues, as well as northern arms. They could the more readily fuse with Angle or Saxon, Celt or Gaul.

Here, then, was the aboriginal Briton, with a speech abundant, flexible, artificial, still telling of his home in the mystic East, but with the weird and solemn tones and idiom which become the children of the old oak forests of the North—the nation of the mistletoe and the Druid;—a wonderful tongue, a faint echo of which, in the imitations of Ossian, has since sighed and moaned through all Europe. This grand old stock had the traits of the primitive races; it was proud and unyielding, hard to develop or mix, but softened somewhat by the story of Christ.

Here were the Saxons, with their large and well-formed hands,[2] crafty hands, full of nerves as the heads of another race;—the race of intellectual manual labor; the race of freedom, tall and strong; the fair-haired, blue-eyed, shapely race, who love home, and one wife to rule it as lady and mother.

They spoke a language of the heart, rich in dear brooding tones of warm affection—in simple hearty words for home things and feelings, for every dimple that smiles on the face of home; rich in simple hearty words for the nature in which they lived, their flocks, and herds, and crops, the sun, moon, stars, the clouds, the seasons, the weather, the tides; for this was a people at one with nature, and they kept in their purest forms the sounds which are the audible representative of nature—the common heritage of the Arian races. Come what might, here were sounds that could not die, while the love of nature and of home was warm in the hearts of the race.

And here too were the Normans—every man a prince—the born rulers of the world, the knights of old romance, whose marrow grew in open boats on the stormy northern seas, who fought with the heart of lions, who loved as they fought, and sung their own combats and loves to the music of the language of sunny France. They spoke a language which was the queen of the Romanic languages, the language of chivalry, of compliment, of courtesy, the language of the camp, the joust, the court. The last stage of the Latin, with half its strength shorn, and divorced from simple nature, it was yet fit to be the speech of gallant chevaliers and fair dames all the world over, as well as on the soil of *la belle France.* The immediate result of throwing these nations together, was a chaos of language, hissing, sputtering, bubbling like a witch's caldron. For a century, every man blurted out the sounds which suited his whim, and explained himself with his sword. The laws of the Saxon tongue were broken. The laws of the Norman tongue were broken. The Celtic would not mix.

But apparent chaos is the condition of a new Cosmos. One who had watched this chaos of language after the Norman conquest, might have seen gradually emerging a new life, as the smoke that had poured from the coffer of the fisherman in the Arabian tale, cloudy and shapeless, thickened slowly into a gigantic shape, and one of the genii stood before him.

Perhaps the first fact which would strike the observer of this new

[2]Sir Gareth had "the fairest and the *largest hands* that ever man saw."—*Mort d'Arthure*, 1, 232. "The German's wit is in his fingers."—George Herbert, "Jacula Prudentum," p. 302.

being—this infant language, is its prodigious appetite and digestion. It is a man-child, and has the stomach of an ostrich. It is a universal imbiber. No words come amiss to it; whether it is the home-made, week-day, Saxon or Celt, festival Norman, the Sunday Latin and Greek of the Church, foreign dainties brought in by the merchant Portuguese, or strange knickknacks found in the East by Crusaders—nothing comes amiss to the new speech; it will try its jaws on all utterances. And its digestion proves equal to its appetite. The *sesquipedalian verba* of Greek and Roman are taken up if expressive to his sensitive ear, analyzed if they have an expressive root; or, it may be, he craunches them, as Swift's lady does the wing of lark, bones and all, between his teeth, and grinds them to monosyllables in a trice.

It imbues all words with its own spirit. By some modification of articulation, adjusting it to its own laws of sound, by some variation of meaning or association, each word is given a new citizenship, and becomes obedient to the laws of the new language—a loyal member of the new body; just as when some powerful helix, connecting the poles of an electrical battery, stands ready with its hollow coil, and every bar of steel which is dropped through receives at once a new power, and becomes henceforth a magnet.

In this respect, the English differs from the Anglo-Saxon and other Germanic languages; they like home-made words and cannot away with foreign manufactures. This quality fits the English to be a universal language—to be the exponent of a race, who are to be the freemen of the world, and to extend their citizenship to all nations. Here is already a prophecy of our great republic.

The second fact which would strike the observer of the new language is, that it is a root-speaker. It drops the terminations of the Saxon, and the Latin, and uses the simple fundamental syllables common to all the Arian race, which are naturally expressive to them of substantive thought. It rejects the various indefinite relational syllables, and takes up or makes separate words to express each shade of relation. Relations and notions are at last on the same footing in speech. This people is not content to speak the substantive ideas, and leave you to guess their relations from a few indefinite articulations for cases, or modes; they will be as precise about relations as any thing else; they will say just what they mean every time they speak, to the minutest shade of relation.

Grammar and logic become one to this people, and both are at one with nature. They will not be obliged by mixing up notions and relations in the same word to say what they do not mean. They cease to use grammatical gender, for example, which mixes up men, women, and things, on the hint of a sound. They will not be made to call their women things, as the Germans do every time they call them wife. Here at last is a language with hands. Here at last is a people who do not fly along on the wings of verbal suggestion, but have true hands and fingers, and an edged brain, and shape speech with art to suit their ever active thought. In this respect also the English differs from the Anglo-Saxon.

The observer might notice a third fact about the new language; it ceases to compound its words. The Saxon compounded freely like the German, and the rejection of the habit is the strongest mark of the despotic dominance of the analytic spirit in English. For it is the desire of all thinkers, especially of all poets, and orators, to fix the permanent stamp of their own thought upon every object they speak of. A compound is such a stamp. But the same cause which prevents our new language from using permanent indefinite terminations for inflections, prevents also the formation of new permanent compounds. This distinguishing mind, ever alert, chooses to say, each time it speaks, exactly what it then and there wishes to say. It will not take up an indefinite general descriptive, nor will it mix in one what it knows to be two, and means to keep two. It had rather split the one, than glue the two. In this radical point the English differs from the Saxon, and agrees with the Norman.

The observer might notice a fourth fact in regard to the new language. It uses a new gamut of sounds. There is a stable adjustment of mind and vocal organs in the Arian races, so that an idea naturally expresses itself every where by the use of the same organs. The consonants of the root syllables, and the relational consonants, remain letters of the same organ through all ages of all languages of the Arian stock. But there are smooth, middle and rough letters of each organ. New speech begins with the vigorous, the broad, and loud, and strong, and rough, and gradually becomes more refined and attenuated. The consonants of any radical sound change. The vowels change also. Diphthongs attenuate into vowels; the broad sounds flatten; the harsh sounds soften; the strong sounds weaken; all runs into whispers and i s (ees). The Greek, for example, which must have run and roared with every sonorous variety of musical utterance in the time of Homer, has insensibly thinned away, until the modern Greek has nothing but ee (i) to give us for three of the vowels and three of the diphthongs of the written tongue. The new life and vigor of the English shows itself in reversing this course of attenuation. It gives the weak strength; the flat, roundness; makes the thin vowels broad; delights in new and sonorous diphthongs, and decisive strong consonants, nor does it fear a masculine harshness. It has the phonology of a vigorous youth.

It has moreover a peculiar gamut of vowels. It took up the Anglo-

Saxon sounds for the objects of nature, and of home, and the heart; it took up the Norman sounds for artificial manners; but in adjusting them to each other, so as to make a scale of sounds, each was varied by the new instrument which sounded them—the vocal organs of the Englishman; and inspired with a new quality and tone, to render them expressive of the new soul which was speaking in them, the vital spirit of the English race. The result has been strongly stated by Grimm. He says that in the richness and fulness of its free middle tones, it has a real power of expression, such as perhaps no other human speech could ever command. He adds, that these tones cannot be taught—they may be caught.[3] The separate sounds of single words may be caught, but to speak English is one of the fine arts. The same letters in different words—the same words in different connections, vary freely by shades of tone so delicate, that no notation could give them—no teacher could repeat them as a matter of artifice, without the life and soul to inspire them. To read a page of Milton to the height of the great argument, or a scene of Shakespeare, with its proper harmony and spirit, demands a happy genius and organization, and could never be taught or caught. While the capacities of the language for harmonious and powerful expression are not used to the full by either of these mighty masters of it. It has combinations of sound grander than ever rolled through the mind of Milton; more awful than the mad gasps of Lear; sweeter than the sighs of Desdemona; more stirring than the speech of Antony; sadder than the plaints of Hamlet; merrier than the mocks of Falstaff.

Our observer might perceive, in the fifth place, that the syntax of the new language was as new as its etymology and phonology, and a further expression of the same analytic spirit. It flings away all that is complex and artificial in languages, like the Latin and Saxon, where sentences are made by an adjustment of final sounds, where every word has its mortise or tenon, and a whole sentence is dovetailed, so that speaking is like putting a Chinese puzzle together, or a perpetual game of dominos. The syntax turns on the thought, not on the sounds, and in its general laws is a pure logic carried to the limits of the most refined analysis. No language has ever been spoken where words did the reason so much and obstruct it so little; so little impose their laws on thought and wrest reason from its natural processes. These remarks apply only to the general laws of syntax.

For our observer who is watching the growth of the new language, will, in the sixth place, see gradually taking their places in it, idiom after idiom

---

[3]"Nicht einmal lehrbaren, nur lernbaren." *Ursprung der Sprache*, p. 50.

of every variety and shade of structure, the ganglions of the linguistic body. This is the field where the free will of the individual man does its freest work in language. In its general laws a language is the result of the relation between the general traits of a race and the nature in which they live; but free will disports itself in the idioms. These are the contributions which genius makes to its national tongue; genius, whose motions always hover on the verge of mystery, basks in idioms.

The inexplicable coils of words instinct with electrical life, which send a thrill to the people's heart no one knows how; hard knots of words where the soundest sense is tied up the tightest; touches of nature that make the whole world kin; leaps of thought which grammarians balk at; every means, simpler or more vivid than reason can command, which poetic genius, or patriotism, or any breathing or beaming of the free soul has found to convey thought or feeling; every form of speech which the linguistic sense of the people recognizes as a stroke of genius which it cannot willingly let die, adds to the stock of idioms, and to the peculiar treasures of a national language.

It is the glory of the English speech that its idioms speak for truth and freedom, and law and religion. It grew up in the midst of struggles for religion,—in the midst of the contests of freemen,—in the midst of a people fond of nature and home. Its idioms have been dyed in the blood of martyrs, or taken their festive colors in the secret heart of patriots or poets; they are tinted less in the colors of fancy than in the veritable hues of sky and cloud, wood and field, and ocean, wrought into unity of meaning under the solemn and earnest gaze of imagination.

We shall only mention further, in the seventh place, that the English language may be known as new by its stamp and flowering in literature.

A people do not come to consciousness until they have a classic language. Barbarians have feelings, instincts, sentiments, but not reflections or ideas to be the basis of literature; the people is still unorganized, public spirit is still to be born. As soon as it is born, it will make itself heard in a speech which is then and there classic. Now, to use our old figure of the birth of an animal, the first organ that is seen in the embryo is the heart. Some book, written or unwritten, must be the heart of a classic language. Homer was the heart of the Greek language; the laws and ballads of Rome, the heart of the Latin. The Bible was the heart of the English.

We yield to no one in love for Homer. College recollections of it still hallow the memory of him whose enthusiasm gave life to the antique lines. We are told that tropical fruits must be eaten under the trees to know their proper taste; but I am sure that when our Greek Professor visited the classic shores of the Mediterranean, neither orange, nor date, nor olive, gained in flavor, as did the songs of Homer. Years ago, while fresh from this bracing air, stricken by sickness, with the heart of an exile, I spent solitary months beneath the palm trees under the tropical sun, on the beach of a tropical sea. Day by day as I walked the beach, I heard again the song which Homer sang; and it gleamed and flashed with a new light, as I gazed on the strange brilliancy of that tropical sea and sky; and it rippled, and ran, and roared with new music, as I listened to that many-voiced sea. A new love and sympathy for this wondrous song grew up in my mind. It seemed the very echo of nature from the seat where beauty and music sit enthroned in the heart of genius. It is worthy to be the heart of the language of Greece. But the Bible was the heart of the English.

The laws and ballads of Rome (the heart of the Latin language) have been stronger food for heroes than the hearts of lions. The trumpet blast which rings through the pages of Livy and Plutarch has roused the heroism of all succeeding generations. Here are the stories of heroes whom Shakspeare rejoiced in more than in all the great names of Greece. Here are the heroes whose trophies gave the old knights of France no sleep,—who inspired the men and women of the first Revolution, when Madame Roland carried Plutarch's *Lives* to church, and wept that she was not a Roman. This has been called the Bible of France, and it is worthy to be the heart of its courtly language.

But our Bible was the heart of the English. A thousand years this book had been waiting the advent of the English race. As in the geological eras, so in the history of man, in the progress of redemption, advance is not in the continual development of a single race. Singularly developed individuals of a race give promise of a higher type; a new race springs up and realizes the type, while the old race decays. To the Jews, for example, the Christian Apostles came as the harbingers of a new type. The new race came, but not from the Jewish or other Shemitic stock. A new and different race were to embody the advancing ideal, while the Shemitic stock, having borne its flower and fruit, stands barren and decaying, as if exhausted by the ripening of such a fruit. In the English at last came the race which was to be the race of the Bible.

It was in no spirit of scholarship or literary enthusiasm that the English Bible was made. The Saxon race had received Christianity with an intensity of feeling like their old Berserker madness. Not Dante had such appalling visions of hell, or such rapt musings of heaven. Wyckliffe and his fellows wrote to save the men of their own blood from everlasting burnings, to show them the way to everlasting joys. They put their whole souls in the work. The spirit of the English race was in them. The Spirit of the living God was with them. The special providence which guided its growth may be considered a kind of inspiration. It is more than accurate. It is felicitous and moving. It is full of living idiom, which no scholastic art, no unconsecrated genius could suggest, idiom instinct with devotion, full of harmony and a majestic simplicity. It is no copy of the common speech. It was always above it, an ideal, which the English heart has recognized from the first. These true prophets laid themselves so closely to the heart of the Bible, that the yet plastic language which they spoke, run in the moulds of the Hebrew and Greek, repeated the idioms, and caught the spirit of inspiration. Far as the throbbings of this mighty heart were felt, so far the language grew into organized English, so far the English grew into strength; and to this day every part of the language is pervaded by its influence. No one has ever yet known how to move the English people, whose style has not its life-blood from this great heart of the English speech.

If we choose to carry on in a loose fashion the figure of growth,—in Chaucer we see the senses complete. His lungs are in full play. He shouts as he walks afield, and greets the rising sun. His eyes see, his ears hear. He knows the smell of clover and new hay, and the taste of the tankard.

"And always roaming with a hungry heart,
Much had he seen and known, cities of men
And manners, climates, councils, governments;
Himself not least, but honored of them all:
And drunk delight of battle with his peers."

"Ever with a frolic welcome took
The thunder and the sunshine, and opposed
Free heart, free forehead."

"Since Chaucer was alive and hale,
No man hath walked along our roads with step
So active, so inquiring eye, or tongue
So varied in discourse."

But Shakspeare is the exponent of the English language in its ripe manhood.

We need not try to point out the merits of Shakspeare. We only remark in pursuance of our theme, that this genius of Shakspeare was a new gift to the world. It is not to be found in Saxon. It is not to be found in Norman. It is no development of Saxon or Norman. It is not classical. It is not romantic. It is new. It is Shakspearian. It is English. Criticism which long stood aghast before him, has now made itself new laws from the study of him, and judges all genius by its relations to him. Again, this genius of Shakspeare is marked by the same characteristics which have been pointed out in the English language. The unbounded stomach, under the craving of which we have seen the language taking up words from every quarter, is equally plain in Shakspeare. Nothing comes amiss to him. All moods of both sexes of all ranks of all nations in all ages are food for this hungry heart. Spirits are his familiars. Nature has no mood strange to him. No animal or green thing but has its speech for him; there are books in the running brooks, sermons in stones, and good in every thing.

The same analytic spirit which in the language uses only roots, and dissects and displays every relation of things, and refuses to stereotype compound associations, is also prominent in Shakspeare. He lays open the finest movement of all human hearts and minds. Landseer did not enter more intimately into the innermost nature of a dog. All things in his pages, as Goethe says, are like watches with crystal faces, through which every cog of every separate wheel is displayed.

We saw that the English has a new gamut of sounds, unrivalled in their compass and nearness to nature. It is Shakspeare who has best proved this. This master musician best knows how to "run with a quivering hand in a thousand moods over all the chords of the soul." His syntax and his idioms are characteristically English. Simplicity and fitness rule every general syntactical combination, while an all-pervading and transforming imagination creates at every line some wonderful plexus of words, which seems, like a ganglion of nerves, not simply to transmit, but concentrate and intensify the action of the mind. And finally the great heart of the English speech, the Bible, sends its vital currents through every page, through every phase of his speech.

The glory and influence of Shakspeare are not bounded by the shore of Britain. A great German Philosopher of History, Baron Bunsen, pronounces him: "The great prophet of human destinies on the awakening of a new world. His histories are the only modern Epos, as a poetical relation of the eternal order in a great national development. They are the Germanic Nibelungen, and the Romantic Divina Commedia both united and dramatized, and the dramatic form was the natural organ of the Epos of an age ripe for the realities of life and full of action."

And the greatest master of language,—its most profound historian, and its most trustworthy prophet, I mean of course, Jacob Grimm, has said: "It is not without significance that the greatest and most transcendent poet of the new time, in distinction from the old classics, used the English speech. This speech of his may, with full right, be called a speech for the world. It will go on with the people who speak it, prevailing more and more to all the ends of the earth. In richness, reason, and compression no living speech can be put aside it."

Such is our birth-right. The treasures of this prevailing tongue are ours. This noblest development of ideal language, this grand daguerreotype of the English race, the study of philologers and philosophical historians, this language of the Bible and of the Protestant religion, this tongue of freedom is ours. We speak the tongue which Shakspeare spake, and Chaucer, and Milton, and Bacon, and Locke, and Sidney, and Webster. The glories of these great names, the glories of this conquering language, are ours. Let us acknowledge ourselves debtors to our mother tongue. Let us study it with earnestness, and treat it with reverence and love. The English scholars have been the worst enemies of the English language. They have studied Latin and Greek till they have lost command of the English idiom; some of them till the free English heart has left them, and they have gone over to Rome altogether. How many of our colleges even now study the English Bible, and Shakspeare, and Milton, as they do Homer and Horace?[4] And yet these English books are infinitely more worthy to be known, and this language a better field for philological study. May it not be said, when the historian of this language sums up the proud story of its progress, that the last and most difficult of its conquests was that of the brotherhood of American scholars?

---

[4]The philological study of Milton and Shakspeare is a regular part of the course for the Junior year in Lafayette College, and it is pursued to some extent in Columbia College. The experience of these two institutions has abundantly established the practicability and value of the study.

Standard English: Its Pronunciation, How Lerned

The most activ students of the English language ar fonetists, students of vocal sounds and fonetic laws. The elementary facts on which fonetic science is based, ar the pronunciation of individuals, and the movements of the vocal organs by which the pronunciation is affected. These ar very difficult to ascertain with precision, and of course each person can most conveniently study his own articulation. Professor Whitney was, I believ, the first to attempt a scientific description of his own nativ pronunciation, as distinguisht from his cultured habits. In 1875, in the second series of his *Oriental and Linguistic Studies*, appeard a paper entitld "The Elements of English Pronunciation," which sets forth an analysis and description of the elements of his nativ pronunciation.

This has been followd by similar papers from Mr. Sweet, the hed of the London fonetists, and others. They hav stil further elaborated the description of their speeches and attempted to giv a sort of fonagram of their colloquial frases and connected discourse. This work has excited great interest among filologists and teachers of modern languages. In 1885 Mr. Sweet publisht in German a *Primer of Spoken English*, in which all the English is givn in fonetic writing as this colloquial Londonese.

Prof. Whitney spoke of his paper as a contribution to English dialectic utterance, and again as the "Confessions of a Provincial." But Mr. Sweet and his followers urge their confessions upon the world as the best of English. They urge foren teachers to uze these instruction books, and they urge spelling reformers to adopt their pronunciation and spelling in place of the common orthografy.

When the talk is of standard English Mr. Sweet himself merely says that he knows nothing about it. But when great leaders ar agnostics, the followers ar negators.

So Aug. Western, author of a book on English fonetics, says that he "does not agree that the language teacher should endevor to represent that form of

---

"Standard English: Its Pronunciation, How Lerned." *Transactions of the American Philological Association* 19 (1888): 70-78.

speech that wil be most redily understood by all educated nativs, simply because such a form doesn't exist. Any one who speaks a local dialect wil both understand and be understood by all educated nativs better than a forener who has lernd an artificial standard of the language." Ther is no such thing as a standard language, over and abuv the local dialects, with these fonetists.

Their difficulty seems to be sumthing like that of the nominalists about general notions. Ther ar right-angld triangls they say, obtuse-angld triangls and acute-angld triangls. These uze up the hole set and leav nothing for a triangl in general. So every man is either a Londoner, or a Scot, or an American, or something, and each speaks his own dialect, and ther is nobody left to speak standard English.

The scientific fonetist is at loss to know to whom he ought to apply his apparatus of fonometers to giv him standard English. And anything which can not be mesurd with a fonometer is nonexistent to hiz science. Thackeray said that he uzed no part of his hed abuv his eyes in his literary work. So these fonetists uze no part of their heds abuv the ears.

But a standard language implies sumthing more than observation. It is an ideal to be attaind by the reason. It implies history, and the winning of authority. It implies induction.

How, then, does a standard language come into being?

Persons, or tribes in the state of nature, take their language by tradition from those about them. They catch up from their parents and their playmates the words and frases which their hear oftenest, and acquire a natural speech without any special exercise of reason or reflectiv purpose. Such speech is the result of social necessities acting under the common laws of association. Every tribe, every family, every person, has natural peculiarities: dialects, idioms, idiotisms, ar free, and in a certain sense ther ar as many dialects as ther ar persons. Of language in this state it is wel enuf said, that it grows; it is not made, but grows. Each person talks for himself and knows no better speech than his own.

A standard speech may appear thru the influence of government or of literature. When tribes ar organized into a nation proper, sum tribe becums the ruling one. Then the laws, the public documents, the formulas of the courts and of important business, the charters, the conveyances of land ar prevailingly promulgated and writn in this dialect of the ruling tribe, and all other tribes ar compeld to uze this dialect more or less, and to recognize it as in sum sense a higher and more important form of speech than their own. It finally becums the common speech of courtiers and officials everywhere, a standard speech.

But another way, and a more important way in which standard speech becomes establisht is thru the influence of literature; under the influence of reason, and the intuitions of beauty and order. Whenever deeds ar done or to be done which exalt the faculties of large numbers of men, the creativ power works in language under the guidance of beauty. The poet, the orator rouses to heroic acts or recounts inspiriting achievements in wurthy forms of speech. The happiest forms of the popular dialect which had grown up by association ar selected and combined into speech more perspicuous, more vigorous, more regular, and more harmonious than had been known before. Successful compositions of this kind ar preservd and make part of the education of the nobl and cultured. They ar imitated and accumulate from generation to generation, til the time cums for Homeric poems and classic Greek, or for Chaucer, Shakespeare, and Bacon.

It has been sumtimes said that sum book is the hart or soul of every proper language, that Homer was the hart of the Greek language, the Bible of Luther the hart of modern German, the English Bible the hart of English.

It is certain that no great language has been left to the laws of association and grown to its forms of power and beuty unaided by reason. The steps and stages of progress in literary languages ar mostly recorded in books. The part of a language which is standard in the eminent sense is at first small; the happy idioms of the Bible, the ballads, Chaucer. Then for generations there is slow increase, one new idiom from this author, two or three from that, til Shakespeare gathers them up by the hundred and adds his hundreds more. How many generations has it taken to incorporate the frases of Milton into the speech, so that one uzes them without quotation or allusion, and his "Babylonish dialect" is standard English?

Close upon the creativ contributors to the language in literature proper cum students of language and literature, who make dictionaries and grammars for the standard speech based upon inductions from the literature. Such students do not restrict themselves to books, but gather new data from observation of living speech, of great orators, actors, gentlemen. Then cums critical study of the laws or rules working in these facts of language, with a view to teach them to new generations and to improve the speech.

Work of this sort is at first of narrow range, and small bulk, and hasty induction. Personal authority is more lively in it than reason. Mere grammarians or dictionary-makers ar of slight esteem. But great authors, Dryden, Pope, Addison, Swift, enounce maxims of style and definitions of words, and pronounce sentences of outlawry on certain words and frases, and of pardon or approval on others. By and by a French Academy or Dr. Johnson is able to produce a great dictionary, including standard words enough to constitute a language, a work supported at every word by an authoritativ body of authors and enforced by the power and personal authority of a dictator in the relm of letters. Such a book is a record of standard English. It is not perfect, of course, not infallibl. From its decisions an appeal always lies to the classic English authors and to reason. In the English language ther hav been a succession of dictionaries and grammars making continual, tho slow, advance in recording the standard speech. These books also ar authorities, and help to shape the speech. They ar like the decisions of the judges in common law. In deciding what law is, they make law for the future. So the students of language teaching laws of language make them effectiv in the language of the next generation. Ther is standard speech, as ther is common law.

This standard English is an ideal, somewhat different from colloquial speech, not spoken in perfection by any one, not even perfectly recorded or described in any book. It has its history. It is still making history. Its definitions and idioms hav been more studied than its pronunciation and spelling, but these too hav their standard forms. At the meeting of this Association at Hanover in 1884 I presented a paper on the influence of writn English and of the linguistic authorities upon spoken English. It was an examination of the pronunciation in Walker's dictionary and showd that a very large number of changes in pronunciation has taken place since that book was writn, and that they hav most of them been in accordance with the recommendations of the dictionary, and many of them contrary to the law of least effort.

The following classes of sounds wer mentioned as having changed in England, and more in America.

1. *a* preceded by guttural *g* or *c* softend by the intervention of *e* . "When the *a* is pronounced short as in the first syllables of *candle, gander,* &c., the interposition of the *e* is very perceptible and indeed unavoidable: for though we can pronounce *guard* and *cart* without interposing the *e*, it is impossible to pronounce *garrison* and *carriage* in the same manner."
2. *e* before *r* pronounced *a* in *clerk, sergeant, servant, merchant,* &c.
3. *e* pronounced *i* in *yes, pretty, engine,* &c.
4. *i* pronounced *i,* in an initial syllabl unaccented before a syllabl beginning with a consonant: *didactic, digamma, dilate, fidelity*, &c.
5. Words ending in silent *e* after a short vowel: *crocodile, columbine, eglantine, metalline*, &c.
6. The unaccented vowels pronounced in England with the obscure sound ar now in large numbers distinguisht in America.
7. *s* pronounced as *z* between two sonants by Walker often has its name sound: *disable, disdain, absolve, resignation, nasal*, &c.
8. *d* + *i* and *d* + *y* sounded *j* by Walker, and *t* + *i*, *t* + *y* sounded *ch*, ar now often *dy* and *ty*: *soldier, educate, nature*, &c.

A large number of anomalous words which Walker notes as having a deplorabl pronunciation hav becum regular: *ac'ceptable, ặlienate, annihilate, apostle, apothecary, apron, asparagus, authority, been, bellows, chorister, confessor, construe, cucumber, catch, caviare, chap, chart, china, dictionary, oatmeal, ostrich, schedule,* &c., &c.

A comparison of later pronouncing dictionaries shows that ther is a constant and rapid change in the direction of what ar recognized by the authorities as analogies of the language, and of etymological truth. In Walker's day, *catch* was almost universally pronounced *cŏtch* in the capital; *chap* was calld *chŏp,* and described as "one of those incorrigibl words the pronunciation and orthografy of which must ever be at variance"; *chart* was "almost or quite universally pronounced" *cart*; *china* was *chāne*; *cucumber* was "too firmly fixt in its sound of *cowcumber* to be alterd," and "must be clast with its irregular fellow esculent *asparagus*," (*sparrow grass*); *dictionary* was "a few years ago universally pronounced *dixnary*, and a person would have been thought a pedant who pronounced it as spelt, but now *dixnary* is rather vulgar." Hundreds of such pronunciations hav givn place to regular and distinct articulation of the writn words. The law of least effort has yielded to the teaching of the schoolroom. Physiological laws exert less effect than ideals, than reason. Tradition yields to culture.

Our pronouncing dictionaries hav heretofore givn the full, distinct sounds of English words as utterd by traind orators speaking them with emfasis. In American schools these sounds ar carefully taught, and constitute the primary concept of the word.

Teaching pronunciation has two parts, first: giving a clear and distinct concept of the sound to be utterd ; second, training the vocal organs to make the sound correctly upon a volition to utter the concept. We do not in speaking wil to move each separate muscl, we only wil to make the sound, to utter the concept.

And teaching conversation, or any connected discourse, implies more than this. As we talk we wil to sound our concepts. But the law of least effort works, and in conversation especially we do not use energy enuf to put the organs of speech thru the proper movements, or send up volume of voice sufficient to bring out the resonance of the vowel chambers. The same letter in different words, the same word in different relations to accent, emfasis, and feeling, varies freely by shades of sound so delicate that no notation can giv them. The speech is, as J. Grimm says, nicht einmal lehrbaren, nur lernbaren. It cannot be taught, it may be caught.

It has been common to teach foreners the standard pronunciation, and let them catch the conversational weakenings. But the new fonetists propose to teach conversational pronunciation as primary English. The sentence is taken as a unit, and sentences ar caught by imitation of their colloquial utterance in London. It is denied that ther is any such speech as the standard speech of the dictionaries.

In answer to this it has been said that the standard speech is embodied in literature and recorded in dictionaries and grammars. For pronunciation we look to the rhythms and rimes of poets. These assure us of the number of syllabls in the words they use, of their accent and the resemblances of sound in the accented syllabls. The new fonetists pronounce *difference* difrŭns. But one of the best known stanzas of Wordsworth reads:

> "She lived unknown, and few could know
> When Lucy ceased to be;
> But she is in her grave, and, oh,
> The difference to me."

And Tennyson says in another verse almost as famous:

> "For woman is not undevelopt man,
> But diverse: could we make her as the man,
> Sweet love were slain: his dearest bond is this,
> Not like to like, but like in difference."
> "The Princess," vii., 262.

And again :

> "Or will one beam be less intense
> When thy peculiar difference
> Is cancell'd in the world of sense?"
> "The Two Voices," 41.

Ornament is to be taught as *ŏŏnŭmŭnt*. But no great poet has rimed with dropt *r*s, as *born* with *dawn, doors* with *cause,* as Mr. Sweet does, or with *–ment* as *mŭnt.*

> "She was a phantom of delight
> When first she gleam'd upon my sight;
> A lovely apparition, sent
> To be a moment's ornament."
> Wordsworth, "She Was a Phantom of Delight"

"Each month is various to present
The world with some development."
Tennyson. "The Two Voices," 75.

Many facts about pronunciation which cannot be lernd from the poets ar lernd from observation of living orators and actors, and recorded on the ground of wide induction.

A person who has been traind to standard pronunciation is easily distinguisht from an untrained speaker, even in his colloquial utterances.

His variations from the standard sounds ar weakenings; the concept is present, the organs move. An attentiv listener close before him can distinguish each letter. Illiterates leav their organs in the neutral position, and positively make the neutral vowel of *but* or *burr* for any unaccented vowel, and make no movement to articulate many consonants.

Colloquial pronunciation is not fixt for familiar sentences, much less for literature. Contractions, weakenings, ar used or not according to the feeling of the moment, the ernestness or levity of the speaker, the connection suggesting distinctness or plesant rhythm, the persons addrest, and other causes.

The clear tones, in short, should be dominant, the others tastefully used in particular connections and moods. American habits in this matter differ much from those of London, as shown by the new fonetists. When one of their periodicals prints one of my letters in their spelling, I feel as if they misrepresented my tone and manner as well as pronunciation.

Untraind popular orators from England, whose oratory is only a loud utterance of their colloquial articulation, ar not easily understood by American audiences, but when English scholars do us the honor of addressing the Philological Association, nobody notices their pronunciation as peculiar. A Frenchman or German who was grounded first in the London colloquial, and had no guiding concepts of the standard pronunciation, would be thereby markt in America as a forener, and an illiterate one.

It is very desirabl for the science of language to hav minute and accurate accounts of the conversational speech of Londoners. Such accounts ar also of much use to persons who wish to pass for nativs of the metropolis. Similar accounts of the speech at Oxford and Cambridge, at Edinburgh and Dublin, at New York, Boston, Chicago, San Francisco, would hav like value. But in order of teaching these should be secondary to the classic speech.

It is also possibl and desirabl to determin a standard conversational utterance, so far as to record in the dictionaries the common weakenings and the limits of allowabl weakenings in each word as secondary to the ruling concept. Such a record is to be attempted in the *Century* dictionary. It must be establisht by induction, as an ideal from wide and select observation, shaped under the direction of laws of economy and eufony. It must not accept dialectical peculiarities.

Since the colloquial speeches of different regions of English speaking peopls are different no one of them should be substituted for the standard speech of literature as giving the ruling concepts for pronunciation.

Standard English, the heir of all ages, resting on a solid foundation of literature and observations, recorded in dictionaries and grammars, is a permanent and authoritativ institution, a stronghold of the unity and power of the Anglo-Saxon race. It has a right of possession not to be devested by singl localities or passing fashions.

Is There an Anglo-Saxon Language?

Several of the English scholars, who are most active in the study of Early English, wage war on *Anglo-Saxon*. They attack the word. Mr. Sweet, in his edition of King Alfred's Version of Gregory's *Pastoral Care*, published by the Early English Text Society, announces that he uses "Old English" for the "stage of the English language commonly known by the barbarous and unmeaning title of Anglo-Saxon." They are still more hostile to the suggestion which goes with the word, that the speech called Anglo-Saxon is different from modern English so as to deserve a separate name. They say there has been but one speech spoken in England by the Teutonic tribes and their descendants from Cædmon to Tennyson. This speech was at the first called *Anglise*, English, by those who spoke it, and the name has never changed, and there is no reason for changing it; the early periods may be called Old English. The scholars who are pressing these views, are in positions to secure them a general hearing, and they have well earned the right to a most respectful one. They introduce them into publications of the Early English Text Society, and the series of school-books issued from the Clarendon Press. Mr. Freeman urges them in his elaborate histories, Dr. Morris in his philological works, and men of all arms in the *Saturday Review*.

The questions to be decided are partly questions of substance and partly of the use of language.

I. What is the real relation between modern English and Anglo-Saxon? There have been occasional enthusiasts since the time of Verstegan, who have identified them; but the more thorough study of the ancient speech has clearly established its remoteness. It had been often thought to be a rude form of colloquial English, and its strange appearance had been attributed to the irregular spelling of illiterate and careless service. Thus President Jefferson, who was a student of the language, and who first introduced the study of it in our colleges by establishing it in the University of Virginia, and composed an essay to exemplify his method of study, proposes to reform the spelling. He says—"the writer having no exam-

"Is There an Anglo-Saxon Language?" *Transactions of the American Philological Association* 3 (1872): 97-110; rept. in *Englische Studien* 1 (1877): 367-78.

ples of orthography to recur to, thinking them indeed not important, had for his guide his own ideas only of the power of the letters, unpractised and indistinct as they might be. He brought together, therefore, those letters which he supposed must enter into the composition of the sound he meant to express, and was not even particular in arranging them in the order in which the sounds composing the word followed each other. Thus *birds* was spelt brides; *grass*, gaers; *run*, yrnan; *cart*, craet; *fresh*, fersh. They seemed to suppose, too, that a final vowel was necessary to give sound to the consonant preceding it, and they used for that purpose any vowel indifferently. A son was suna, sune, sunu." Thus changing the spelling to modern English, and disregarding the final vowels, he declares groundless all distinctions of gender, all case endings except the genitive singular and dative plural, and most of the forms of the verb; in short he considers the whole grammatical system a series of "aberrations, into which our great Anglo-Saxon leader, Dr. Hickes, has been seduced by too much regard to the structure of the Greek and Latin languages, and too little to their radical difference from that of the Gothic family."

"Remove," he says, "the obstacles of uncouth spelling and unfamiliar character, and there would be little more difficulty in understanding an Anglo-Saxon writer than Burns' poems?" Such views are no longer held by scholars. The speech of *Beowulf*, Cædmon and Alfred, is recognized as a literary language, carefully written, competent to translate the Latin classics, and having original works of importance, both in extent and kind. The comparative study of the northern dialects shows it to be a German speech lying perfectly parallel with the other Teutonic tongues, so that its grammatical forms can be clearly traced, and a historical orthography established, extending even to the quantities of its vowels and the place of the accent. The modern discoveries of the laws of letter change point out the relations of the Anglo-Saxon spelling and pronunciation to ours, and enable the scholar to distinguish the errors of scribes from the records of varying sounds.

This classic Anglo-Saxon differs from our English:

1. In phonology. It has sounds which we have not; y is the Greek upsilon, the French *u*; *h* represents the guttural aspirate, the Greek chi, the Germans *ch*; *hl*, *hn*, *hr*, *wl*, *wr*, are frequent initial combinations. The sounds which are common to both speeches are differently used. Words spelt with the same characters are pronounced differently. The weak vowels *î*, *û*, have become diphthongs: *wrîte* is pronounced *rait*. The mixed vowels *ê*, *ô*, have shifted to their weaker element; *fêt* is pronounced *fît* (feet); *gôs*, *gûs* (goose.) The laws of phonetic change are different. The Anglo-Saxon vowels were very sensitive to the influence of the letters

near them. A vowel is changed by the vowel of the following syllable to a mixed vowel between the two. Consonants difficult to utter break the vowels before or after them into a kind of diphthong, other consonants assimilate the vowels. So that in the declension of a noun, or the inflection of a verb the root vowel wavers from case to case, or person to persons. There are refined laws of assimilation of consonants which may be compared with the euphonic laws in Greek. All these changes have ceased. All this sensitive life is gone. The few relics of it which remain in such forms as *men* from *man*, *elder* from *old*, *told* as a past of *tell*, and *sought* of *seek*, strike us as anomalies. Our English vowels are "ded as a dore-nayle."

2. In vocabulary. A Frenchman, M. Thommerel, has counted the words in Johnson's dictionary, and found 43,500, of which 29,000 are of Romance origin. If two-thirds of *Johnson* are Romantic, we should guess that at least four-fifths of *Webster* must be. We do not know how large a part of the Anglo-Saxon dictionary still survives. A modern Englishman may look long in Cædmon or *Beowulf* without recognizing a word. An examination of two pages, 74 double lines, of Cædmon, containing 442 words, shows 168 words completely gone, so that no spelling, or other modifications, can bring them within the ken of a mere modern-English scholar.

3. The inflections have almost all disappeared. The Anglo-Saxon is a synthetic language, with five cases, four declensions of the noun growing out of the joint influence of stem endings and genders, two full declensions of the adjective for its definite and indefinite use in all genders, three numbers of the personal pronouns, six conjugations of the verb.

4. In the derivation of words. The free production of compounds, which belonged to the early speech, ceases in English; and the prefixes and suffixes of derivation are many of them no longer living, and their places are taken by others of Romanic origin.

5. The syntax is also that of an inflected language. The government of cases is highly complicated. Verbs and prepositions may require not only accusatives, but datives, or genitives, genitives and datives, accusations and datives; the same word requires sometimes one case and sometimes another, according to the sense. The use of the moods is also complicated and subtle. The rules for the subjunctive and participle rival those of the Greek in their number and nicety. The arrangement of the words in a sentence is also free, and often different from the English, and like the German, separating agreeing words and holding the sense long in suspense to the extreme embarrassment of the English reader.

6. The versification has changed. The old alliterative meter with its peculiar laws has passed away. Chaucer and his successors use the metrical forms of France and Italy.

7. The modes of thought are different. Students who are familiar with synthetic languages, and skillful in matching inflection endings find Anglo-Saxon literature difficult. Though they know the meaning of the separate words, and see how they must be put together, they often do not after all see what the sentence can mean. It is the thinking of a strange race, which died out, and is not embodied in modern literature.

These specifications may be summed up in the statement that the Anglo-Saxon presents a language and literature copious enough and peculiar enough to have dictionaries and grammars of goodly size especially devoted to it, and histories of its literature. A German can read it more easily than an Englishman. It would seem then that it deserves to have a name of its own.

In answer to this it is urged that these changes have been gradual; there is no break in the language, but a constant, unbroken progress from the beginning till now.

It is true that the change in the traditional colloquial speech of the common people of England has been gradual; we might go back to Adam with no absolute saltus. But literary language has its periods. Such a language is an ideal, formed in the application of speech to purposes which exalt the faculties of the speaker, to oratory, to poetry, to the record of heroic acts, or to national annals. The creative power then works on language under the direction of the intuition of beauty. The happiest forms of the popular dialects are selected and combined into a speech more perspicuous, more regular, more vigorous, more harmonious than had before been known. Successful compositions are preserved, and make part of the education of the noble and cultivated. They are imitated. A literature grows up, which the people read and remember, and a classic speech, which a few can write and speak. Such was the classic language of Greece, and such the Latin, and the Anglo-Saxon. Such languages need a certain elevation and cultivation of mind to preserve them. Each generation must attain it for itself, or the speech will decline. Such languages die. The descendants of those who spoke them revert to dialects. A new life may quicken in the people after many generations and great dialectical changes, and a new classic language be formed, which is no development of the old classic language, but a new growth. Such are the Italian, the Spanish, the French, all created from dialects which are descendants of the speech of the people of Rome, none of them developments of classic Latin.

Such also is the English, with a difference which removes it still further from the Anglo-Saxon than any Romance language is from the Latin. It is mixed with a large proportion of the language of a different race, and the masters of the new literature spoke this Norman French, studied it, and were educated by its masterpieces. Chaucer knew nothing of Anglo-Saxon. His originals are found in France. And the thought and spirit of the new literature continued to be drawn from the Romanic side; so that if the early English authors had not kept the old idiom in use, there would now be left almost no Anglo-Saxon in the significant vocabulary of science and literature. The affiliation is well grounded, which is made in the name of the German *Jahrbuch für romanische und englische Sprache und Literatur*.

If literary or classic speech is to control the classification and naming of the languages in which it is found, the Anglo-Saxon is clearly to be separated from the English, and separately named. The former is a synthetic German speech with its own periods of early irregular idiom, classic cultivation, decline and fall into dialects, the latter an analytic, mixed speech of Romanic cultivation, with other periods of growth, and classic regularity, and progress. And a chaos separates the two languages. It is only when attention is directed to the history of etymological forms that unity can be plausibly claimed for them. What few inflection endings we have, are of Anglo-Saxon origin; and they have been gradually falling away since the time of Alfred. But while the importance of these forms in tracing the descent of languages is probably not over-rated, their weight in establishing identity or similarity may easily be. An Englishman can read French much more easily than German, or Anglo-Saxon. He has less grammar to learn, and unlearn. The French grammar is, on the whole, more like English than is either of the others.

A comparison of English with German suggests another way of stating these differences. The modern German is a development of the Old High German of the ninth century. There has been some weakening and falling away of the unaccented syllables; but in all the substantial powers of language there has been constant growth, a constant forming of new words from the old roots to express the new thoughts of successive generations. Fast as science or art, eloquence or poetry, have found new facts, or dreams, or cadences, the old significant Teutonic syllables have been marshaled into combinations to represent them. Not so the English. The Anglo-Saxon of Alfred was stronger than any contemporary Teutonic speech. It was especially rich in the vocabulary of morals, religion, and law. But it decayed not only in its grammatical and poetical forms, but in its power to express the substance of thought, and when it died out into dialects, its capacity for freely forming new words was lost. English has made no attempt to frame its Saxon elements into new words to keep pace with the advance of thought. It has grown by the introduction of new words of Romanic origin or by coinage from the ancient Latin or Greek.

These considerations go to show that a separate name for Anglo-Saxon will do no wrong to historical or philological truth, and that the convenience of students, and makers of dictionaries, grammars, and other linguistic and critical works demands some single name. One, at least, of the new school, Mr. Tancock in his etymological vocabulary in one of the Clarendon Series, uses *English* simply for all words back to Beda, and yet he distinguishes French and Old French. Others use *Old English* for all obsolete words and forms. In any considerable philological works, like Dr. Morris's *Historical Outlines of English Accidence*, this is surely a grave defect. Even popular discussion or instruction needs names for two periods of Anglo-Saxon, its classic period and its decline, and for at least two periods of English. A full historical grammar must notice other periods, the oldest Anglo-Saxon, for example, and at least three periods of English. The proposed use of *Old English* does not distinguish, but confounds all the periods of Anglo-Saxon and the two early periods of English. It is bad in substance since it unites unlike objects and separates like. It unites Chaucer with Cædmon and separates him from Shakespeare.

We may further specify. The mere leaving out useful information is something. The student wishes to learn as a matter of general information, whether any old word which may be mentioned, belongs to the period of Chaucer, or Layamon, or Alfred.

Then the relations of these periods to modern English are very different. Conclusions which may be safely drawn from a word, if it is in Cædmon, may fail altogether, if it is only known in *Piers Plowman*.

Then the inflection endings are so different in the different periods, that unless you know at what time a word occurs, you cannot be sure what form it was intended to represent.

Then the Anglo-Saxon is printed with all the long vowels marked, while the later language is without marks. In a book calling many periods *Old English*, it cannot be told when a word which might be Anglo-Saxon, is printed without marks, whether it is because the author thinks the vowels are all short, or because he takes the word from some writer of a period later than Anglo-Saxon, or whether it is an error of the press.

When such a book has different spellings of the same word, it is not plain whether they are mere irregular spellings of the same period, or regular spellings of different ages, or partly errors in the book.

These and like defects might be easily avoided by the use of a series of names for the different periods, such as *English of the first period* for classic Anglo-Saxon, *English of the second period* for late Anglo-Saxon, and so on. Dr. Morris, apparently feeling difficulty here, often calls Anglo-Saxon oldest English. The periods might be named from prominent persons, the *English of Alfred*, of *Layamon*, of *Chaucer*, and the like. But such forms are cumbrous. And all of them encounter a substantial difficulty when applied to the discussion of the elements of modern English. This is, as has been before pointed out, a mixed language; and one element of it is the same as the language which was used in England before, and should be, and will naturally be, called by the same name. If the old language is called *English*, the Romanic part of our language is called *foreign*, a naming bad in substance as stigmatizing one part of our speech.

The reasons urged for this nomenclature are in great part sentimental. It is thought to magnify the English language and race to represent them as Low German, having an unbroken history parallel with that of the High German, and reaching through a more famous career to a more venerable antiquity. But Americans are taught to believe in mixed races, and it magnifies the English most in our eyes to represent it in the old fashion, as formed by the junction of two great languages, the bearers of the best cultivation of the Teutonic and Romanic races. It is the fashion now to laud and honor the Germans. It was not long ago the fashion to speak of the Anglo-Saxons as an effete race at the time of the conquest, and to ascribe everything valuable in the organization of the church and state, in art and literature, in war and adventures of discovery, to the Norman side; the language of the court, the camp, the study derived its grace and dignity from its Norman parentage. Fashions change, but surely no Englishman need apologize for his Norman blood, or tongue. And scientific linguists will prefer a nomenclature for England different from that of Germany, and plainly indicating that the history of German there and on the continent has been different, and that English is a child of a Norman father and a Saxon mother.

II. As to the word *Anglo-Saxon*, it seems to answer its purpose well enough. We begin with *English* as the name of our modern speech. *Saxon* and *Norman* are good names of the two kinds of words in it. *Old English* is the name of the growing speech, with which the older synthetic Teutonic speech is not to be confounded, either in its classic, or decaying state. To call this old speech *Anglo-Saxon* unites it with the Saxon element of English, and at once classifies it with, and discriminates it from, its nearest kindred of the Continent, the Old Saxon. This is the old nomenclature.

As soon as the new mixed race was fairly born, and the Normans and all were known as English, writers who had occasion to speak of the two kinds of Englishmen called them Saxons and Normans. The first example of it yet found in books is the oft-quoted passage from Robert of Gloucester (A.D. 1298):

"Of þe Normans beþ heyemen þat beþ of Engelonde,
& þe lowemen of Saxons as ich understonde."

When the attention of scholars was drawn to the writings of the ancient period, and works began to be "newly collected out of the Auncient Monuments of the sayd Saxons, and published for testimonie of the same" in the latter half of the 16th century, the same word *Saxon* was naturally carried back to the ancient language. When grammars, and dictionaries, and philological works like that of Verstegan, were published in the 17th century, some variation between *Saxon*, *English-Saxon*, and *Anglo-Saxon* is found; but *Anglo-Saxon*, which is used by Somner in the earliest printed dictionary (*Fol. Oxon.* 1659), by Hickes in the *Institutiones Grammaticæ* (4to, Oxon. 1689), and by Junius, finally prevailed, and has been steadily used by the scholars who have worked in this field since the rise of modern comparative philology. A library of books, reprints or original editions of the ancient texts, dictionaries, grammars, histories, translations, criticism, now exists in which these names are used. The most eminent scientific philologists of all nations have used them. It is unnecessary to enumerate Rask, and Grimm, and Koch, and Heyne, and Grein, and Kemble, and Hadley, Marsh, Earle, Ellis, Latham, and the like. Dr. Morris's *Historical Outlines of English Accidence* (1872) is the first philological work of importance which has not used them. Their use has been established through the whole period of modern English. Mr. Freeman says, "The most grotesque instance of this confused sort of nomenclature is to be found in the technical language of unscientific philologers,—" "—the English language has never either changed its name or lost its continuity. In the eyes of the scientific philologer, it is the same English language throughout all its modifications. But by unscientific philologers, the language, from some utterly mysterious cause, is not called English until the two processes of which I speak are accomplished. Before those processes begin, it is 'Saxon,' or 'Anglo-Saxon;' while they are going on, it is '*Semi-Saxo*'—a name perhaps the most absurd to be found in the nomenclature of any human study."

He means by the "two processes" the loss of the ancient inflections and the introduction of foreign words; what he means by "scientific philologers" and "unscientific philologers," it is not so easy to say, or who his "scientific philologers" were, since Dr. Morris's book had not appeared at the time of his writing this surely rhetorical rather than historical paragraph.

Our nomenclature, as we have shown, is a growth of the necessities of the modern mixed speech. England, *Englaland*, was the general geographical name of the country of the Teutonic settlers in Britain, and English, *Anglisc*, *Englisc*, the name of the people and language used by the missionaries who converted them to Christianity, and afterwards by the people themselves. These words naturally continued to be used in their old geographical national sense after the conquest, and so became the name of our mixed race and language. *English* could therefore not be used to distinguish the Teutonic elements of English. It has been proposed by Professor Haldeman, and others, to use the old form *Anglisc* for the distinctive name; and it might answer the purpose. *Anglian* would perhaps be more easily made current. But the speech to be named is West-Saxon after all rather than Anglian, and *Saxon*, *Anglo-Saxon*, are the words in use. They are objected to as unhistoric.

Saxon is not a current name for the language in the old speech. It is, however, the name by which the Teutonic ravagers of Britain were earliest known to the Romans and Britons, and by which they have been known ever since to the Celts or Britain. It is found in Latin writings of Britons and foreigners; in Prosper's *Chronicon Imperiale*, of the 5th or 6th century (Duchèsne, Rer. Franc. Scriptt. i. 199: Freeman i. 557); in Paul Warnefrid of Lombardy of the eighth century (Latham, Pref. Dict., and see below); in Eginhard who died in 839 (Vita Karoli, 25; Annals, 808: Freeman, i. 530); in Asser, a Welshman in the court of Alfred. Alcuin (*Ealhwine*), a Northumbrian (A.D. 735–804), in his poem *De Pontificibus et Sanctis Ecclesiae Eboracensis* (Wright, B.B.L., 44) speaks of his countrymen in his punning fashion as

"*Duritiam* propter dicti cognomine *Saxi*."

And in the Latin writings of the Anglo-Saxons the same use occurs. Beda (Hist. Eccl. i. 14, 22), Æthelweard (A.D. 1090), Henry of Huntingdon (A.D. 1154), Florence of Worcester (died 1118), Roger de Wendover (died 1237), abound with it, but mostly in the early period, or where Asser is followed; the later chronicles repeat the language of the earlier. It also occurs in the Anglo-Saxon speech in Alfred's translation of Beda (i. 14, 15; iii. 7); so also in one passage of the Anglo-Saxon chronicle (A.D. 605); *And swâ wearþ gefild Augustinus wîtegunge þe he cwađ,*

Gif Wealas nellaþ sibbe wiđ us, hy sculon æt Seaxenâ handa forwurþan. Its appearance here is explained by Mr. Freeman as a Welsh use; it is perhaps simply an ancient one. The country is sometimes called *Saxonia* (Cod. Dipl. i. 28; Beda, Hist. Abb. Wirem, p. 329, and elsewhere: Freeman i. 533). The language is often called *Saxonum linguam* (Beda, Hist. Eccl. iii. 7), *Saxonice*, *Saxonicibus*, *Sermonibus*, and the like, in the charters, (Cod. Dipl. v. 144, 161, 185, and often,) and Chronicles, from Asser's life of Alfred, through his followers, down to the times of Geoffrey of Monmouth, and Robert of Gloucester. See Roger de Wendover (A.D. 1237; Flores Historiarun, pp. 7, 40, 65, 184, 324, and elsewhere). There never has been a time from Alfred's day to this in which *Saxon* has not been familiar to scholars as a name of Alfred's speech. The word *Saxon* was kept familiar to all the ancient people by its continual use in their popular speech as a distinctive name in speaking of the West-Saxons, East-Saxons, and South-Saxons, and though in the books which are preserved, *Englisc* is the familiar general name of the tribes, there seems to have been felt a defect in it for precise and formal expression. Thus when Beda says at the beginning of his history, *Historiam gentis Anglorum*, &c., Alfred translates it *Angel þeôde and Seaxum.*

From the same feeling the word Anglo-Saxon probably arose. The earliest examples of it yet pointed out are in the Latin of foreign writers. Paul Warnefrid (8th Cent.), before mentioned, uses *Angli*, *Angli-Saxones*, *Saxones Angli*, for the inhabitants of England, *Vetuli Saxones* for the Saxons of the Continent (ii. 6; iii. 25; iv. 23; v. 30, 32, 33, 37; vi. 15, 28, 37: Freeman, i. xxxv). Mr. Freeman also refers to Lambert of Herzfeld (1066), Prudentius of Troyes (Pertz, i. 441, 449, 452; see also, iii. 32, 71), Orderic (666 A., 525 B., 722 B: Freeman i. 536). It is frequent in the Latin charters given by kings who style themselves *Angul-Saxonum rex* (*Alfred, Cod. Dipl. v. 134; Eadward, v. 146, and often; Æthelsan, v. 187; Eadmund, ii. 268; Eadred, ii. 304; Eadwig, ii. 318; Æthelred, iii. 340; Cnut., iv. 18). Here also are found *Anglo-Saxonia* (vi. 166), *Angul-Saxonia* (v. 169), as names of the country. *Anglo-Saxon* in one form or another is also frequent in the Latin chroniclers, in Asser, Aldred's contemporary biographer, Florence of Worcester (A. 1066), Simeon of Durham (x. Scriptt. 137). It is also found in the vulgar tongue: Eadred is endowed *mid cynedôme Angul-Seaxnâ* (Col. Dipl. ii. 304), Æthelstan is described as *Ongol-Saxnâ cyning*, (Cod. Dipl., v. 218), and the same word with its Teutonic genitive comes up in the midst of Latin; thus of Eadmund (Cod. Dipl. ii. 268) "qui regimina regnorum Angulsa xnâ & Norđhymbrâ—gubernabat;" of Eadred (same) "sceptra-diadematum Angulsaxnâ cum Norđhymbris, & Paganorum cum Brettonibus gubernabat." It is not improbable that this word may have been used at first as a contraction of *Angli et Saxones*, but the forms just mentioned suggest a word formed in the common dialect in analogy with *West-Saxons*, *East-Saxons*, and *South-Saxons*, and *Old-Saxons*. Alfred uses *Eald-Seaxan* in his Orosius, i. 1. 12. We find in Widukind (i. 8: Freeman, i. 772), a mention that certain Saxons settled in Britain, to which he adds, "et quia illa insula in angulo quodam maris sita est, Angli Saxoens usque hodie vocitantur." Others probably interpreted *Anglo-Saxons* as the *Saxons of England*, even in the ancient period, and since the revival of the word in modern English, it has been commonly taken in that sense. Surely there is no historical reason against that "desynonymizing" of the three words *English*, *Saxon*, and *Anglo-Saxon*, which has actually taken place, applying *English* to the present mixed language, restricting *Anglo-Saxon* to its original sense, the Teutonic people and language of Alfred and that part of English derived from them and co-ordinate with Anglo-Norman, and leaving *Saxon* as the general name of Old Saxon and Anglo-Saxon. Nor need we fear that students who are grounded in the elements of English, will not be naturally led from the study of the Saxon elements to the study of the Anglo-Saxon tongue.

From a scientific point of view it does not seem to be a good time now for special English scholars to discard this old set of names. They had better wait a little, till the science of language shall adopt some uniform systematic nomenclature for all languages and dialects.

A Universal Language

No thought is more firmly fixed in the minds of students of language than that language grows, and that particular laws of language are laws of growth. They do not believe in the power of individuals, however great, to modify the laws of language, and they are apt to despair of effecting even slight changes. They often deplore particular defects; they write papers which point out illogical idioms or blundering and absurd spelling; but usually they close with the reflection that language is a growth, and that we must let it grow.

In this the linguists fall in with other scientists. Evolution, development, is the atmosphere of the science of to-day. In this atmosphere it is absurd to talk of one man making a language; it is doubtful whether one person can make a book of national importance. The *Iliad*, the *Odyssey*, *Beowulf*, *Kalevala*, are believed to be growths from old ballads; the Shakespeare folio is too great to have been written by Shakespeare.

A universal language must be a growth. Some national language must expand until it covers the whole world. Of late years the English language alone has been much spoken of as likely to grow so great. Hardly any philosophic linguist attempts to forecast the future without some discussion of the destiny of English; and De Candolle calculates that within a hundred years English will be spoken by 860,000,000 of men, German by 124,000,000, and French by 96,000,000. At present the populations either speaking the English language or under the domination of English-speaking peoples number more than 318,298,000, or one-fourth of the population of the globe. The English-speaking races occupy one-fourth of the dry land of the earth, and own nearly two-thirds of the tonnage of the ships. They live in all regions; they handle all articles of trade; they preach to all nations; they command one half of the world's gold and silver, and distribute more than two-thirds of the Bibles and Testaments. More than one-half of the letters mailed and carried by the postal service of the world are written, mailed, and read by the English-speaking populations. The expectation that English will come into universal use is not based upon anything in the nature of the language, but rather on the character and circumstances of the people. The English people have been the great colonizers of modern times.

"A Universal Language." *Forum* 5 (June 1888): 445-53.

They have taken possession of America, of Australia, of South Africa, the regions which are to be the seats of new empires, and they control and assimilate the populations which flow into them and which grow up in them.

All the modern language of civilized nations have grown up under influences which have led to differentiation of the meanings of words, to extension of vocabulary, and to compression and simplicity in the forms of words. The older inflected languages express an object and its relations in a single word. One or two of the syllables describe the object, the prefixes and suffixes suggest various relations in an indefinite fashion. *Môna, mônan, mônum, mônena,* are Anglo-Saxon forms of the same word. The first syllable, *môn,* môeans measurer, and describes the moon. The other syllables mean, in a vague and indefinite way, all sorts of relations in space, time, power, and thought which the moon can be imagined to have. But the discriminating intellect, working from the vague to the definite, analyzing, scrutinizing, is continually adopting separate words to express more clearly and emphatically each common relation, adopting prepositions to express each kind of relation between actions and objects, auxiliary verbs to express relations to tense and mode, and pronouns for personal relations.

But after the prepositions are established the case endings become superfluous; when the pronouns are used pronominal endings are tautological. These endings are, therefore, dropped; the languages thus change from what are called synthetic languages to analytic languages. Collision and mixture of races promote this process. The English language is the most perfect illustration of it. It begins its historic career as the literary language of the Teutonic tribes of Britain, a mixed nation of Angles, Saxons, and Jutes. We find, by comparing it with Gothic and Old High German, that it had already lost a large part of its inflection endings. A collision and mixture with the Danes followed, and then the Norman Conquest. This was the most important event in linguistic history. It brought together picked men of the two great modern stocks, the Germanic and Romanic, under the most favorable circumstances for the development of language. They lived together for a century without much mixture of speech. The Normans did not try to learn English with care; they picked up a little of it for practical needs. They knew nothing and cared nothing about being correct. It was condescension to try to make themselves understood. They never learned the case endings. Why should they take pains to get *môna, mônum, mônan, mônena,* all right? *Mône,* moon, was enough for them. The Anglo-Saxons fell into the same neglectful habits. There had been five declensions of the noun, with from three to five cases distinguished in each number, and hosts of irregular forms. Of all these forms only one was like the Norman, the plural in *s*. That they understood, and that has survived. The genitive in *s* has also survived. So far as prepositions have come into use to express the relations of the case endings, the substitution is a differentiation, a more exact expression of the thought.

The greatest gain to the language in this dropping of inflections is the simplification. There were five ways of expressing the genitive case in regular declension, besides irregular ways. The verb was worse than the noun. In the French verb there are now 2,265 terminations which must be learned by heart, 310 regular, 1,755 irregular, 200 for the auxiliaries; and all these must be connected in memory with their proper verbs. To simplify all this, to have but one set of terminations for all verbs, is an inestimable gain. A large approach to it was made in English by the collision of Saxons and Normans. The same want of attention in the Normans led to the dropping of the signs for gender, which had accompanied every noun and adjective in Anglo-Saxon. This distinction of gender is not really helpful to thought in any way once in a thousand times, and is a grievous burden to the memory. It takes more time to learn the grammatical gender of the words than it does to learn their meaning.

The same general reason led to a great abbreviation of words. Just as children catch at first the accented sounds in words, so these careless strangers were content with English sound enough to be understood. The Anglo-Saxons called the heads of the family and of the table *hlâfordas,* loaf keepers, but the Normans called them "lords," neither knowing nor caring what the word meant; so they called *heafod* "*hêd*," head, and *hafoc* "hawk." This compression, this monosyllabic habit, suited the Anglo-Saxons well. They had used it freely upon the words from Latin and Greek which they caught up from the priests. *Presbyter* is *préost,* the first time it appears in Anglo-Saxon; *episcopus* is *biscep*; *kyriake* is *circe,* church; *eleemosyna* is *ælmes,* alms. Now they began to take up Norman words freely in the same way. They took up pretty much all that are worth having, doubling the number of their descriptive words; and our language has ever since been gathering freely from Latin, Greek, and the languages of all nations with whom our people come in contact. There are perhaps 20,000 words of Anglo-Saxon origin in our present English; we have 250,000 words in all. There is also a condensation of idiom. Direct and compact phrases and sentences are gathered and remembered and make part of the wealth of the language.

Such is the process of growth which the students of language look for in the universal language. Our present English is a type of it. Jacob

Grimm, one of the most profound historians of language, and an enthusiastic lover of his native German, says:

> The English speech may with full right be called a world-language. It will go on with the people who speak it, prevailing more and more to all the ends of the earth. In richness, reason, and compression no living speech can be put beside it; not even our own German, which is torn, even as we are torn, and must first rid itself of many defects before it can enter boldly into the lists as a competitor with English.

Carrying out these laws of change, the English of the future will be completely simplified in its inflections. The relics of Anglo-Saxon declension will be made regular, the plurals "oxen," "mice," "feet," "men," and so forth, will pass away. Generations of children will be allowed to grow up saying "foots" and "mouses" and "mans." The irregular verbs will all fall into line, as they have been doing one after another since a time beyond which memory runs not back. The newspapers try in vain to force new irregularities upon the language, like "proven" for "proved." The condensation of the old words will be carried out regularly in the written as well as the spoken words: we shall write "tho" (though), "tung" (tongue), "tizic" (phthisic), "catalog," "thru" (through), and the like. We shall accept more thousands of words from Japan, China, Africa, and elsewhere. We shall pick up and invent thousands more of compact phrases and idioms.

This process may go on gradually with the advice and consent of the cultured class. There may also be new collision and mixture of nations comparable to those of the Saxons and Normans, and producing new vulgar dialects which may afterward rise to greatness. Such a dialect has in fact already arisen in eastern Asia—business English or Pigeon English. It is usually described as a grotesque or absurd jargon of English used in the cities of China in dealings of foreign merchants with the Chinese, "a ridiculous and silly expedient." It is not printed, but is taught in Chinese schools. Some students of language, however, have taken it more seriously, and claim for it the honors of the coming universal language. Mr. Simpson has done so in an article in *Macmillan's Magazine*, November, 1873, and Professor Sayce seems to agree with him in his *Introduction to the Science of Language*. In absence of inflections and general condensation it answers well, but it has a very limited vocabulary, and in that respect belongs rather to shop or technical dialect than to folk-speech proper; for it should be noticed that the views of growth which have been before stated apply to language proper, to standard folk-speech, and not to technical scientific language, or the peculiar vocabularies of arts or shops. These last are made or modified freely by agreement among the specialists concerned. The botanists, for example, have a regular system for naming and describing plants. The system is the result of laborious study and wide discussion. The privilege is given to a finder of a plant who is able to name and describe it according to the system, that his naming shall be accepted. So he who discovers a planet may name it, if he will select a name according to the system adopted by the astronomers. The chemists not only have an elaborate scientific language, but a system of writing in it by single letters representing words, and by signs of relation, so that a train of reasoning in chemistry looks something like an algebraic demonstration. Algebra and other branches of mathematics have their special languages, spoken and written. In all these modern scientific languages the object aimed at is the expression of fact, of truth. Objects are named by their essential qualities, and sets of names are systematically framed to indicate by their forms the scientific relations. The great advances of modern thought are rendered possible by the advances in scientific terminology. No one could grasp and handle the facts and relations of mathematics or chemistry or other great modern sciences, if they were written out in popular language.

Language proper, which grows, is the means of communicating the whole man, his needs, his wishes, his joys and sorrows, loves and hates, hopes and fears, passions and thoughts. Objects are named from the way they affect us, not from their essential qualities. Then genius shapes the words to beauty; the poet, the orator, arouse to heroic acts or record heroic achievements in language in which sound and sense have been fused. They add the powers of music to those of sensible signs and of the natural language of the emotions, and produce idiomatic combinations reflecting and expressing with strange perfection the most complex and subtle states of mind and heart. It requires many generations of great speakers to originate the idioms of a speech like English, and they can be mastered only by wide acquaintance with its literature. What could be made of Shakespeare by looking out in a dictionary the meanings of the words he uses? In fact very few persons do fully respond to the language of Shakespeare and know all its meaning and beauty. Many great philosophers do not; they get more from a book of mathematics or chemistry. Several noteworthy attempts have been made to produce a general language of the same type as the language of mathematics or chemistry or botany. That is to say, the attempt is made to give to all the objects of our thought names which express their essential qualities, to classify them and express their relations to each other by their forms, and to make words expressive of all possible relations. Bishop Wilkins, one of the founders of the Royal Society of London, presented to that body an essay of this sort, which was published by the society in 1668 in a handsome folio. It contains not only a language such as has been just described, but also a real character for writing it, the letters of which are taken from pictures of the organs of speech while uttering them, reminding one of Mr. Bell's visible speech. This book most likely suggested to Leibnitz the practicability of a universal scientific language. He several times speaks of it, and seems to have seriously contemplated undertaking it. Such a language would be a universal language, much as the arabic figures are, or mathematical signs.

Other attempts at a universal language for correspondence and business purposes have been made. These do not undertake a reorganization of thought, but only some selection and modification of language which may be easily learned. Volapük is a great success of this kind. It was published in 1879, by its German inventor, Johann Martin Schleyer, a Roman Catholic priest. It was first taken up in Austria, then in Holland, Belgium, and France, and since through Europe, except England. 210,000 persons are estimated to have studied it. Such a language should be constructed according to the laws which govern the growth of great historic languages, and Volapük is, in great part, so constructed. It has perfect uniformity, one way of expressing each relation, one declension, one conjugation, no exceptions, no irregular nouns or verbs. It simplifies the phonetic forms; "world" is changed to *vol,* "speech" to *pük, a* takes the place of *s* as a possessive sign, and so "world's-speech" becomes "Volapük." The vowels always have the long sound, and the accent is always on the last syllable, vō̆-lâ-pük. Each word is to have one meaning. The elementary words are to be taken from the modern languages, so as to be intelligible to the largest number of people. The largest proportion, forty per cent, are from English. All this promises a language very easy to learn. An Englishman, however, sees at once that Volapük is not simplified English. It plainly differs from English in being an inflected language, and in making words freely by composition.

Abraham ädalagom bäledani, for "Abraham saw (an) old man," is nothing like Pigeon English. It is German in its make; *log* means "eye," and the rest of *äda-log-om* puts together the proper relations for "saw." *Bäl* means "old" in some sense, and the rest of *bäledani* means "aged one" in the accusative case. There are four case forms. The verb has twelve tenses, eight modes with variations, and various voices and quasi-voices, so that over half a million of verb forms may be made from a single root. The Greek verb has 500. These forms are in great part completely unknown to students of English, and many of them are strange to classical scholars. Derivatives and compounds are freely made, and it is not easy to tell in an original writer what their meanings are, as every English speaker will conjecture who has reveled among the German polysyllables. We can think of a thousand things they might denote, but what particular thing they do denote we can only conjecture. It would seem impossible that such a word-system could be used by Englishmen. It is said, however, that the system may be learned in five minutes. It may be so; it can certainly be forgotten in five seconds. One may learn the theory of the keyboard of a piano in five minutes, but when can he play in concert?

If these German masters of Volapük were to produce a literature in it, and use all these verb forms and other forms everywhere, students of this literature would have a terrible time of it. And if the forms of expression used in the literature became standards which must be followed to write correctly, it would be next to impossible to write. But in the uses of common life it is not necessary to bring in all the niceties. A Greek child of three years talks very good Greek. Addison was surprised that the children in France spoke French so well. Any one who has been stranded in a country with unknown speech knows how easy it is to catch enough to make his wants known, and how far a few words will go, when one does not fear mistakes or try to conform to standards. It is easy enough to begin writing an English Volapük, using only forms corresponding to the English, and picking the words from the brief vocabulary. It will be intelligible to a German master, very much as the Englishman's pronunciation of the Volapük sounds is, though it may make him smile. There is, moreover, a great fascination to a bold, original, imaginative linguist, like our American Volapükist, Mr. Sprague, in using his wings in this new medium. He becomes an improvisatore, without fear of critics or comparisons, and will chant noble rhythms, sonorous, canorous as Dante's, or utter himself in oratory or witticisms as the spirit moves him.

Scholars will be apt to judge that the success of Volapük is not due to its inflective and composite structure, or any linguistic qualities, or indeed to the ease of learning it, but to external circumstances. The demand for a universal commercial medium, a universal telegraphic language and news reporter, is such that many persons see money in it. There is a large number of persons seeking clerical employment who are eager to acquire any new knowledge or dexterity which may enable them to obtain employment or advancement. The same reason which induces thousands to learn stenography and type-writing leads also to trying Volapük. It is claimed that there is, or will be, a great demand for Volapük clerks.

It would be easy to prepare a commercial vocabulary selected from English words now current, spelled according to a simple and reasonable system, and with the verbs and nouns made uniform in their inflection. This would make a universal commercial language, intelligible at once to the ninety millions of English-speaking people all over the world, and fifty times more easy for other peoples to learn than Volapük is at present. The difficulty of introducing such a speech is national jealousy. If Volapük can overcome this, it may well spread. If it does spread it will, of course, be much modified, and almost certainly will slough off a large part of its inflectional apparatus. It will be watched with the highest interest by all linguistic scholars. It is impossible that any artificial language should be worked out and established in use in our day without making most important additions to the knowledge, the resources, and the powers of the race.

On Lexicography

March's close contact with Noah Webster undoubtedly influenced many of his ideas about lexicography and, for that matter, about spelling reform. As noted in the Introduction, March had heard Webster speak at Amherst, where March had studied under Webster's son-in-law, William Chauncey Fowler. It is difficult to exaggerate Webster's profound effect on American thinking about language, especially regarding the equal status given American English as compared to British English. Webster's openness to and encouragement of the more simplified American spelling (reflected as early as his *American Spelling Book*, 1783) was important, to be sure; this book has never been out-of-print and its total sales have been estimated to exceed 100,000,000. *The American Spelling Book* was one of three parts to be included in *A Grammatical Institute of the English Language* (1785), along with a grammar and a reader.

But the publication of Webster's two-volume *American Dictionary of the English Language* was even more influential, especially in its premise that English grammar, spelling, and even usage should be based on language as it was actually used by its speakers rather than on inflexible rules. In 1806 Webster published *A Compendious Dictionary of the English Language*, with 5,000 more terms defined than Samuel Johnson had in his 1755 work; it was the first work to distinguish between *i* and *j* and between *u* and *v* in its alphabetical sequence. This work was barely published before Webster embarked on research for his *magnum opus*, his *American Dictionary*, which was published in 1828 when he was 70. He spent much time in Cambridge (England) and in Paris delving into materials in some 20 languages that were unavailable in the United States. The edition of 2,500 copies designated for sale in the U.S. and 3,000 for sale in England was exhausted in about a year even though it was attacked widely for its "Americanisms," notably American spelling and usage. The work contained about 70,000 entries, some 30,000 to 40,000 not found in any competing dictionary, and received a second edition in 1840.

March was certainly aware of the principles underlying the preparation of a major dictionary that departed from previous lexicographical principles, not only from his undergraduate exposure to Webster's ideas but also from his close comparisons of Webster's influential work with such competing dictionaries as that by Joseph Emerson Worcester (1784-1865). His expertise in lexicography culminated in subsequent posts as director of American readers for the *Oxford English Dictionary* and consulting editor for *The Standard Dictionary.*

English Lexicography

An American Dictionary of the English Language. By NOAH WEBSTER, LL.D., etc., etc. Revised and enlarged by Chauncey A. Goodrich, Prof., etc. With pictorial illustrations, synonyms, etc., etc. Springfield, Mass.: G. & C. Merriam. 1860.

A Dictionary of the English Language. By Joseph E. Worcester, LL.D. Boston: Hickling, Swan & Brewer. 1860.

It is said that the dictionary department of the British Museum occupies nearly a mile of shelf-room; a fair proportion of these works are English dictionaries and glossaries, and yet the demand for more is as urgent as ever. There are two reasons for this constant renewal.

The first is the continual change of the language. Mr. Herbert Coleridge has just published a glossarial index to the printed English Literature of the 13th century. It appears as part of the machinery to be used in the preparation of the complete *English Dictionary* which is to be published under the care of the Philological Society of London, and it may be relied on as accurate. A writer in one of the German Quarterlies[1] finds that the proportion of obsolete to living words, gathered from an examination of the words beginning with R in this specimen is 31 to 49, and that there are 163 of Teutonic origin (including Scandinavian) to 77 of French or Latin origin, while in the authorized version of the English Bible, judging from a corresponding portion of Cruden's *Concordance*, 74 are Teutonic, and 211 French. Besides these changes in the household speech, the general relations of which may be seen stated pretty definitely in Marsh's *Lectures on the English Language*, pp. 118+, the continual making or adoption of new words in science and art soon calls for a new dictionary. The insensible but ceaseless change in pronunciation and spelling also demands after a time a new standard in those matters.

A second reason for publishing so many dictionaries is found in the progress of philological learning. There are three definite stages in the

---

"English Lexicography." *American Theological Review* 27 (August 1860): 444-56.

[1]*Jahrbuch für Romanische und Englische Literatur*. Berlin: March, 1860.

growth of any inductive science. First, a period of mere accumulation of facts; then a period of the discovery of the general outlines of a science and the use of the facts rather as illustrations, than proofs; and last comes the full development and proof of all the intermediate principles and laws of the science from a sufficient induction of well established facts. Philology, which rested so long in the first of these stages, has within the last thirty years been advancing with marvelous rapidity through the second to the last stage. In no language have the popular general dictionaries at all kept pace with it. We believe that our American dictionaries may challenge a comparison with any others published for general use in any modern language. They are inferior in proper linguistic merit to some of those published in Germany; but their compass, unscientific it may be, but convenient, their cheapness, and their general popular value, make them on the whole equal to any, while they are vastly superior in every respect to most.

The Americans are said to be better linguists than the English, to speak foreign tongues more easily and accurately, to translate more skilfully; and our mixed races and free-and-easy intercourse with all mankind, look that way. We have some reason to be proud of our classical grammars and dictionaries, and of our investigation of the language of the aborigines of this country; Crosby, Harrison, Anthon, and Pickering are good names every where. But Noah Webster had a genius for linguistic investigations which has not been surpassed by any English lexicographer or grammarian. The dictionaries before his time were in the first stage of philology, unorganized accumulations of facts. Webster caught the spirit which was beginning to move in France and Germany, and advanced from Horne Tooke to the second stage. He grasped the general principles of etymology; that certain root-sounds have a definite sense which is the radical sense of all words into which they enter; that the growth of words goes on according to regular laws both of sense and sound; that the various meanings of a word should be developed from the radical meaning according to the regular laws of philological suggestion; that all languages have like roots and laws, so that a comparison of all should be made to throw light on all, and on language in general; that letters of the same organ interchange so that the recognizing of kindred words is no guess-work.

Noah Webster's life was nobly spent in reörganizing English lexicography in view of these principles. But he was not a linguist only, he was a patriot in the times of the revolution, a friend of Hamilton, Jay, and Pickering, an active supporter of Washington and the constitution, and he kept in mind the wants of the American people. The merits and defects of his great work are accordingly characteristic of America. His independence is so,—running sometimes into love of innovation; any Englishman of that day would have simply amended and enlarged Johnson and Walker.

This is on the whole a great merit. We have already said that it advanced the philological stand-point a whole stadium. It has also aided greatly in the improvement of the language. It is often said by those who love old ways, and still adhere, or imagine they do, (nobody does,) to the complex spelling and huddled pronunciation of Walker, that we do not want an American dictionary. It is true that we do not want Americanisms as such; but where the greater independence of our character, and the more acute linguistic feeling of our people, bring us to the scholarly regularity and simplicity which all thinkers commend, more rapidly than the English, we are stupid indeed to be ashamed of it. Our lawyers pride themselves on the fact that our character and circumstances enabled us at once to rid ourselves of a thousand useless complexities in the common law practice, and the English are slowly following us, as they are able. There is no reason why we should drag on the "ick," "our," and "ll,"[2] any more than the lumber of the law.

The encyclopedic character of the dictionary is also characteristic of America. It is often said that the scientific explanations are in great part out of place; that men of science will consult special treatises, and that others do not care for them. We think this is a mistake. We read every thing, and know every thing to the talking-point; but do not pretend to know many things in precise detail. This may be a defect of character, but it demands encyclopedic dictionaries. There is a wholesome demand for such books even among scientific men. They cannot purchase treatises on all the subjects of which their daily reading and conversation lead them to wish occasional general knowledge. It is this very feature which has most promoted the universal sale of *Webster* and *Worcester*. The poorest citizen of the United States reads his newspaper and hears his "congressman" give an account of himself, and his preacher deliver learned sermons; and he needs and buys his large dictionary.

[2]A writer in the *Boston Christian Examiner* for May, 1860, who uses the words "Sanscrit," and "Keltic" with apparent familiarity, speaks of "*equaled*" as being introduced by Dr. Webster on the usage of his own writing-desk. The word occurs five times in Milton's *Paradise Lost*, and is spelt every time with one l. It is well known, or should be, that the uniform "ll" in books recently printed in England is due to the printers. The same writer rejects the comparison of Hebrew with English as a Matherism (Cotton Mather). We will not ask in what lexicographers he studied his Hebrew Bible; that is plainly taking too much for granted; but did he never happen to look into Bunsen's *Philosophy of Universal History*?

The great compass of vocabulary, the illustrative engraving, are both called for by the same national peculiarities; and the comparative philology, even the Hebrew and Ethiopian words, are not lost on book-buyers. *Webster*'s corresponding Hebrew words are sometimes laughed at; but we suspect they have been looked at as often as any others, except the Latin and Greek. Our ministers all study the Bible, most of them, more or less of it in the Hebrew. There is probably more Hebrew scholarship, in extent, we know not if in depth, in this country, than in Germany, certainly much more than in any other country. The earnest study of the Bible by all classes during the formative period of our language and its whole growth has given to our devout speech a cast of the Hebrew idiom. As to particular words, no one supposes that the English are often derived from the Hebrew; but the striking resemblances between them which have long been noticed in our English dictionaries, and which are now carefully pointed out by the best Hebrew scholars, Gesenius, for example, excite the more thought. A more extended knowledge of language will enable us to base these resemblances in some historical connection, genuine, however remote. It seems to us that no scholar who compares the resemblances in language and other marks of race of the Shemitic and Indo-European stocks to each other, and then to other stocks, can doubt their comparatively near consanguinity. *Webster's* dictionary, then, is suited to the uses of the American people, and well deserves the popularity it has attained. It is in its definitions, however, that its greatest worth is found. His attempt to deduce all of the meanings of each word from one fundamental idea according to uniform laws of suggestion, naturally led him to describe the ideas to be defined and not to be content with synonyms, and also led him to anticipate the changes of meaning in individual words, and to be prepared with distinctions carefully elaborated. His success has been universally acknowledged both in this country and abroad. The *Edinburgh Review* for April, 1859, in a discussion of this subject says: "We should like to meet with a lexicographer equally brief, terse, and lucid in his definitions with the indefatigable Dr. Noah Webster; but we should prefer one who would give us fewer words, and a greater number of illustrative quotations."

We have already said that the progress of modern philology has left *Webster* far behind. It has rapidly wrought out subordinate principles and details, and brought together historic proofs from every quarter. The first great advance was in taking up the relational words and parts of words in the Indo-European languages as a separate study. The primitive prepositions, conjunctions, suffixes, prefixes, and pronouns, were found to have a peculiar character and history, and a striking phonetic relationship to each other. They could be easily examined in many lights, and traced with certainty to an indefinite past. Their small number however is perhaps the most important point, for that has permitted a thorough study of them through the whole range of their languages. A man who is to write a book on the terminations—t, d, th, will collect and clear up his facts, concentrate his thoughts and bring out principles and laws, which he who flutters from word to word will never see. Meantime another class of inquirers have been tracing the actual meanings and various forms of words through the manuscripts of the middle ages, and books as rare as manuscripts, and so setting aside many ingenious and formerly probable derivations of particular words. Laborers in both these directions, and in the physiology of speech, and the comparison of languages, have discovered new laws of the growth of languages, and more precise statements of their rules and analogies; and the students of modern philology now look to find in a dictionary, which they will accept as satisfactory, a thoroughly scientific method, and an incorporation of the whole history of the words, as well as their relationships.

We have said that *Webster* does not satisfy them. We must say the same of *Worcester*. His is a noble book; a monument of thorough and intelligent labor which its author may well be proud of; a credit to the American press, and to the American people, who having *Webster*, still demand more; but its merits are the same, in general, as those of *Webster*. It has not advanced the philological stand-point. This country hardly affords the means to do it; we have not the manuscripts, or old books; nor could one man do such a work. The Philological Society, which we have referred to before, by the aid of scholars in every part of England and America, will have all the earliest printed books in English, and all the classic English authors since, thoroughly read, and quotations made from each, containing all the words, phrases, idioms, and varieties of form in it now obsolete, and all there occurring for the first time in our literature; also all passages which give information of the first use of a word, or a new use of an old word, or which discuss or reveal the etymology of a word or the rationale of a name, or which contain happy definitions or explanations, or throw light on the relations of synonyms, or on the early uses and successive modifications of meaning through which any words have passes.[3] They also invite assistance from every quarter for the etymological department, which they promise to treat with a thoroughness, and scientific method, as yet entirely unknown in English lexicography.

We give a few examples of the kind of matter which they wish:

[3]*Proposals of Phil. Soc.*, pp. 8-10.

PROVERBS.

"In olde termys it is found,
He that lovythe me, lovythe my hound,
And my servant also."
Early Engl. Misc. (Warton Club) p. 62 (15th cent.)

IDIOMATIC PHRASES.

Strong death=violent death.

"The he (king Gowan) destroyed al this lond and the cristen peple that was in much Britayn so that no man was so hardy for to name God, and he that so dyd anone he was put to *strong death.*"—1480, Caxton's *Chronicle*, c. 52.

To save his bacon.

"He was resolved to take a course like the soldier in Terence, *to save his Bacon.*"—Trans. Milton's *Defence of the People of England*, ed. 1698, p. 561.

IMPERFECT NATURALIZATION.

Criterion.

"Lastly, from this philosophy it is also manifest that sense is not the *κριτήριον* of truth concerning bodies themselves, if confidently pronouncing that these supposed qualities of bodies represented such by sense are merely phantastical things."—Cudworth's *Intellectual System*, p. 47. (1678.)

THE FIRST INTRODUCTION OF A WORD.

Tulip.

"And now within these foure years (1578–82) there have been brought into England from Vienna in Austria divers kinds of flowers called *Tulipas.*"—Hakluyt's *Voyages*, vol. ii. p. 165, ed. 1598.

Humiliate, Civilization.

"I asked him (Johnson) if *humiliating* was a good word. He said he had seen it frequently used, but he did not know it to be legitimate English. He would not admit *civilization,* but only *civility.*"—Boswell's *Johnson* ætat. 63, (1772.)

SYNONYMOUS WORDS.

Symulacres and *Ydoles.*

"But betweene *Symulacres* and *Ydoles* is a great difference, for *Symulacres* ben ymages made aftre lyknesse of men or of women, or of the sonne or of the mone, or of ony best, or of ony kyndely thing; and ydoles is an ymage made of lewed wille of man, that man may not fynden among kyndely thinges; as an ymage, that hath 4 hedes, on of a man, another of an hors, on of an ox, or of sum other best, that no man hathe seen aftre kyndely disposicioun."—1366, Sir John Maundeville, *Voiage and Travaile*, reprint, 1839, p. 164.

Keenness and *Subtlety.*

"Few men of genius are *keen,* but almost every man of genius is *subtle.* If you ask me the difference between *keenness* and *subtlety,* I answer that it is the difference between a point and an edge. To split a hair is no proof of subtlety, for subtlety acts in distinguishing differences, in showing that two things apparently one are in fact two; whereas to split a hair is to cause division, not to distinguish difference."—Coleridge, *Table-Talk*, p. 148.

Fancy and Imagination.

"The *fancy* brings together images which have no connection, natural or moral, but are yoked together by the poet by means of some accidental coincidence; . . . the *imagination* modifies images and gives unity to variety; it sees all things in one, il più nell uno."—Id. ibid. p. 327.

"The *fancy* sees the outside, and is able to give a portrait of the outside, clear, brilliant, and full of detail. The *imagination* sees the heart and inner nature, and makes them felt; but is often obscure, mysterious, interrupted in its giving of outer detail."—Ruskin, *Modern Painters*, vol. ii. pp. 157, 158.

EARLIER MEANINGS.

Brat=child (without contempt.)

"O Israel, O household of the Lord,
O Abraham's *brats,* O brood of blessed seed,
O chosen sheep, that loved the Lord indeed!"

Gascoigne, "de profundis." (Trench, *Glossary*, p. 22.)

Imp=youth (in a good sense.)

"The king returned into England with victory and triumph; the king preferred there eighty noble *imps* to the honor of knighthood."—Stow, *Annals*, 1592, p. 385.

Paramour (in a good sense.)

"To his moder then gan he (Christ) say,
'For this mylke me muste day,
It is myn kynde therwith to play,
My swete moder, myn *paramour.*' ?"

Songs and Carols from a 15th cent. MS., Warton Club, 856, p. 48.

It will be seen that this great book is likely to be a thesaurus, or statistical history of the language, for the use of philologists; certainly not a dictionary for the people. After it shall be completed, there will be just as much need as there is now of works on the same general plan as *Webster* and *Worcester*. The owners of *Webster* owe it to the public to give us thoroughly revised and improved editions of it, and such editions will continue to pay as long as they are faithfully made. The main defects of *Worcester*, aside from its want of a thoroughly scientific method, grew out of the necessity of differing from *Webster*. There appears a bias against *Webster* in smallest matters, a disposition to occupy space with his supposed mistakes, which is a defect; but in regard to general treatment, and definitions especially, the necessity of differing in order to avoid a trespass on the copy-right, is a very serious draw-back. The merit of *Webster*'s definitions is such, that, until another philological genius shall appear, with so superior a method that it will be right for him to work into his own book the particular statements of *Webster*, we cannot hope to have a popular dictionary which shall equal *Webster* as a whole.

Yet the successive additions to *Webster*, which are pieced on at the beginning and end, do not equal in general convenience the continuous order of *Worcester*; and, this last, as having some new etymological details, as giving more information about pronunciation, and, as the latest, largest, handsomest book, will be sure to crowd its predecessor from much of its use, or compel the publishers to re-cast it speedily. We trust they will re-cast it at once. There is plenty of room for great improvements without changing its popular character, or increasing materially the bulk or cost of the book. A dictionary of this kind ought to be in one volume, not too large to be lifted with one hand. *Webster* and *Worcester* are now full-grown. The improvements which we now have in mind, would constitute an attempt to tell us how all the words stand related to the general usage of the language, that is, to its principles and laws. Dictionaries should be repositories of facts, of usage; but not simply of separate facts or usage in regard to individual words. General facts or truths, general usage or laws of the language, should be every where recorded.

To illustrate from the department of pronunciation: what is meant by saying that usage must decide it? Not that a count of Englishmen is to be taken, and the majority or plurality of tongues is to rule. The great majority have no fixed way of speaking; but would shift from day to day on hearing a new mode of speech, or being told they are wrong. Some do and must count more than others. In old times the king set the fashion for the court, and the court for the nation. So Vaugelas defined good usage in France, "C'est la façon de parler de *la plus saine partie de la cour,* conformément a la façon d'ecrire de la plus saine partie des auteurs du tems;" and in England, Chesterfield's advice in his *Letters to His Son*, to avoid the pronunciation of "obleege" as affected, restored the i in oblige to its original rights; though, according to Walker, before the publication of the *Letters*, twenty years after they were written, the proper sound of the i had come to be used only by the lowest vulgar. So Fowler tells us that the pronunciation of *wound,* as if spelled *woond,* was "a provincialism until Lord Chatham, in the height of his popularity, used it in the enthusiasm of debate, whether by mistake or not, and thus gave it currency, first on the stage, and then among the people." The stage has been a weighty authority in England. Walker watched the actors. Kemble is said to have corrected the Prince of Wales for saying *obleege.* "It will become your royal mouth better to say oblige."

In America neither President, nor Senators, nor actors, as such, are authority. In some very fashionable circles there may be a setting of the mouth by the lion of the day; but such circles have a very short radius. In some neighborhoods the "first families" still preserve, in certain words, as a mark of gentility, the traditional pronunciation of the times of Queen Anne; and the servants, still more conservative and aristocratic, hold to that of the time of Elizabeth; but the mass of the American people have dictionaries, and use them. They make small account even of their teachers and preachers, when they find them in conflict with *Webster* and *Worcester*. This universal reference to book authority is an important fact. The true American, especially the Yankee, seems to have a natural set against the authority of *persons*. He is apt to speak or act contrary to any such authority for independence's sake; but let him see it in a book, then he knows it, as he phrases it, "on his own hook," and feels as independent in the use of it, as though it were an original invention of his own. It is the Protestant spirit: no man's dictum, but our own reading of the book. We are reasoners from first principles in law, politics, theology; and the mass of the people are fully up to the idea that there are principles, that there is a right and wrong in regard to language; and if the dictionaries pointed out which is the correct *pronunciation*, for example, according to analogy, nine out of ten of our teachers and preachers at least would prefer to go with preponderating analogy, rather than with preponderating personal authority. At any rate, we are sure that information about the laws and principles involved in doubtful cases of this kind, would be just as acceptable to the multitude of dictionary users as to students of philology. It is only by the cultivation of such a spirit that we can hope to see regularity and uniformity in language prevail. Mere usage, as distinct from laws of usage, can never be a guide to uniformity.

We will make the following suggestions for a new *Webster* or *Worcester*:

1st. Pronunciation. The different modes should be given with the authorities for each, as in *Worcester*; and the one which is preferable on the ground of common use should be indicated; but there should be some designation, by style or type, invariable order, or otherwise, of the pronunciation which conforms to analogy, and this should be given with every word, whether there is any *authority* for it or not.

2d. Spelling. All forms known to have been in use should be given with authorities; that form which is now in most general use should have its indication as such; but there should be a designation by type, order, or otherwise, of the spelling which most conforms to analogy, and to etymological truth; and this spelling should be given with every word, whether there is any *authority* for it or not.

3d. Etymology. (a) The historical portion of the etymology should be distinctly separated by its type, or otherwise, from the comparative philology; and it should be a special point, uniformly labored, to point out the connection of the successive steps in the history of each word from its first known germ to its present use. Then the corresponding words in other languages may be given in different type, uniformly arranged according to the nearness of their kinship, in as great numbers as the publishers are willing to print. (b) With each word should be printed, in different styles of type, or otherwise, plainly and uniformly distinguished, its prefix, root, suffix, euphonic letters, orthographic expedients; and (c) wherever there is obscurity, a statement of the meaning, to show how the root, prefixes, and suffixes are combined in the sense. (d) If a combination of root and prefix or suffix in any word is against law, that also should be marked, and a legitimate combination given. (e) If a combination of root and prefix or suffix in any word is not used in the legitimate meaning of such a combination, that, too, should be marked. (f) If the change in the run of meanings is out of the ordinary etymological association of ideas, that, too, should be noted and explained. (g) If the euphonic letters or orthographic expedients are irregular, it will be shown in the spelling, and should be explained, if possible, by pointing out the origin of the blunder.

4. Relational words, prepositions, prefixes, etc., should have thorough separate discussions; be systematically treated in the categories of space, time, cause, etc., and their uses under each category carefully illustrated by many examples. Their uses in phrases and idioms should be given and explained with special care. Here lie the vital energies of the language.

A book which should try to give such details as these would not, of course, be received without much dissent; but it may be hoped that the criticism of it would be taken up by philologists, and turn on the discussion of the laws of the language, and not be, like too much of that on *Webster* and *Worcester*, a mere ebullition of odium orthographicum, or œorthoëpicum. This, as Archdeacon Ilare says, in a note-worthy article on English Orthography in the *Philological Museum*, (i. 640,) like the odium theologicum, to which alone it is second in virulence, rests mainly upon ignorance. "We spell so and so without well knowing why; except that all the world spells so; and we are angry with any body who spells otherwise, because he pretends to have a reason, when we have none. * * * * What we cannot grasp we peck at; and through a dread of having to acknowledge any deficiency in ourselves, we eagerly accuse our neighbors of the most revolting faults." It is time that this spirit should feel itself out of place in discussions of language. Let us have articulate reasons.

Review of *Noah Webster*, by Horace E. Scudder

*Noah Webster, b*y Horace E. Scudder. Boston: Houghton, Mifflin & Co. 1882.

The second volume of "American Men of Letters" is devoted to Noah Webster, and very fitly. He was not great in belles-lettres; but there is no American who has devoted himself more completely to book-work, or left a deeper mark by it on the English language, or won a wider fame. Mr. Scudder's book is not a common biography. It does not trace the life of Webster from year to year and from place to place; nor is it an attempt to present an elaborate picture of him at his literary work, such as we have of Southey and Gibbon, and of his brother lexicographers, Johnson, Grimm, and Littré. It is more like a very long magazine article on Webster and his times. A good many important facts in his life are given in one place or another, too often without dates, and they are told in a pleasant style, and in such order and form as to be interesting to a casual reader, if not altogether satisfactory to a statistician. There are somewhat extended descriptions and estimates of his principal works.

A large part of the book, however, consists of discussions of the literary and scholarly condition of New England and New Englanders, and other matters which might belong to a description of the times of Webster, but which are so little connected with him as to look like padding, and to make the impression that the writer has found Webster himself rather a meagre subject. This effect is increased by the attitude and tone of the author. Mr. Scudder writes of Webster and his times with a certain playful condescension. Webster distinguished himself at Yale College. President Stiles's mention of this leads Mr. Scudder to say: "Each college made believe very hard that its students were scholars, and its scholastic life the counterpart of historic universities." That is hardly a graphic description of Yale and Harvard. In 1812 Mr. Webster betook himself to Amherst with his apparatus, and devoted himself wholly to researches for his dictionary. The ten years that he spent there were the great years of his literary life. Mr. Scudder's description of it is: "He had withdrawn himself into the wilderness." That is hardly a graphic descrip-

Review of *Noah Webster*, by Horace E. Scudder. *Nation* 34 (May 25, 1882): 449-50.

tion of Amherst. Webster records that he was musician in a college military company which escorted General Washington from New Haven; whereupon Mr. Scudder:

> "The last sentence is a faint hint at an amusing and pardonable little vanity of Webster's, who, as the reader will discover later, liked to think he had a hand in pretty much every important measure in the political and literary history of the country in those early days, and remembered that when the great Washington appeared, Webster was ready with the prelusive life."

Webster graduated in 1778, nineteen years old. His father was a descendant of Governor Webster, of Connecticut, and still lived on the family farm. His mother was a descendant of William Bradford, the Plymouth Governor. They sent Noah to college, but after he graduated he had to teach school for a while. Mr. Scudder pursues him through life with pleasantries and criticism turning on his being a schoolmaster. He gives him faint praise as a statesman, though Jefferson mistook his work for Hamilton's. He says "such men as Belknap and Hazard [Mr. Scudder's representative authors of the day] looked with disdain upon him; they felt rather than said that Webster was not one of them." "So, when living in Hartford, Webster was not identified with the circle of Hartford wits." One of Webster's latest works was an edition of the Bible "purified from obsolete, ungrammatical, and exceptional words and phrases"—as to which Mr. Scudder tells us:

> "He is a schoolmaster in this business, squaring Elizabethan English to suit the regularity and uniformity of language which have been the dream of all schoolmasters." "He had not, in such a work as this, the qualifications of a scholar; he had simply the training of a schoolmaster."
>
> "I wonder if one of those scholars [the recent revisers] who signed the non-committal endorsement of Webster's Bible may not, in the midst of his recent labors, have contrasted in his mind the learned company to which he belonged with the schoolmaster who offered a Bible 'purified from the numerous errors.'"

In taking this attitude and tone toward American life and toward the hero of his book, Mr. Scudder does not seem to be influenced by any unhappy temper or by want of knowledge. He has fallen in, shall we say ? with the fashion of depreciating the greatness of our history and the qualities of our people. It is the fashion also for biographers to assume the air of specialists pronouncing impartial judgments from lofty heights above their subjects—an ungracious fashion. The air of a great specialist may be assumed, but the substance of his utterance cannot be. Cautious and moderate praise of our great lexicographer from Curtius or Whitney would do him honor; condescending commendation from Mr. Scudder is belittling to him. An old-fashioned enthusiastic account of Webster by a thoroughgoing hero worshipper would make a more truthful impression of his character and his relations than this volume by Mr. Scudder.

Review of *Webster's International Dictionary of the English Language*

Webster's International Dictionary of the English Language, being the Authentic Edition of *Webster's Unabridged Dictionary*, Comprising the Issues of 1864, 1879, and 1884, now thoroughly Revised and Enlarged under the Supervision of NOAH PORTER, D.D., LL.D., of Yale University, with a Voluminous Appendix. Springfield, Mass.: G. & C. Merriam & Co., 1890, pp. xcviii, 2011.

"*Webster's International Dictionary*, the Authentic Unabridged, revised and enlarged." This looks like the origin of a new species. The genus *Webster* appeared in the form of *An American Dictionary*, with American writ large, and a patriotic preface setting forth the necessity for it. The volumes of 1828 have grown to great bulk, and, under the skillful hands of G. & C. Merriam, given rise to many varieties. The *Unabridged Webster* has become an authority among all English speaking peoples. And so the time has come for an *International Dictionary*. The copyright upon the original *Webster's Unabridged* has expired and strange publishers have reprinted it and are selling it at cheap prices as the genuine *Unabridged*. The first use that many a man will make of the Authentic *Unabridged* will be to look up *authentic*. The editors would have saved many a worry if they had given their title as an illustration under the meaning of *authentic* which they intend it to bear.

The Merriams are, in good comity and morals, entitled to claim for the *International* its due succession to the authority, the rights, and honors of the *Unabridged*. The success of the *Webster* books has been greatly due to them. The *International* has been prepared, they say, to meet "the severer requirements of a new generation." The work upon it has been in progress over ten years, not less than one hundred persons have done paid editorial labor on it, and more than $300,000 was expended in editing, illustrating, type-setting, and electrotyping it before the first copy was printed.

Review of *Webster's International Dictionary of the English Language*. *Educational Review* 1 (1891): 288-92.

The general character of *Webster's Dictionary* is familiar to every one. It tries to give under each word just what the common reader is likely to wish to know about the word and about the objects denoted by it. Students of language have criticised it often as going beyond the province of a dictionary, mixing up the encyclopædia with it, and the like. But beyond all question it is a very convenient kind of book. Webster himself had genius in this line, a peculiar felicity in hitting on the right facts to bring in, which has been caught by the revisers and enlargers of his book. So that one who uses many dictionaries recognizes the *Webster* type at once. Several English dictionaries have been made like it with good success, and the Germans, who esteemed it so chaotic and unscholarly at first, are now publishing a German *Webster* by Moriz Heyne, one of the most efficient collaborators of the great Grimm *Lexicon*.

The first matter in the dictionary to which attention is drawn is the vocabulary. In the early editions the effort was to add new words. They ran up from 60,000 to 110,000. But now the *Century* promises 200,000 words, and Dr. Murray more than a quarter of a million. These are too many to be handled in a single volume. The old *Webster* was as large as could be raised with one hand. The *International* has been obliged to use higher powers than were required to work the drag net, to use reason, judgment, to reject and to select from these hosts. We have compared considerable portions with the *Encyclopedic* and the *Century* and Dr. Murray, and are well pleased. No words are rejected which it is plain that readers will look for; there are very few here which are not interesting to some class of readers.

Going over the columns in this way, however, the enormous number of technical terms in the natural sciences forces itself on the attention. The thousands, tens of thousands of names of natural objects, not names used in real life, but closet compounds of words fished from the Greek dictionary, many of them never uttered by any human being, stagger one when he meets them in such force. In spite of a strong prepossession in favor of having such words in *Webster*, a doubt has arisen whether this side of the vocabulary may not be overdone; whether there has not been a change, since the plan was formed, in the popular interest in these sciences of classification. Has not the Darwinism, which so stimulated interest in all living things, become rather an old story? Are not our lively minds, readers and thinkers, now turning to the proper study of mankind, man, and looking up technicalities in psychology, ethics, political economy, civics, history, literature, linguistics? It is true, however, that there has been copious cutting out of natural names and much care of the others. We do not find any single word which we wish to comment on as showing bad judgment in the admission or rejection.

The same selection and condensation has been used in the definitions. Nothing could well be better than a large part of them. But any verbal definition or description may fail to give a good idea of the object named. Here, then, are pictures to help out, greatly improved in fitness for their purpose, and greatly increased in number compared with the old *Unabridged*. For objects that cannot be pictured there are quotations which show the thought in its relations; the current phrases help out also, and they are given in large numbers. We have noted the special difficult words which have come up during the examination of the dictionary. The first word was *authentic,* which was mentioned above, the next was *copyright.* Wondering how long time the *Webster* copyright ran, I looked in the *Century* first and then in a cyclopædia without finding it, and was about to take up a law dictionary, when it occurred to me to try *Webster*. There it was, all right, simply, precisely stated: Twenty-eight years with a renewal of fourteen. This is an experience which I have had a hundred times with the old *Webster*: a search through all the cyclopædias in the college library in vain, a find in *Webster* at my elbow. This quantitative definition of copyright, true scientific work, exact figures, has been added in the *International*, and is a fair specimen of it. Then *pons asinorum* turned up in the New York *Tribune.* A good many college graduates seem to remember no other demonstration in geometry than the forty-seventh in Euclid, and no other title than *pons asinorum,* and they put the two together. The dictionaries are all alike about the meaning, but the *International* pleased me well by having a diagram of the fifth, the true *pons,* looking quite bridgy.

About the same time the *Sunday School Times* wanted to know whether *tireless* was a good word. It is not in the *International*, though it should be, as it is found in Bishop Heber and other classics, and is a good word every way; *untireable* will not do; nor *undauntable* for *dauntless; irresistible* might do for *resistless;* this use of—*less* is well established—*exhaustless, quenchless, etc.*, are questionless,—and it ought to be given under the suffix—*less,* but it is not in the *International.* The absence of *tireless* was doubtless an oversight as it is not in the other dictionaries, except the *Encyclopædic. Worcester* uses it, to be sure, to define *untirable. The Independent* asked about "peevy," the name of a tool for handling logs. The *International* knows it not, nor does any other dictionary, except *Bartlett.* It is a common tool in these days of telegraph poles and log-rolling generally, and its inventor, Mr. Peevy, deserves a dictionary immortality. An inquiry from England about "*condition,*" as used in

American colleges, found the verb *condition*, but not the noun *conditions,* back studies. *Tangerine,* the fruit, is given, but not *ekemis* and *elemi,* names of figs; *Kodak* and *hoodoo* have not reached the dictionaries, nor *sheeny,* which figures in one of the New York pictorials, and is in *Bartlett.* But the *International* is very good on American uses of words, and all the "questionable" current speech.

On the philological side there is considerable change in the new book. The brief history of the language by Professor Hadley, a masterly sketch, has been skillfully touched up by Mr. Kittredge, of Harvard. The introductory discussion of pronunciation has been greatly deepened and widened by Professor Samuel Porter, and stated in the language of Mr. Bell's system so far as that applies. Professor Porter is an independent thinker, and a minute and accurate observer. This introduction is a capital treatise of phonetics. A body of rules for syllabication in agreement with pronunciation is given, and the vocabulary words are carefully printed in syllables, and accented. This will please the teachers. The great phonetists may say, if they must, that syllables are imaginary divisions, and the philological dictionaries, like Dr. Murray's, may decline to indicate syllables even in the pronunciation; but they are very real in the school-room in teaching, spelling, and pronunciation. The *Webster* convention about them, even if it is nothing more than a convention,—a view which we do not accept,—has been a powerful influence upon the speech of America for distinctness and uniformity, and it is indispensable in the school-room.

The *International* respells the words for pronunciation, an acceptable addition to the old *Webster*, and it indicates the pronunciation of the unaccented syllables with a nicety never attempted in the old dictionaries. The means of indication are very ingenious, and easily understood by any one who pronounces the key words correctly. There is seldom more than one pronunciation given in the vocabulary, but there is a table of words differently pronounced. The vowel gamut is English. The scientific terms and other book words which have no folk-pronunciation are pronounced like Latin, as heard in the English method. The great number of scientific men of foreign blood among us, and of the Germanized scientists of home blood, and the Roman pronunciation of Latin in the schools, are fast rendering this pronunciation of scientific terms strange; it has always been very rare. But it would not have done for a *Webster* to displace it.

The *International* is English also in adopting lightened pronunciation, obscure and abbreviated syllables, more freely than the old *Webster*. The Southern English pronunciation of this sort has been heretofore ridiculed among us, and vigorously corrected whenever it has appeared in our schools. But the London phonetists have lately made a vigorous crusade for it as spoken English by eminence. There ought really to be a distinct recognition of two kinds of pronunciation: one, the standard literary English of oratory and pedagogy; the other, allowable weakenings in conversation. Prof. Whitney has made a notable attempt to represent both in the pronunciation of the *Century* dictionary. His scheme is certainly scientific, and it seems to be successful, a good advance beyond the single obscured pronunciation indicated as the only one in the *International.* This will embarrass many a teacher in the spelling classes, and tend to weaken the distinctness of articulation characteristic of the American schoolmistress. She will be slow to understand that *cent* does not spell *cent* in *recent,* and shrink from *resunt* as much as from *sullur.*

The etymology of the *International* is excellent; simple, clear, and according to the latest authorities. We mean the etymology in the body of the work. It is notable, however, that its relation to the rest of the work has been inverted. The world has changed since the great eponymus of the American dictionaries retired to Amherst with his houseful of lexicons, and devoted his ten best years to making a synopsis of all the languages. The well-known appendixes of proper names and phrases and all sorts of useful knowledge are retained in full force, revised and enlarged by the ablest scholars.

"Foreword" to March's *Thesaurus Dictionary of the English Language*

In London, 1852, appeared a volume entitled, *Thesaurus of English Words and Phrases, Classified and Arranged so as to Facilitate the Expression of Ideas and Assist in Literary Composition*, by Peter Mark Roget, M.D., F.R.S. It was intended to supply a collection of the words and idiomatic combinations of the English language, "arranged, not in alphabetical order as they are in a dictionary, but according to the ideas which they express," so that any one who has an idea may here find the word or words by which it may be most fitly and aptly expressed. This book has been for half a century a familiar part of the machinery used by authors, preachers, lecturers and the like. The number of such persons has lately increased rapidly. Writing also fills a larger place in our schemes of education. The students of our universities have little time for Socratic dialogue; they hand in essays day by day, and close their careers with original theses as heavy as articles in the quarterlies. Observation of the needs of the book-buying public, especially that part of it which has found use for *Roget*, has led to the thought that its material may be prepared and supplemented for a much wider sphere—one that comports better with a largely extended language and modernized form of expression.

The first shortcoming in *Roget* is that there are no definitions of the words or explanations of the phrases. The book is really an index of words to be looked up in dictionaries and cyclopedias, unless one comes to it with his mind thoroughly stored with words and meanings. Besides the single words there are collected phrases, kennings, and longer familiar quotations in English and foreign languages. These are all helpful to the literary worker. There has been a great accumulation of them in the latest dictionaries, in the *Century*, the *Stanford*, and in the *Oxford Dictionary*. The *Standard* has gone farthest in the collection of groups of words, giving, for example, groups of names of apples, and coins, and structures, and animals. The *Oxford* prints the most numerous phrases, and adds quotations containing them which ex-

"Foreword" to March's *Thesaurus Dictionary of the English Language*. Philadelphia: Historical Publishing Co., 1902, 1906, 1925, n.p.

hibit their biographies. The time seems ripe for a Thesaurus, bringing together groups of them, accompanied by concise definitions giving in each group the meaning of each word as used in the group.

Then there is difficulty with the machinery for finding any particular word or phrase. Early vocabularies often consist of groups arranged by their ideas. That of Ælfric, a tenth century Anglo-Saxon work, begins with farmers' tools all in a heap; then come ecclesiastical matters, then political, then diseases, then wild beasts, insects, vessels, a room and its contents, and so on. Nothing could be done with the materials of the *Oxford Dictionary*, or the *Century*, or *Standard*, on any such plan. Dictionaries are sometimes arranged according to a philological system. Ettmüller's *Anglo-Saxon Dictionary* has the words classified under their roots, and the roots and words arranged according to the scientific order of the sounds. The beginner has to master this order of sounds, and then to guess under what root his word belongs—or rather under what root Ettmüller thinks it belongs. He has, in fact, to learn the language to its depths before he can use the dictionary.

Roget's arrangement is primarily one of nameable objects. "It is impossible we should thoroughly understand the nature of the *signs* unless we first properly consider and arrange the *things* signified," as his motto, taken from Horne Tooke's *Diversions of Purley*. He classifies nameables, after the manner of the English psychologists, into matter, mind (intellect, volition, affections), space and abstract relations, and divides and subdivides these until he makes out an even thousand divisions, and into these he puts all the words. In order to find any word it was necessary to think out in which subdivision its idea belongs. This is worse than Ettmüller. It was necessary to add a verbal index, alphabetically arranged, with references to the groups by number. It is not easy, indeed, to find a word after you know the number of its group, for the group may contain hundreds of words in no manageable order.

The machinery of a serviceable dictionary is found in the alphabet. The invention of alphabetic writing has been often pronounced the most important ever made. It is not the least of its benefits to mankind that it affords the means of making knowledge accessible. Every one knows the letters of the alphabet. If all thoughts are arranged under their words, and the words arranged in alphabetic order, any one can find off-hand any of the million facts and thoughts which are stored in the dictionary. The use of the simple alphabetic order is almost as important an invention as the representation of words by single signs of their elementary sounds.

The material of this Thesaurus has been brought to alphabetic order. Our publisher suggested that it be called a THESAURUS DICTIONARY, believing that the word "Thesaurus" will easily assume the meaning of *groups*, and "Dictionary" that of *alphabetic arrangement.*

In using the THESAURUS DICTIONARY, look up any word connected with your subject in its alphabetic place in the vocabulary list in larger black type, exactly as in a common dictionary. *Anger*, for example, is found thus on page 45. It is there briefly defined as a violent passion, and two groups to which it belongs are then mentioned in small capitals, EXCITABILITY-INEXCITABILITY and FAVORITE-ANGER. To study the first group turn to EXCITABILITY-INEXCITABILITY in its alphabetical place in the general vocabulary, page 372. There, under this heading, are two parallel columns, the left-hand for EXCITABILITY, the right for INEXCITABILITY, each running on for a couple pages and bringing together some one hundred and fifty words and phrases. These are divided into nouns, verbs, verbal phrases, adjectives, etc., arranged in alphabetic order. The first column contains all words and phrases naturally associated according to the laws of similarity, contiguity and comprehension,—synonyms and the like; the second column contains a similar group related to the first column according to the law of contrast,—antonyms, polar opposites, and the like. By means of cross-references, other groups of associated meaning are brought to the attention.

A large collection of groups like these, printed without alphabetic order and without definitions, notes or comments, constitutes the *Thesaurus* of Roget or the *Dictionnaire Idéologique* of Robertson. It is obvious that this is really an index of words to be studied in other dictionaries, unless the student be thoroughly stored beforehand with words and meanings.

An attempt has been made in this volume to give the less accomplished student further help in his handling of the groups, and his use of them for original work. In the first place the words and phrases are defined. The dictionaries try first to state, with exactness and clearness, the thought for which each word stands. The student of literature or oratory knows that putting together these dictionary definitions does not give the full force of the great passages. When words are idiomatically put together, the combination is not agglutinative; relations between the words appear, and the result is not a mechanical compound, but chemical, or, rather, vital, especially when the melody of the voice is added.

The definition is an idea, a solid intellectual center; the emotions which have been felt with it rise in memory with it, and give it an aureole, a halo, a nimbus, a glory, spheres of radiance. A word is thus a living power, with an individuality embodied in its root and affixes. It has a history; it has a character derived from its history. Every familiar phrase in which it occurs, every great passage in literature in which it is found, every great occasion with which it is associated, every honored name with which it is connected adds to its charm. Every happy phrase in Gray's "Elegy in a Country Churchyard" adds to the charm of every other. Every resonant word in the Declaration of Independence, or in Webster's Speech for Liberty and Union, has new power, and when the great orator repeats the magic words of Milton and Shakespeare he redoubles their harmonies. Every kind of favorable influence combines to strengthen and beautify the moving idiom of our English Bible.

In order to aid workers in literature to perceive and enjoy these associations, the definitions here given are often turned so as to suggest the original thought of the word, the beginning of its history, especially if it is derived from the name of some person or place worthy of renown. In the group of words we have mentioned under *Excitability* are *Quixotism*, chivalry run mad in amiable madness, as in *Don Quixote* of Cervantes; *Agony*, like that of a wrestler in the Olympic games: *Patience on a monument*, defined as "smiling at grief," and given its Shakespearian grace by reference to *Twelfth Night* ii. 4. There is *Stoicism*, dignifying the "Stoic of the Woods, the man without a tear," in Campbell's *Gertrude of Wyoming*, and there are Chaucer's "making a virtue of necessity;" *Inextinguishable* laughter of the gods, from Homer, *Iliad* I, 268; *Volcanic*, like the chimney of the forge of Volcan; the Bible's *itching* ears; Shakespeare's *itching* palm; *Mens aequa in arduis*, "equanimity in difficulties," the trait of Warren Hastings recorded on his portrait at Calcutta.

In the reign of Queen Anne Englishmen spoke of living in the Augustan age of the English language; they thought it had reached perfection, and they wanted a dictionary that should record the words then in use and be a standard for future generations. Dr. Johnson's great dictionary was widely accepted as such a standard. Authors of eminence were careful not to use any word not in *Johnson*. Critics pounced upon every writer who strayed from the standard. Slang was deadly sin. The golden age was to be kept pure from it forever. There are still survivors of this period. Not long ago the *Sunday School Times* sent out an inquiry about *tireless* and some eminent authors answered that they had thought it good, but since it was not in *Worcester* or *Webster*, they would not use it.

But we have changed all that. We see that a language must change with each generation. If it is to live it must be supplied with a constant inflow of new words, of which a vital part comes from the feeling and imagination of persons who utter themselves in slang. A living language is a lake from which there is a constant flow of words to the ocean of oblivion, and which has a constant supply from the fountain of popular talk.

During the last half century more new words and phrases have poured into the English language than in any century before; new arts and new sciences have swollen the inflow. In this volume many new words will be found added to the old groups, and a number of new groups have been gathered, chiefly words of the expanding sciences, such as biology, chemistry, and electricity. These we cordially commend to the attention and use of all students.

Those who may find expressions which they recognize as living slang worthy of longer life, we advise to use it with some token, as Lord Bacon does, when he says, "It is a dull thing to tire, and, *as we say now*, to *jade* anything too far."

On Orthography

The sporadic proposals to "simplfy" English spelling one encounters today can hardly suggest the animated polarization of opinion in the later nineteenth century over such proposals. Noah Webster introduced some spelling alterations in his dictionaries to distinguish American English from British; he also justified such changes elsewhere in his writings (Webster 391-410). But the proponents of such change, of whom March was particularly prominent along with Max Müller (1823-1900), Walter W. Skeat (1835-1912), James Murray (1837-1915), Henry Sweet (1845-1912), and Otto Jespersen (1860-1945), advocated such widespread changes that it almost became an obsessive cause. Indeed, interest in and support for such change was so enthusiastic that it reached the highest levels of the American government.

An international convention was held in Philadelphia in 1876, as part of the Centennial Exposition, dedicated to "the amendment of English orthography." The Spelling Reform Association, with March named permanent president, was created by the convention, and this group in turn became affiliated with the National Educational and American Philological Association that thereafter issued periodicals and books advocating reformed spelling. Despite concerted opposition (primarily from the publishing and printing industries and ordinary citizens accustomed to traditional spelling) and limited resources, the efforts of the group resulted in numerous debates for one side or the other in editorials, essays, and books.

In 1906 Andrew Carnegie established a fund to support reformed spelling, and the Simplified Spelling Board was created with such distinguished members as Brander Matthews (Columbia University professor) as chairman, Nicholas Murray Butler (Columbia University president), Carnegie, Samuel Clemens, Melvil Dewey (library pioneer), Thomas Wentworth Higginson (author), Henry Holt (publisher), and William James (psychologist and philosopher). The Board established working principles for reform, created an initial master list of 300 words in need of such change, and persuaded President Theodore Roosevelt to issue an order to the U.S. Government Printing Office to adopt such changes and later an additional order for all branches of the federal government to do the same. Though the Printing Office complied, the judicial branch refused to do so, and the 59th Congress in its second session (December

1906) passed a resolution rejecting the changes. Recognizing the degree to which reform was a lost cause, Roosevelt revoked his order except for White House correspondence. With the change of administration, however, even this ceased to be a prominent place for spelling reform to be expressed, though numerous ventures and proposals advocating such reform continue to this day.

The claims and alleged benefits set forth for such simplification did sound utopian, as J. H. Gladstone suggested: (1) reduction in the cost of printing, (2) ease in establishing "correct" pronunciations, (3) reduction of dialects, (4) gain in philological study, (5) substitution of a "healthy" for a "vicious" form of mental training, (6) increased demand for printed materials, and (7) increasing worldwide demand for English (Gladstone 22-30 *passim*). Even Matthew Arnold supported the cause and advocated the creation in England of a permanent Royal Commission to "amend" then-current spelling (Gladstone 79). Objections, however, quickly arose; Henry Bradley, while supporting the need both for change and for compromise, noted that the "ordinary reader" would "turn away" from such "grotesque" spellings, even while finding them "amusing," and that even such an "impassioned" advocate as Skeat never used such unconventional spellings in his published writings or correspondence (Bradley 33). Harry Thurston Peck pointed out the obvious: that it is easier to "propose a new system of spelling than to get any number of sensible people to adopt it" (Peck 67); that the "squabbling" reformers could not even agree among themselves as to which of various competing systems was preferable (Peck 76); and, most crucial of all, that in time language will change anyhow, in spelling as in vocabulary, idioms, pronunciations, and structures (Peck 87).

From our perspective, it is obvious that the normalizing effects of modern worldwide communications has had much to do with creating standardized spellings and diminishing the perceived benefits of spelling reform. One of the chief advocates for orthographic change, Sweet, proved a particularly inept prophet when he claimed that any proposed changes that were to be adopted would be "unphonetic" a century later, when England, America, and Australia "will be speaking mutually unintelligible languages, owing to their independent changes of pronunciation" (Sweet 196). March's own dedication to "simplified" spelling can be seen in his insistence in many of his published papers in using the International Phonetic Alphabet (IPA), created in 1888 by the International Phonetic Association (founded in 1886).

March was indeed a true believer in such change, but he was no more reliable a prophet than Sweet in predicting inevitable, lasting reforms that never occurred. Nor was he any more consistent, for in all but a few of his many subsequent writings, March used only conventional spelling or modest variations. There were, of course, exceptions, as in his 1887 essay, "Spelling and Progress," scanned in at the end of this section so that readers might see spelling reform in its most extensive and sustained form.[1]

WORKS CITED

Bradley, Henry. *On the Relations Between Spoken and Written English.* Oxford: Clarendon P, 1919.

Gladstone, J. H. *Spelling Reform from an Educational Point of View.* London: Macmillan, 1879.

Peck, Harry Thurston. *What Is Good English? and Other Essays.* New York: Dodd Mead, 1899.

Sweet, Henry. *Handbook of Phonetics.* Oxford: Clarendon P, 1877.

Webster, Noah. *Dissertations on the English Language.* Intro. by Harry R. Warfel. Gainesville, FL: Scholars' Facsimiles & Reprints, 1951.

[1]We should point out, as we do in the Editors' Note, that March's "The Opening Address Before the International Convention for the Amendment of English Orthography" (pp. 99-112) uses phonetic symbols too difficult to reproduce here.

The Opening Address Before the International Convention for the Amendment of English Orthography

Scholars spend a great part of their time studying old books and monuments. They are apt to think of writing as a record merely. But it is really mighty machinery working for the future, the agent by which each generation is introduced to knowledge and culture. Philology prides herself on her conquest of the past, her reconstruction of history: but she should aim at the higher praise of earnest work for the future, of contributions to the progress of the race. The improvement of the reading machinery of the English language, the reform of English spelling is a great work. It is doubtful whether the welfare of the race is as much promoted by any invention of the century, whether the steam engine or the telegraph contributes as much to the progress of the people, as would the invention and introduction of a good phonetic system of spelling our language. The difference between a family who can read and one who can not, is vastly more important than the difference between a family that uses railroads and telegraphs and one that does not.

EVILS OF BAD SPELLING.

Our wretched spelling hinders our people from becoming readers in two ways, by the length of time which it takes to learn it, and by the dislike of reading which it induces. Three years are spent in our primary schools in learning to read and spell a little. The German advances as far in a twelvemonth. A large fraction of the school time of the millions is thus stolen from useful studies, and devoted to the most painful drudgery. Millions of years are thus lost in every generation. Then it affects the intellect of beginners. The child should have its reason awakened by order, proportion, fitness, law in the objects it is made to study.

"The Opening Address Before the International Convention for the Amendment of English Orthography, at Philadelphia, August 15th, 1876." Philadelphia: International Convention for the Amendment of English Orthography, 1876.

But wo to the child who attempts to use reason in spelling English. It is a mark of promise not to spell easily. One whose reason is active must learn not to use it. The whole process is stupifying and perverting; it makes great numbers of children finally and forever hate the sight of a book and reluct from all learning. There are reported to the takers of our last census 5,500,000 illiterates in the United States. One half at least of those who report themselves able to read, cannot read well enough to get much good from it. It may be held certain that good spelling would increase by millions the number of easy readers, and by millions more the number of those fond of knowledge. But moral degeneracy follows the want of cultivated intelligence. Christianity can not put forth half her strength where she can not use her presses. Republics fall to ruin when the people become blind and bad. We ought then to try to improve our spelling from patriotic and philanthropic motives. If these do not move us, it may be worth while to remember that it has been computed that we throw away $15,000,000 a year paying teachers for addling the brains of our children with bad spelling, and at least $100,000,000 more, paying printers and publishers for sprinkling our books and papers with silent letters.

ORTHOGRAPHY NOT ORTHOEPY.

We are met to reform orthography, not orthoepy; we have to do with writing, not pronunciation. There are all sorts of English people, and words are pronounced in all sorts of ways. It is the work of the orthoepist to observe all these different ways, and to decide which is the prevailing pronunciation of the most cultured, to decide which is the standard English pronunciation. The orthographer tells how to represent this pronunciation in writing. The orthoepist has many nice and difficult questions to solve. We enter into his labors. We take for granted that there is a standard pronunciation of English. We wish to see it represented by simple and reasonable alphabetic signs.

AN IDEAL ALPHABET.

The essential idea of an alphabet is that each elementary sound have its own unvarying sign, and each sign its own unvarying sound. But in a perfect alphabet the characters should be easy to write and to distinguish, and shapely; similar sounds should have similar signs, and similar series of sound should have series of signs with similar analogies of form; each character should be so shaped as to easily suggest something about the position of the organs of speech in making it; and all nations should use the same characters with similar values. Moreover, derived alphabets, being necessarily bearers of history, should be esteemed better as they incidentally embody more important history. The perfect alphabet will not press any of these incidental qualities so far as to interfere with the essential purpose of an alphabet, the easy communication of thought by signs of sound. Standard alphabets for popular use should have signs only for well established significant sounds. The vowel sounds shade into each other like colors. The consonants are made in many ways. Mr. Ellis had signs for some 300 letters, years ago. Thousands may be distinguished, and need to be, for the purpose of comparative phonology. No minuteness comes amiss to science. Different nations make different qualities of sound significant. Tones make letters for the Chinese. Length was a great matter with the early Indo-Europeans, in the Sanskrit and Greek, and the like. We have come to use stress for the old pitch, and neglect the measure of time; we make letters only on the ground of quality. Many tribes make nothing of the difference between surd and sonant; *p* and *b* are all one to them; both are made with the lips, they say. We can not be sure that any difference is so slight that no nation has exalted, or may exalt it to significance. But the general standard of a great nation must always be severely simple. It is wholly undesirable to admit in it the ever varying glides and finishes and coloring of fashionable or vulgar articulation, or even the more stable and general colorings produced by adjacent letters, as long as they are without significance. The perfect alphabet will not record etymology and history to the neglect of current sounds.

THE REAL ALPHABET.

No language has a perfect alphabet. Alphabetic writing was not invented to answer to an ideal; it is a sort of growth, or development by natural selection, from picture writing, and like other things that grow in minds without ideas, it needs making over for the use of man. Moreover, living speech is always changing, the spoken language always running away from the written.

CHANGES IN SPOKEN LANGUAGE.

Two classes of changes may be distinguished. One of single words. The letters of unaccented syllables are carelessly pronounced, and often drop out, and bring together letters which are hard to pronounce together, so that one weakens, is assimilated, or silent. Carolina tends to become Caroluna, and then Culina and Culiny and Cliny. In most languages the written words rapidly adapt themselves to these changes. As soon as scholars all stop sounding a letter in any word, they stop writing it. Such changes as affect one word at a time must go on slowly, and the written and spoken speech are not drawn far apart. The other is a general change in some elementary sound. It gets to be the fashion to utter some sound in a slightly different way from the old standard; a vowel is made closer than it used to be, or is made with a finish: every body gets to saying a for *a* (past for past) or iu for u (tiune for tune) or ei for e (feite for fete.) The change goes on until the old letter is merged in sound into some other old letter or letters, or till *a* new letter is established as significant. Changes of this class often go far without affecting the written speech. The Greek affords many familiar examples. Several sets of such changes are of interest in English.

1. The regular assimilation of letters connected in discourse, by which intermediate letters spring up between the old ones. Between *a* (*far*) and *e* (*met*) a as in *fat, fare,* has now become established; between *a* (*far*) and *o* (*no*), *o* as in *not* and *nor;* then there are the neutral vowels of *fun* and *burn*. Mute consonants under vowel influence change to continuous or spirant consonants, as *ti* to *sh* in *notion;* and surds change to sonants, as *si* to *zh* in *pleasure*. Six vowels and four consonants unknown to the early Romans have arisen in this way.

2. Another class of changes is connected with the accent. The close vowels *i* and *u* lengthen into diphthongs by taking before them the sound of *a* (*far*). The long *i* (*ai*), as in *mine,* was at first pronounced as in *machine;* the *ou* (*au*), as in *house* (Anglo-Saxon *hus*), was spelt and pronounced like *u* in *rude*. The open and mixed vowels have become closer, *a* (*far*) going to *e* (*fate*) or *o* (*wall*), *e* (*they*) going to *i* (*machine, me*) *o* going to *u* (*rule, moon*). It has thus come about that single characters stand for diphthongs, and that the short and long sounds which go in pairs in other languages are denoted by different characters in ours, and are derived from different sources.

3. These pairs, not having been associated together, have not grown so much alike as in other languages: the *e* of *met* is different in quality from its long as heard in *mey*, the *i* of *fit* from its long as heard in *fee;* so that it is doubtful whether one character will do for both, whether we must not have different characters for each short and long, after the manner of old time-observing tongues.

THE ANGLO-SAXON ALPHABET.

Our grandmother tongue, the Anglo-Saxon, had a pretty good alphabet. There was early writing in runes, but the Roman missionaries, who converted the nation, reduced the language to writing in Roman letters. They gave them the power which they then had in Latin, using *c* always like *k,* and *g* as in *go*. For sounds which did not occur in Latin they preserved runes, or used digraphs after the manner of the Celts. Runes were used for *th* and *w*. They distinguished *a* in *far* from *a* in *hat,* using *ae, æ* for the latter. They also distinguished other nice varieties of vowel shading and finish.

THE MODERN ENGLISH.

Our woes spring from the Norman conquest. Anglo-Saxon and Normans united to make the English nation, and they threw their languages into a sort of hotchpotch. Many of the words of each race were hard for the other to pronounce. They were spelt by the scholars to whom they were native, in the old book fashion, but the people did not pronounce them correctly. Many letters were left silent, or inserted to no purpose, in ill-directed attempts to represent the strange combinations. Then the great shifting already described took place in the whole gamut, so to speak, of the vowel sounds. People hardly knew what was the matter as these changes went on, and before our scholars waked up, the whole habit of writing was so far away from a phonetic one, that people ceased to feel any necessity for keeping sounds and signs together, and the scholars gave up. We attained at last a very fair approach to the Chinese idiographic system. The written words are associated with thoughts as wholes, without reference to the sounds which the separate letters might indicate. Changes in the sounds of words go on with no record in the writing. Ingenious etymologists slip in new silent letters as records of history drawn from their imagination. Old monsters, fertile in the popular fancy, propagate themselves in the congenial environment, and altogether we have attained the worst spelling on the planet. And we have been proud of it, and we are fond of it.

WHAT CAN WE DO?

What can be done for reform. We can produce dissatisfaction with the present spelling. That is easy. We can teach the people what spelling ought to be. That is harder. We can harmonize views as to the changes which are practicable, and the methods of introducing them. And then we can use reformed spelling, and get others to use it.

PREPARATORY WORK.

Much has already been done to prepare the way. Comparative philology is founded on phonetics, and no scholar ever works in this field without lamenting the condition of the English language. Most of our ablest philologists have spoken out about it. Several of the most eminent have published vigorous essays of demonstration, objurgation and appeal. Our venerable chief, the Honorable George P. Marsh, minister of the United States at Rome, Prof. Hadley, the presidents of the American Philological Association, Whitney, Trumbull, Haldeman, stand side by side with Prof. Max Müller, with presidents of the London Philological Society, with Ellis, with Pitman, Bell and other practical workers, and with all scholars, great and small, of other races.

The growth of the historical study of the English language and literature has also been of great service. It has made it necessary to ascertain the pronunciation of the language at different epochs. The difficulty of this investigation, and the singular facts which are unearthed from old gramm?rs and dictionaries, or made out by induction from the poets, or reasonings from the laws of letter change, surprise every one. The huge volumes in which Mr. Ellis has collected the materials for the study of the history of English pronunciation are impressive witnesses against the spelling in which the facts were buried. The publications of the Early English Text Society, which reproduce the spelling of the original manuscripts, similar publications of the Chaucer Society, reprints of the first folio of Shakespeare and of the early editions of Spenser, make every one familiar with many ways of spelling, and so make it easy to read in any spelling. We get used to seeing the same word spelt half a dozen ways on the same page, and are not easily startled by the most ingenious modern professor of phonetics. Modern writers in dialect like Burns and Scott, and the comic caricaturists of fashionable or vulgar slang, Dickens, Nasby, Josh Billings, all help. We make the widest guesses at the sound, which they mean to indicate, we read our Burns in Scottish which no Scot ever dreamed of, but at least they set us free from the common spelling.

Our common-school teachers have been powerful aids in producing dissatisfaction with the old spelling, especially in those parts of the country where there are German children in the schools. German parents cannot be made to understand why their children are kept in spelling books four or five years, and they complain bitterly about it. Our Superintendents, always alert and ready for improvements of every kind, have been long in earnest to find some mode of escape from the spelling plague. Teachers of Latin and Greek, and of French, German and other modern languages help. Teachers of elocution also teach systems of vocal sounds, which are passed along to teachers in the common-schools and kindergartens who train the children in reading. Many of our school primers and readers do good work by trying to introduce children to our present written language through a phonetic system. Dr. Leigh's books of this kind are used in many of our cities from New York to St. Louis, if not to San Francisco, as they might well be. Many persons learn phonetic stenography. There are a large number of teachers of it and periodicals published in its interest. Mr. Pitman's *Phonetic Journal* has a circulation of ten thousand copies.

Most persons forty or fifty years old would be astonished to learn how extensive is the preparation for a change of spelling already made in the younger generation. Add foreigners and other persons who read imperfectly and do not know but Josh Billings spells as well as any body, a great host, and it would seem that three fourths of the persons in America who are counted in our census as able to read, could read with little new embarrassment a reformed spelling having no unknown characters, while the 5,500,000 illiterates might be taught it in half the time of the old one.

SCHEMES OF REFORM.

The remedy for single words which have old silent letters standing, or blundering spelling of their own, is obvious, if not easy. Drop the silent letters. Correct the blunders. It is not easy to apply these obvious directions, because our spelling is so complex that a change can seldom be made without starting into activity some minor analogy which stops the way. Drop the silent *e* of *ripe,* it becomes *rip*. Drop one of the *t's* of *latter,* it becomes *later. Grief* has a silent letter. Is it *i* or *e?* The *l* in *could* is a mere blunder under the influence of *should* and *would;* the *o* is a modern insertion. Shall we then write *cud?* Before we can answer we must decide on the scheme of sounds which we will use. All corrections should bring the words nearer to the ideal alphabet. There are a few words in which we can not go wrong. Such are most of those with a silent *e* after a syllable with a short vowel, *give* (*giv*), *live* (*liv*); and of those in which *ea* has the sound of short *e, dead* (*ded*), *head* (*hed*); but in most words we can do nothing to the purpose till we have settled the alphabet which shall be the basis of general reform. The remedy for the general insufficiency and contrariety of our notation is by no means obvious or easy. There are three general methods of cure, each of which has its show of reason and its able advocates.

NEW SIGNS.

The first is the invention and adoption of a new set of alphabetic signs, which shall have forms better suited to rapid and legible writing than the Roman characters, and have scientific analogies with the sounds which they represent. It must be admitted that it is easy to improve upon the Roman alphabet in these respects. Any one who has seen the alphabet of

Mr. Pitman's stenography, or that of Bishop Wilkins, or of Mr. Bell, will be at no loss for suggestions. It would be a great thing, certainly, if we could have in English a system adapted to all possibilities of vocal utterance, with scientific simplicity and legibility such as to make it finally the alphabet of the world. For my part, I do not regard it as a wild vision to imagine such an alphabet in the future. But it is obvious that any such system must win its way very slowly, first into co-ordinate use with the Roman alphabet, and after a struggle of many generations, to its displacement; so that the improvement of our present alphabet is still to be desired while it lasts. As to the direction in which we are to look for the coming conqueror, it may be worth remarking, that it seems not unlikely that printing by hand-machines may take the place of writing to a great extent, and make rapidity quite secondary to legibility. If the press had not been invented, and books, and magazines and newspapers had to be prepared by penmen for all the readers of the present day, Pitman's stenography, or something like it, would have long since displaced the Roman letters; the hand-machine for printing may open the way for an alphabet like Bell's, of complex signs with large significance.

OUR LETTERS WITH ROMAN VALUES.

The Roman alphabet is so widely and firmly established among the leading civilized nations that it can not be soon displaced. In adapting it to improved use in English, and in supplementing it, two plans may be followed. One is to hold the Roman values of the letters as nearly as they are found in English, and supplement by the invention of new characters, and the use of diacritical marks. This is the system which scholars generally use when they wish to represent in writing the true sounds of English words, and it brings us into accord with other nations. It gives the following alphabet. The letters which have their Roman sound, or nearly that, in familiar use, and so retain it, are *a* (*far*), *e* (*let*), *i* (*pit*), *o* (*note*), *u* (*bull*), *b*, *c* (*k*), *d*, *f*, *g* (*go*), *h*, *l*, *m*, *n*, *p*, *r*, *s* (*so*), *t*. We now distinguish between the vowel and consonant sounds of the Roman *i* and *u*, using *y* and *w* for the consonant sounds; *j* and *v*, old variations of *i* and *u*, were at first used with this power in English, as they still are in many languages, but since the Norman mixture they have acquired other sounds, and *y* and *w* are too firmly established to be easily shaken. We have also come to distinguish the surd from the sonant utterance of *s*, the sonant now being denoted by *z*, or *a* reversed *s*, so that we must add to the Roman consonants, *v*, *w*, *y*, *z*. (ƨ). There are three new short vowels which need signs, those in *fat*, *not*, *but*. For these the signs most easy to introduce are easily recognized variations of *a, o, u,* such as, for example, a, o, u. It has been heretofore found best in languages written in Roman letters to use the same sign for a short vowel and its long, adding a diacritical mark where great precision is needed. This course would probably be acceptable in English with the sounds of ɑ (pɑst fɑr), a (fat fare), o (obey note), u (bull rude), o (not nor), u (but, burn). There is doubt about e (let late) and i (pick pique); variations of e, looking like a or *a* such as, for example, *e*, and of i looking like e, *e* have good promise. For diphthongs there are ɑi (by), ɑu (house), oi (noise), iu (music). It seems to be necessary almost for us to use at first for *ai* some variation of *i,* such as, for example, *j:* and for *iu* some variation of *u,* such as, for example, *u*. Nor is the permanent use of a simple character for these glides to be deplored, if polite pronunciation is to be represented. Finally there are the consonants th, dh, (thin thine), sh, zh, (sugar pleasure), ng (sing), and the combinations tsh (church), dzh (judge), which await their signs in the perfect alphabet. The surd and sonant th had their simple signs in Anglo-Saxon, which scholars would like to revive. The old long *s* has been used a good deal for *sh* by scholars in Germany. The italic *g* g offers a good transition form for g, when it has the sound of *dzh;* and many other characters have been suggested for all these sounds by our modern inventors, none of them quite satisfactory, or giving promise of easy introduction. But we need not fear. The digraphs with *h* are not so very bad, and the single signs will be forthcoming in due time.

In behalf of this system it may be said, that it will be easiest to read for all who read French, German, Latin, Greek, or Anglo-Saxon, and will have all learned associations in its favor. It will be easiest for children and the illiterate to learn. It will make the learning of foreign tongues easy. It will settle the school pronunciation of Latin and Greek. We shall pronounce, of course, as the Romans did; for that will be our natural reading of the letters. No one will think of studying up a pronunciation so remote and difficult as our English method will then become, or of making a *lingua Franca* of good old Latin, after the manner of the so-called continental method. It will revive the speech of our classic old English authors. As we now read *Hamlet* and the *Canterbury Tales*, Shakespeare would understand them with difficulty, Chaucer hardly at all. Chaucer tells us what pains he took with his spelling:

> "So oft aday I mot thy werke renewe,
> It to correct, and eke to rubbe and scrape."

He says further:

> "So preye I God that non myswrite the,
> Ne the mysmetere for defaute of tongue."

The old manuscripts are carefully printed for us; we have only to pronounce correctly and we shall hear the music of the masters.

That this reform of our spelling will be no hindrance to etymological studies need hardly be mentioned, it has been so often explained by our great philologists. We have the records preserved of all the old forms of spelling, and scholars like nothing better than to search them out, and give them to the public, who may find them in their dictionaries. It will however make it harder for foreigners little versed in etymology, to recognize English words akin to their own, or to the other foreign tongues. It is thought that it will be hard to introduce this scheme; that the printers can not use it for want of types, and that no one can read it without study. These objections have force against the sudden use of the whole scheme, but may be met by its gradual introduction and by temporary expedients. Three lines of movement are needed, one to render the new types familiar to the public, a second to carry out a system of uniform use of all the letters, a third to drop silent letters. Something may be done in each line at once, but the first naturally leads the way. The new letters may be substituted for the old ones which they resemble, when the old ones have the intended sound, without embarrassing any reader; and when the new letters have become familiar, they can be gradually used wherever their sound occurs. Printers who have not the new types, can use the old ones of which they are variations, adding a dot: a · for *a,* o · for *o,* u · for *v,* and the like. Every one of these distinctions, accurately made, is clear gain, however it may be expressed by types.

REFORM ACCORDING TO ENGLISH ANALOGIES.

The other system is to follow the analogies of the present English spelling, to give each of our single letters the value which it has oftenest, and to supplement with those digraphs which now most commonly represent the sounds which would have no single letter to represent them.

Two powerful reasons may be urged for *a* trial of this method.

1. It can be easily read by every one who can read in the present spelling.

2. It can be printed with common types.

It may be further said, that it is in the line of the regular development of our language. It is the tendency everywhere in language for minorities to conform to majorities. The unusual modes of spelling would naturally, according to this law, give way to the most common mode, and this would ultimately be the only mode of denoting each sound. So that in adopting this system we should only be hastening the natural process by which cosmos comes out of chaos; and this, our scientific men say, is the true office of the reformer.

Many of the objections to this scheme would be removed by regarding digraphs which represent elementary sounds, as single characters, and naming them as such by their elementary sound without making mention of the separate letters. They should be cast as one type. Then the type founders would soon invent shapely abbreviations, which would be good enough signs, and record some English history to boot. In reducing the scheme to practice difficulties arise. The uses of our letters are so various that the conflict of rival claims among the digraphs is hard to decide, and, however it be decided, the aspect of large numbers of words is so completely changed that easy reading is out of the question. Then this kind of spelling is associated in many minds with buffoonery, vulgarity and illiteracy. It excites odium, ridicule and violent opposition. In spite of all this, there are many persons to whom it is more acceptable than any other scheme. It has been carefully labored by Mr. Ellis, Mr. Jones, and others, and the use of it may obviously contribute to genuine reform in the present stage of the movement.

PRACTICAL MEASURES.

No earnest comprehensive effort has yet been made to ascertain and harmonize the views of those interested in this reform. Committees of the English and the American Philological Association would be now in a position to attempt it, and probably the attempt will be made during the coming year. If the assent of a few of the most eminent representatives of scholarship can be combined with that of the leading practical workers, an indefinite number of subscriptions of assent from others can easily be obtained. It would be too much to hope that any complete system can at once be agreed upon: but it seems almost certain that some important particulars may be, since the report of the Committee of the American Philological Association was not only made unanimously and adopted without opposition, but is apparently cordially assented to everywhere, even by those who have been looked to as champions of our present spelling. This report contains the following propositions:

"The ideal of an alphabet is that every sound should have its own unvarying sign and every sign its own unvarying sound."

"The Roman alphabet is so widely and so firmly established in use among the leading civilized nations that it can not be displaced; in adapting it to improved use for English, the efforts of scholars should be directed towards its use with uniformity and in conformity with other nations."

It can not surely be impossible to take a first step in the course thus distinctly marked out.

AN ASSOCIATION OF REFORMERS.

But even before any agreement on schemes of reform, a national or international association of those interested in the matter may be formed. A nucleus of permanent workers might accomplish much by collecting the names of a large number of members, organizing subordinate societies, urging the reform by lectures, through the press, by private correspondence, and in many other ways.

LEARNED SOCIETIES.

Many learned societies may with propriety aid by passing resolutions in favor of reformed spelling, and by introducing it into their Transactions. The Philological Society of London, the American Philological Association, National and State Teachers Associations, the Associations for the Advancement of Science in Great Britain and America, and other similar bodies, may be looked to with hope. Both the Philological Societies have had the matter before them; the American has appointed and continued from year to year a committee representing our great universities and our best scholarship—whose report for the last year has already been mentioned; the London Society allows a certain latitude to its members in the spelling of their papers in their transactions. National and State Teachers Associations have also appointed Committees to investigate and report, and to co-operate with the Philological Association.

GOVERNMENT ACTION.

The Legislatures of our States, of the United States, and of Great Britain may introduce the new spelling into public documents. A considerable number of documents published by the United States contain linguistic material connected with the aborigines, which ought to be printed in uniform phonetic spelling to be easily used by scholars. The legislature of the conservative old State of Connecticut has the honor of leading the way. The following joint resolution passed both their houses without dissent.

"*Resolved by this Assembly:* That the Governor be, and he hereby is authorized to appoint a Commission, consisting of six competent persons, who shall examine as to the propriety of adopting an amended orthography of the public documents hereafter to be printed, and how far such amended orthography may with propriety be adopted, and report thereupon to the next session of the General Assembly. That such Commission shall receive no compensation for its services. Approved July 20th, 1875."

The Governor appointed Senator W.?W. Fowler, by whom the Resolution was offered, Professors Whitney and Trumbull of Yale College, the Secretary of the Board of Education, Hon. B.?G. Northrup, Professors Hart of Trinity College and Van Benshoten of Wesleyan University, a Commission of which any State might be proud. This Commission has been continued by the legislature in the hope that concurrent action may be taken by other States. The two houses of the Pennsylvania legislature were passing a similar joint resolution without dissent, when some one noticed that under the new constitution it must have the form of a bill. This preliminary action has been of great importance in awakening interest and gathering up a certain authority for the movement. The actual use of improved spelling in such documents and transactions would give it authority without kindling popular hostility.

FREEDMEN'S AID AND BIBLE SOCIETIES.

As appeal may be made with much reason to all associations which are formed to support our free institutions and to promote Christianity, such as the freedmen's aid societies, the home missionary and the Bible societies. The freedmen will not learn the present spelling. The missionaries among the pagan populations in California and elsewhere cannot use the press to reach them. We print Bibles and other good books in strange dialects in the hope of reaching a few thousand Asiatics or Africans. An English Bible in reformed orthography may well reach millions in a single generation who otherwise would never read it.

PUBLISHERS.

Publishers must be brought to take an interest in the reform. Some will doubtless do so from pure benevolence and love of progress; but they ought also to have money in it. There are writers among us, scholars and popular authors, who may insist on using in their own publications more or less of reformed spelling. A single new letter is worth introducing, or a single reformed word. Many newspapers and periodicals could be easily opened in this way. Several papers are now printed in a reformed alphabet, and they may be encouraged. Merchants and other advertisers may insist on printing their business advertisements and circulars in the same manner. Dictionaries must be made, and other standard works of reference in which publishers will invest. Is it not possible that the publishers of primers and spellers may adopt a uniform statement of our alphabetic sounds, and change the names of the letters to the sounds which they oftenest represent. That would be great gain, worth holding a convention for.

TEACHERS.

Teachers are our best hope. They need the reform most. They understand it best. They must teach it to the generation who are to use it. The way should be made easy for them. Primers, spellers, readers, and all other school-books, and other printed apparatus of the best kind should be furnished in reformed spelling. It may be made a matter of discussion and instruction in their institutes and conventions, and in their printed periodicals. The superintendent will lead the van. Win the schoolroom and the cause is won.

RAPID PROGRESS.

Want of faith and want of concert are the greatest obstacles to rapid progress. Scholars, especially, think how slow changes in language have been, and how little influence the learned class have exerted upon them; they sleep in the fields of Giant Despair. But year by year the power of reason increases in every form of activity, as year by year the means increase of collecting and concentrating the assent of thinking persons. What with our railroads and telegraphs and newspapers, and our societies and associations, with their meetings and conventions, it is not extravagant to say that a wider and more powerful concentration of opinion can now be effected in a single summer than would have been possible in a hundred years three centuries ago. Changes of pronunciation, general changes of spoken language, depend in great part on little known causes which work upon whole nations through their physical organization, and which we may well despair of controlling; but orthography is independent machinery over which the consent of reason has full control. Several modern languages have had their spelling reformed by the influence of learned academies, or by government; and surely no language needs reform more than ours, and no race are more ready reformers.

A Reign of Law in Spelling

We are slaves to the printers. Write as we may, they spell for us when we print, and their spelling is the worst in the world. As long as spelling was mere fashion, and variations in it were fancies and whims, the reign of the printing office was tolerable. But science has at last reached the English language, worked over its history, pointed out its laws, brought it under the authority of scholarly conscience. There is now a known right and wrong in it, in its idioms, its forms, its spelling. And the time has come, therefore, for those who have scholarly conscience and see the right and wrong, to put in a plea for liberty.

This plea may well be addressed to the editors of our periodicals. The greater part of the thoughts of our best thinkers and ripest scholars appears first in our magazines and newspapers. The editors receive the manuscripts, read the proof-sheets, and decide what spelling shall be used. To them we submit our plea for liberty. We call upon them to act as judges, interpreters, and administrators of law and reason, not as mere arbiters of fashion, or autocrats who know no law but their own caprices. There are editors and editors. There are some, certainly, who heartily sympathize with the spirit of this plea, but who are troubled about the laws which they are asked to recognize. They see the Germans improving their spelling year by year, under the direction of the department of education. It orders all the school books to be printed in corrected spelling, and the thing is done. Our editors wish that we could have our improvements in language established in some such way. They wish that Congress would pass laws about spelling, or that amended words might be adopted, like amendments of the Constitution, three-fourths of the States voting for them. But as it is, they recognize the dictionary as sovereign in this realm, *de facto* if not *de jure*, and take its dicta for the only laws.

It is true that a dictionary ought to be a *corpus juris orthographici*, and scientific dictionaries are fast becoming such. But the science of language is only a few years old. A scientific dictionary is grounded on a study of all the classic authors, and is the work of generations. The old dictionaries are mainly aggregations of sundries, and some of them the

---

"A Reign of Law in Spelling." *Forum* 6 (1888): 424-31.

work of collectors with no scientific convolutions in their brains. English used to be thought no true language, but a barbarous mixture of dialects, most of them unknown dialects; German was little known, and Anglo-Saxon, Icelandic, and Celtic were far-off rumors. Greek, Latin, and French had their laws, but the rest were jargon. There are dictionaries now popular which hold this pre-scientific view. Stormonth says that the phonetic changes in English cannot be exhibited as they are in French. He knows nothing of the work of Sweet, and Nichol, and Murray, and other scientific students of English, and his etymologies are wonderful. But *Webster's Unabridged* is a different kind of work, and so is *Worcester*; and there is *Skeat*; and the *Oxford Historical Dictionary* of Dr. Murray and our *Century* dictionary are in progress. The next generation will have English dictionaries of the right sort, but no scholar now can take any dictionary for a fetich.

This plea shall begin with the most moderate claim. Let the editor accept the authority of *Webster* and *Worcester*. There is still a large number of words with variant spellings which are admitted into the dictionaries used by authors and familiar to printers. Between these the editor must make his choice. The plea is that he make it on grounds of reason, not of this year's fashion among his neighbors, or his English exchanges.

An editor is obliged to choose from "Shakespeare," "Shakespere," "Shakspeare," and the rest. Those who mean to follow the most common spelling in general literature, print "Shakspeare." The students of old editions, the old English Shakespeare Society, and the German Shakespeare Society print "Shakespeare," and the New Shakspere Society is good authority for "Shakspere." So too an editor has to make choice between "ian" and "ean" in "Shakespearian" and "Shakespearean," or "Shaksperian" and "Shaksperean." Both forms are current and approved, and will appear in his proof-sheets day by day. These are specimens of a host. The Grecians have brought almost the whole of the Greek proper names into doubt. Will the editor let "Sokrates" be printed as it stands in the manuscript of the eminent professor whom he has persuaded to send him an article? or "Epikouros," or "Aischylos"? Will he print "Celt," "Celtic," or "Kelt," "Keltic;" "Tartar" or "Tatar"?

A good editor, even of the simplest news sheet, ought to have his reasons. With proper names, indeed, it is an accepted principle to let persons decide the spelling of their own names, and that opens the gate to whim and fancy. The *Cyclopædia of American Biography* tells us that a son of the stout old presbyterian, Dr. Cox, who is now an episcopalian bishop, has adopted the spelling "Coxe." And there are "Smiths" who spell themselves "Smythes." Our great poet, too, who down in Stratford signed his will "Shakspere," as the folk there called his family, up in London, when he printed his dedications to Southampton, and applied for a coat of arms for his father, magnified himself into "Shakespeare." Such fancies an editor may accept. But in general he should be governed by principles, and his principles should be laws of language. It was for a long time the prevailing rule to decide the forms of all words by authority, the ultimate appeal being to kings and lords, or great authors or orators or actors, whose word was law.

Possibly Noah Webster may have been the first to insist that the decision is not with any rank or class, but with the whole people who speak the language, and that their verdict is embodied in the laws of language, so that the proper spelling is that which conforms to these laws. This is good democratic doctrine, and good scientific doctrine. Webster lived, to be sure, before the rise of the modern science of language, before the days of Bopp and Grimm; but he was an able man, fairly comparable with Dr. Franklin, who was one of the great men of the world, in a certain commanding attitude of common sense.

The two spellings "controller" and "comptroller," are common and approved by authority; "comptroller" is perhaps more common in New York and "controller" elsewhere. A New York editor who cares for nothing but the usage of his neighbors may well enough print "comptroller," but he will not do so if he recognizes himself a debtor to his mother tongue and cultivates a scholarly conscience. "Compt" is no way to spell "cont"; it is misleading as to the sound, and wasteful of time and space; it is also deceptive as to etymology. It is imagined to be derived from "compute" instead of from *"contra,"* and seems to tell us that this officer is a computer of rolls, instead of one who keeps a counter or check roll. Every editor has to choose between "program" and "programme." "Program" is the spelling of the printing offices of the country districts and the free West. The "patent insides" are apt to betray their metropolitan origin by their "programmes." "Program" is a good dictionary word, and has been since the time of old Bailey. "Programme" is the French form of the same original. The final "me" modifies the sound in French, but in English is a meaningless superfluity.

There are many words like these in which two spellings are in familiar use. There are others which an editor with awakened conscience would class with them, though they are not so familiar; for example, "tho" and "though." "Tho'?" is familiar, to be sure, to every reader of English poetry, but the word stands without the apostrophe in Worcester's dictionary, as it does in many classic pages. When our first great American epic, *The Columbiad*, shall become a household book for our editors, it will make "tho" the household spelling, and save the printer half his types and the children many a mistake.

Do our editors know that they have free choice between "iland" and "island"? Worcester's dictionary tell us in the last edition that "iland" is the correct spelling, and it stands as such in its proper place in the new vocabulary. And well it may. There is no "s" in the Anglo-Saxon word, which means "land in water," and has no connection with "isle," from the Latin *insula.* In middle English it never has "s," if we may trust Stratmann's dictionary. "Island" there means land of ice, and in modern English it is rare and late. Looking at the translations of the Bible, those inestimable treasures of the worker in words, one finds when he looks in the concordance for "island," that the article upon it is not in its proper alphabetic place, but in the alphabetic place of "iland." That may lead him to suspect the fact, which is that there is no "island" in the New Testament of Wiclif, Tyndale, Cranmer, or in the Geneva, Rheims, or King James, except once in the latter—Rev. vi. 14.

The first folio of Shakespeare begins with "iland," but "island" is pretty frequent. In Milton's *Paradise Lost* "island" appears but once, possibly an oversight, though the blind bard was very careful of his spelling, and has added a page of errata to the first edition. It seems plain that a scholar's dictionary, grounding, as it should, upon an induction from classic usage and the laws and history of the speech, ought to give the form "iland" the preference, as *Worcester* does, and that a scholarly editor ought to use it. So if a poet or a scholar prefers to write "sovran," as Milton did, instead of the modern blunder, "sovereign," why should not a scholarly editor or proof-editor let it be printed? For that also the new *Worcester* stands as popular authority. The printers of the Shakespeare folio spell "soueraigne," bloated French, which gave rise to the false English.

Besides words given in the dictionaries, an editor will now-a-days often be called upon to accept or reject words in the manuscript of scholars which are frequent in classic books, but have not been taken up by the lexicographers. No complete study of the forms of English words in classic books has yet been made. The spelling in the dictionaries has been the record in great part of the guesses or whims of the lexicographers. We may be sure that Dr. Johnson, who fixed the standard spelling of so large a part of our language, would have fixed it differently in many words if he had known the history of the words and the laws of the language. The compilers of the *Oxford Historical Dictionary* are making a thorough study of the whole field for the first time, and it shows us that there are many well-approved forms of the words heretofore unknown to the lexicons. The past tense and perfect participle of regular verbs ending with a surd sound are pronounced as though they ended in "t," and in the early classic books are spelled with "t": "leapt," "whipt," "prest," "dropt." In the dictionaries all these words are spelled, or spelt, with "ed": "leaped," "whipped," "pressed," and the like; some have the form in "t" also given. But many scholars use it with all. Our illustrious scholar, poet, diplomatist, statesman, whom the general suffrage of English-speaking men would rank as high as any one living as a authority for usage of the English language, is seen in his latest book of poems to be one of these. In "Heartease and Rue" the classic form is regularly used: "missed" is "mist," and so with other like words. Another is Mr. Furnivall, director of the Early English Text Society, the Chaucer, the New Shakspere, and the Browning Societies. Why should any scholarly editor refuse to a humbler poet or essayist the liberty of spelling which is given to Lowell and Furnivall?

Professor F. W. Newman, of University College, London, has lately printed what many regard as a great work—*Christianity in its Cradle*. He drops final "e" in all words in which it is "not only superfluous but misleading." It is usually so when it is silent after a short vowel. "Ine," for example, ought to rhyme with "vine," "wine," "line," "pine." "Genuine," therefore, is misleading, it should be "genuin;" so "engin," "imagin," "doctrin," "definit," "infinit," "motiv," "talkativ," and many other words. The mute "e's" in English average four per cent of all the letters on every printed page. Many of them were once pronounced, but after these became silent, others were written. In the old manuscripts they came to be used as freely as penman's flourishes, like the long-tailed "y's" which stand for "i's." In the early printed books they were used to space with, slipped in or slipped out to make even lines. We need them no longer. If there were good dictionary authority for dropping them they would soon disappear.

There are no dictionaries good enough yet, but if an editor or publisher has the scholarly conscience, and seeks the support of scientific authority in favor of progress, there is authority for him far higher than that of any dictionary. It is found in the joint action of the Philological Society in England and the American Philological Association. The American Association's committee on spelling reform, consisting of professors of language in Yale, Harvard, Lafayette, Columbia, the University of Pennsylvania, and the University of Wisconsin, have made reports since 1875. In 1880 the Philological Society of England took up the matter, and in 1881 issued a pamphlet of "Partial Corrections of English Spelling." After two years of discussion and correspondence between the societies, "a joint scheme was put forth under the authority of the two chief philological bodies of the English-speaking world." An alphabetic list of words amended according to this scheme was published in the *Transactions of the American Philological Association* for 1886. The corrections are made in the interest of etymological and historical truth, and are confined to words which the changes do not much disguise for general readers. These amended words are recommended for immediate use. The list has been reprinted by the Spelling Reform Association, and they wish to put it in every printing house and every editor's office. The English Society is the one which has prepared the material for the great *Historical Dictionary*, and is fully equal to the French Academy's dictionary workers in linguistic authority. Our American professors are authorities too. Whitney, Trumbull, Child, and Haldeman are honored names wherever the study of language is pursued. Lounsbury, Allen, and Price are good names too. Let our scholarly editors show cause why liberty of spelling should not be given through all the words included in this joint recommendation of the philologists. Why not let our great librarians—Cutter, Dewey, and the rest—use "catalog" in the popular journals, as they do in their own publications. It will throw the old petrified printing into disorder, but chaos is here the condition for the coming cosmos.

In many other countries spelling reform is a matter of constant interest. In Germany, besides government action, societies of radical reformers are active, and spread their branches wherever there are Germans. The Dutch, the Swedes, the Danes, the Norwegians, are all reforming both by official action and voluntary societies. In Portugal also there is movement, and in France. There has been for twenty-five years a society in Switzerland for the reform of French spelling, but it is only since 1886 that a society has existed in France. Leading linguists—Prof. G. Paris, Prof. A. Darmesteter, and others—are trying to introduce partial corrections into the general press, and a great teachers' congress has lately declared in favor of reform. The English Spelling Reform Association is officered by leading university professors and educators, and includes among its members many of the eminent authors and scientists best known in America: Tennyson, Darwin, J. H. Gladstone, Max Müller, Sayce, Skeat, Ellis, Morris, Murray, Sweet, and the like. They press the reform in the interest of education. Dr. Gladstone has made elaborate investigations in the schools of England and other countries to ascertain the time devoted to teaching spelling. His book, giving the statistics, has been published by Macmillan & Co., in successive editions. He finds that 720 hours at least are lost to each scholar, and that an Italian child of nine years will read and spell as correctly as English children at thirteen, though the Italian begin his lessons two years later. The Germans and Swedes have a like advantage. This extra time is given to civics and useful sciences. The illiteracy of English-speaking nations is startling. There were 5,658,144 persons of ten years and over who reported themselves illiterate at our census of 1870, and 6,239,958 at the census of 1880. The nearly illiterate are probably as many more. England is worse off than we are. But the other Protestant countries of Europe have almost no illiterates. One of the causes of this excessive illiteracy among English-speaking peoples is the badness of English spelling. The reform of spelling is a patriotic and philanthropic reform.

Two works have just been published by Alexander Melville Bell, upon *World-English, the Universal Language*. They are well fitted to attract attention. Mr. Bell is perhaps the most eminent of all the scientists who have applied themselves to the study of speech on the physiological side. His *Visible Speech* has modified the thought of all students of phonetics. A certain air of practical power and wisdom surrounds his name in the popular mind, from association with the invention of the telephone by his son, and with all the wealth he has won from it. He should give the world something worth while in the place of Volapük. But Bell's universal language is simply standard English phonetically spelled.

Ten Years of Spelling Reform

The Spelling Reform Association is now ten years old. It was formd at an International Convention for the Amendment of English Orthografy, held in Philadelphia, August 14–17, 1876. The erliest mover for this convention was said to be Mr. E. Jones, of Liverpool, England, an activ and sagacious filanthropist, who had devoted much time and money to this reform, and had an excellent alfabetic scheme to propoze.

The first public action came from Mr. Wellington Wilcox, of Randolph, Illinois. He also was an ernest reformer, and had convinced the teachers of his region of the need of reform, and of the excellence of an alpfbetic scheme which he had adopted. To the Randolph Association belongs the honor of first issuing a call for a convention. It was soon followd by a more impozing call, in which Prof. Geo. P. Beard, of Philadelphia, led, and in which Mr. Jones and many American reformers joind, reprezentativs of various lerned bodies, or schemes of reform. It would be plezant to reherse their names, each, after a fashion, a

"—wel of English undefiled,
On Fame's eternal bead-roll wurthy to be filed."

Ar they not all recorded in capitals in our book of Bulletins?

Dr. S. S. Haldeman prezided at the convention. He was that year Prezident of the American Philological Association. Of all the subjects into which he thrust his incisiv pen and voice, he had penetrated deepest into fonology. He had carried off the Trevelyan prize, by his *Analytic Orthografy,* over 18 European competitors in 1858. He coud make all the sounds in all the dialects of America and of the outside world. He had workt with all the spelling reformers, and was always redy to work. His deth, in September, 1880, was the greatest loss our Association has sustaind.

Under his lively direction the convention of 1876 was a great success. It naturally suggested the formation of a permanent asociation. Secretary

---

"Ten Years of Spelling Reform. Adress of Prof. F. A. March, LL.D., Prezident of the Spelling Reform Association, at the Eleventh Annual Meeting, July 15, 1886." *Bulletin of the Spelling Reform Association* 22 (September 1886): 45-56.

Dewey was the prime mover and organizer, and under his energetic management the International Convention soon resolvd itself into the Spelling Reform Association. It must be esteemd one of the happiest circumstances of the new asociation that in this first convention leading advocates of the principal schemes of new alfabetic notation wer prezent, and redy to urge their schemes. It was soon evident that no one coud convert a majority of the others. In this emergency it was propozed by Mr. Jones that the decizion upon a reformd alfabet should be referd to the American Philological Association. The propozition was receivd with universal and cordial asent, and the convention proceeded to the practical work of arranging for the disemination of knowledg of the reform and promoting its progress among the peopl, with a unanimity and ardor beutiful to behold.

This cordial concurrence in an apeal to the filologists was doutless due in part to the supreme confidence which each of the inventors had in the superiority of his own scheme, and its certainty of aproval by the filologists.

It is, however, wize in principl. The authority of experts is a characteristic of our time. In it reazon supersedes the warfare of prejudices and stupidities, the so-calld strugl for life. Arbitration supersedes war. There ar few better matters in which to aply this principl than alfabetic discussions. They seem so eazy that the most ignorant scool-boy thinks he can understand them. The bright teacher or editor hears of the reform on Saturday, incubates Sunday, has his scheme redy on Monday. And so conflicting at the analogies of our spelling that every scheme has sum good things to say for itself. But the facts ar so numerous their relations so complex and far-reaching, and the interests involved so numerous and peculiar, that a sagacious decizion requires the most extensiv lerning and penetration, and large, sound, roundabout sense. The study of fonology is the foundation of the scientific study of language, and many of the best minds in the world spend their days and nights in it. The decizion of one such mind must overweigh a hole asociation of others. Then a bench of experts wil make a decizion speedily, while general discussion and voting on such a subject last forever, and produce a chaos of conflicting decizions. The Spelling Reform Association in England, founded in 1879, which has attempted to proceed by general discussion and majority votes of preference, is stil debating its alpfbets, and taking its *plebiscita*.

Another fundamental principl adopted at the first by the American Association is that spelling reformers recognize a standard orthoepy. "We ar met," they said, "to reform orthografy, not orthoepy; we hav to do with writing, not pronunciation. There ar all sorts of English peopl, and words ar pronounced in all sorts of ways. It is the work of the orthoepist to observ all theze different ways, and to decide which is the prevailing pronunciation of the most cultured, to decide which is the standard English pronunciation. The orthografer tels how to reprezent this pronunciation in writing. The orthoepist has many nice and difficult questions to solv. We enter into his labors. We take for granted that there is a standard pronunciation of English. We wish to see it reprezented by simpl and reazonabl alfabetic signs."

The alfabet of standard orthografy is recognized as different from an alfabet for scientific fonology. "An alfabet intended for use by a vast comunity need not attempt an exhaustiv analysis of the elements of utterance, or a reprezentation of the nicest varieties of articulation." "The general standard of a great nation must always be severely simpl. It is not desirabl to admit in it the ever-varying glides and finishes and culorings of fashionabl or vulgar articulation; or even the more stable and general culorings produced by adjacent letters, as long as they ar without significance."

The American Association has acted on theze principls. It follows the pronouncing dictionaries. It abjures peculiar orthoepy. This pozition is esential to spelling reform in the English language. The Londoner has a different way of sounding many of the elementary letters from that of a Scotchman, or that of an American—the *a* in *man,* for exampl, the *e* in *there,* the *o* in *note.* If an alfabet is adopted which goes behind the historical distinctions, and ads new characters which discriminate the speech of London from that of Edinburgh and of Boston, it wil separate the English language into several dialects, and no Londoner wil be able to read an American book. The Londoners do not seem to think of any such impending privation. They take for granted that natural unsofisticated Londonese, the speech of the gentleman and scolar of the metropolis, is what is ment by standard English; that if it can only be set forth in print with all its glides and finishes, all its runs of unaccented, indistinguishabl murmurs, and varied droppings and insertions, the rest of the world wil accept and try to imitate.

So far as the spelling reform is concernd we may be sure this is not so. We shal never be able to reform our spelling by substituting coloquial Londonese for the prezent standard spelling. It ought to be one of the "General Principls" of every spelling reform asociation that no new alfabetic distinctions shal be recognized which wil promote divizion among the English-speaking nations.

The temptation to tamper with pronunciation, if not to thuroly overhaul it, is almost irresistibl to the spelling reformer.

The practical reformer, shrinking from his queer-looking words, finds that he can secure a comparatively natural-looking page by slight changes of pronunciation. Mr. Isaac Pitman, whoze alfabet is on the hole admirabl, has a queer-looking type for *a* in *father.* He shuns the use of it. In a specimen of his printing selected by himself we find he uzes it but once, tho the pronunciation of the dictionaries would call for it 22 times. And so this noble sound, the leader in all alfabets, is buried in Pitman English.

In a similar manner Mr. Pitman favors the insular English *o* in *not;* mainly, it would seem, becauz he uzes the common type *o* for it, and new types for *o* in *no,* for *au* in *author, nor,* and for *u* in *but, sun.* He lets the *o* stand in unaccented syllable, and sumtimes elsewhere, for all three of theze so different sounds. He prints it in the specimen just referd to 53 times, where the dictionaries would giv it only 24. If so eminent a leader as Mr. Pitman yields to temptation in this way, what can be expected of the minor alpfbetic inventors?

The young fonologists also find it hard to rest with the pronunciation of the dictionaries. The microscopic investigation of living speech is just now the fashion, one of the most novel and inviting fields of original reserch. Why not uze the spelling reform to prosecute such reserches? It is certainly important scientific work. Who knows whether spelling reform wil ever cum to anything else? Can it ever cum to anything before these thuro investigations hav been made? With sum such views, most likely, the English Spelling Reform Association has been sending out elaborate circulars of inquiry about obscure and variant articulation. They may perhaps acumulate data for science, tho the answers of the laity to such questions hav the same sort of value as their reports of meteors as big as barrels, or of sea-serpents. But meantime the children ar wailing over the old spelling; filanthropy does not join in theze excursions of fonology. Where spelling reformers marshal their forces for fonologic achievement, filanthropists decline to enlist. Standard pronunciation and standard alfabets ar peculiar problems. A standard speech is an ideal. It implies induction and history as wel as observation. It implies authority abuv coloquial dialects. It has a right of posession which can only be devested by the consent of all the dialects.

Our Association leavs theze problems to experts. It has adrest itself mainly to diseminating its views of the irationality and mischievousness of the old spelling, and to urging the use of the amended spellings recommended by the experts.

The story of our work has been often printed, is familiar to most of our members and friends, and is accessibl to all in our publications, especially in the Circular of Information of the U.S. Bureau of Education, No. 7, 1880, and its supplement. I shal giv only the briefest outlines. Let any who ar interested in further details ask our Secretary for documents. Our most successful work has been done in exciting and concentrating dissatisfaction with the old spelling and desire for reform. The time (1876) was favorabl. The prevailing spirit among filologists had changed from the literary and archæologic to the scientific, progressiv, practical. The country was ful of spelling-bees. We held meetings in sum of the principal cities. We secured local comittees, and promoted auxiliary asociations in all sections of the cuntry. We issued a Bulletin. The members wrote articls for newspapers and magazines, and vizited and adrest teachers' asociations and other organizations. The State Teachers' Associations of Pennsylvania, New Jersey, Ohio, Massachusetts, Illinois, Iowa, Michigan, Indiana, Wisconsin, Missouri, Virginia, ar specialy reported in our documents as moving in the reform. This Association held its annual meeting in 1878 with the American Institute of Instruction, in three other years with the National Educational Association, in the remaining years with the American Philological Association. The county institutes for teachers, and other smaller teachers' associations which pervade the country, hav everywhere had papers and discussions on spelling. The *New England Journal of Education, Intelligence* of Chicago, and other educational periodicals hav had spelling reform departments. A large part of those interested in education hav had their attention calld to the reform.

Atempts hav been made to bring about action by the State legislatures and by Congress.

Comittees hav been apointed to investigate and report upon the matter, especialy on amending the spelling of the public documents, by the legislatures of Connecticut, Pennsylvania and Wisconsin. A memorial to Congress was prepared in 1878, asking for a comittee to report amendments for our public printing, and a consultation with the Guvernment of Great Britain upon a joint comission to consider such amendments. This was very impozingly signd by college men and others, including professors of languages in about fifty of our leading institutions. The department of public instruction of the City of Chicago issued a circular to the principal scool boards and other educational associations of the cuntry, asking them to unite in this memorial to Congress. A bil was reported in accordance with the petition, and might hav past, but it has not been reacht. This action is stil in progress. Colections of writn views upon the reform by eminent persons in literature, science, guvernment, education, and the like, hav been made by Mr. Perry in the *Home Journal,* and by our Corresponding Secretary, Mr. Scott, in the New York *Evening Post.*

A pamflet containing a hundred or so of them is one of our best documents. It is entitled, "Sensible Spelling," and contains convincing testimony that all the modern world of scolarship and culture is in favor of progress in spelling. Our illustrious and venerabl chief, the Hon. George P. Marsh, the American Minister to Italy, said that in his erly life he, like most literary men of that time, was prejudiced against this reform; but the weight of the arguments in its favor had convinced him of its necessity. And a similar declaration is made by Dr. Morris, and by others of our elders. But in all this copious expression of views, I do not know a singl scolar or eminent educator of the new generation who has cum out in favor of the old spelling.

This pozition has been wun in spite of many objections.

There is the etymological objection. It is thought that if we drop the *s* from *island,* we shal not see that it is from the Latin *insula;* if the *g* is dropt from *sovereign*, we shal not see the Latin *regno;* and wurse things than theze might happen.

Then we shal no longer be able to distinguish homonyms: *rite, right, write, wright.*

Then we shal not be able to read the old books, and they wil becum worthless.

Then if we begin to change we shal be in a perpetual flux.

Then nobody knows what is the proper pronunciation.

Theze and the like objections hav been answerd over and over. The greatest scolars—Prof. Whitney, Prof. Max Müller—hav taken pains to write articls to state that *iland* is not from *insula,* that *soverein* is not from *regno,* that our spelling abounds with deceptions and concealments, and that the etymologist, most of all, needs to hav it reformd. And they answer as wel the other objections. It takes a long time, however, to reach everybody. Many persons who hav not been interested in the matter ar stil ignorant of the state of opinion among the lerned and of the facts of the case. We ar stil sending out the documents, and we confidently invite the attention of all mankind. This batl, however, is wun. We hav only to capture the straglers.

The main purpose of the Association has been to bring amended spelling into general use. It might hav been hoped that ten years of effort would accomplish it. That, however, has not proved to be so. The very badness of the old spelling protects it. One who has lernd to read in it cannot eazily read in fonetic spelling. The change must be slow and carried by attacks from different directions. There is the filological or scientific side, where an ideal alfabet is needed for accurate fonetic printing, to giv the pronunciation in dictionaries, for exampl, or in fonetic discussions. We hav an alfabet of this sort. Then there is the educational side, demanding a spelling for scool-books, specialy adapted to make the transition eazy from a fonetic beginning to the old spelling. Then there is amendment of particular words in the newspapers and every-day use, mainly by dropping silent letters.

The first kind of printing has been urged mainly by fonetic stenografers. Mr. Pitman has been printing in it sum forty years. Mr. Parkhurst and Mr. Longley ar veteran fonetic printers. Dr. Vickroy, for sum years our Corresponding Secretary, and manager for the Southwest, whoze untiring activity and ingenuity wer beyond praiz, has also printed in ful fonetic printing. During the last ten years the circulation of Mr. Pitman's *Phonetic Journal* has more than dubld. It is now more than 20,000 copies. He has publisht also several bound volumes. Mr. Elias Longley has the last year done a noble work in fitting out Bishop Taylor for missionary work in Africa with a bountiful supply of fonetic testaments, and apparatus for fonetic printing. Mr. Knudsen has printed in the same Christian spirit, and in a better alfabet, Mrs. Burns in the Burns-Jones alfabet, and many other persons in many other alfabets. The latest and liveliest is C. W. Larison, M.D., with his *Journal of American Orthoepy*. Each of theze printers, I fear, thinks the Association unwize in not giving an exclusiv support to his own types and spelling; but sum of them hav cordially coöperated with us.

We must hav new types for scientific printing. Accented letters ar uzed as new types in filological publications the world over, and in national alfabets. But our shorthand writers look at them as script, and they cannot bear to lift their pens. They prefer therefore to hav tags at the bottom of the letters. It is important to notice that script and print need not be exactly alike. Facility is a main point with script nowadays. Legibility is the first, second, and third point with print. A printer can set up one type as eazily as another. As to legibility we now hav sum scientific investigation. I refer especially to the work of Dr. Cattell, and of Dr. Javal, which has been brought before us at this meeting. It appears that the line of chief legibility runs horizontaly near the tops of the short letters. It would seem then that we should modify our types at the top, even if we prefer tags for our script. Let scientists investigate and experiment; we ar redy for all improvements. Meantime we go on serenely with the excellent alfabet reported for us by the Philological Association in 1877.

In educational printing Dr. Leigh has been the master workman. His books had alredy been sum years in use in many of our largest American cities. During theze last ten years they hav continued in use, saving a year or two of scool life to thouzands of our youth. A book or two hav been added to this course. A great deal of effort was made in this direction in the erlier years of the Association. The young folks ar plainly the ones to be reacht. Mr. Blackmer, of Chicago, our scolarly manager for the

Northwest, was the publisher of a widely circulated periodical called *The Little Folks*. He spent much care and cost in preparing new types for it. The publications of the Association wer most of them printed in similar types. They wer introduced into articls by reformers in the *Proceedings* and *Transactions of the Philological Association*, in the New York *Independent*, and other periodicals and newspapers. Experience shows that the embarrassments conected with new types ar excessiv in a newspaper office. Scool-books may eazily uze them, if the author or publisher is willing to pay. Almost all our primers and readers hav distinctiv types. The direct influence of the reform upon scools by the introduction of scool-books in amended spelling has not been great, but there has been notabl progress thru improved methods of teaching reading and spelling, and the preparation of charts and books skilfuly adapted to fonic teaching. The English Association ar stil experimenting for a scool alfabet. A Fonetic Teachers' Association has also been organized in France, under the leadership of Paul Passy, Professor of Modern Languages in the Normal College of Paris, and Inspector of District Schools, for teaching English to foreners by fonetic text-books and methods. They hav printed scool-books in their alfabet, and publish a paper in it. It closely resembls our own. They expect to see their method speedily cum into universal use. An A B C Book by a member of our asociation took a diploma of the first class at the Exposição Pedagogica, Rio de Janeiro, 1884. Mr. Sweet, the hed of fonetic and Anglo-Saxon scolars in Great Britain, has publisht a fonetic primer of spoken English for the use of Germans, which has been hartily welcumd. It may be hoped that the adoption of such text-books by foren cuntries will react happily on the scools of England and America.

It can hardly be expected that fonetic writing with new letters wil be taken up by the adults of any generation. It is too much work. It is much if they can be brought to aprove it for their children, and direct it to be uzed in the scools. Nor can such spelling be uzed in newspapers and current business. It is too hard to read. We must hav gradual changes of the common spelling, requiring no new types.

As soon as the Association receivd from the filologists its ideal alfabet and the principls which ar to control the changes, it began to recommend the immediate use of certain amended words. The number of these has been gradualy increast, and in 1883 the American Philological Association united with the Philological Society of England upon a joint scheme of "Partial Corections of English Spellings," running thru the dictionary. These hav been printed by the Associations, and ar recommended for immediate use "under the authority of the two chief filological bodies of the English-speaking world."

This would seem to make the way clear for all who ar convinced of the desirablness of reform, to reform their own spelling. There ar difficulties, however.

It is trublsum to spel in a new way. Even lerned professors ar wurried by it. Business men cannot take time for it. This difficulty cannot be removed. We try to overcum it by a "League," the members of which promis to uze sum particular amended word or words, by way of constant testimony and remembrance, if nothing more.

There is danger, also, in writing to strangers, of being thought illiterate. A recommendation of a student as a teaçher to an average scool board might cost your student the place, if it wer spelt in an unknown spelling. We hav stationery prepared for this emergency, giving notice that the writer spels better than others, not wurse.

If the would-be reformer is a teacher, there ar other difficulties. Hostility of parents, of scool directors, perhaps the loss of a pozition, may thretn; and there is not always a Prezident Gilchrist to fall back on. He tells the pupils graduating from the State Normal School of Iowa, that if they loze a scool by uzing the amended spellings, he wil find them a better one.

If the reformer is a contributor to the press, an author, an essayist, perhaps a poet, he fears to divert the atention from his thought. The important truth, the beutiful verse, may loze its power and charm, if it wears a strange dress. He may even feel as tho he wer making a ridiculous exhibition of himself, apearing in the public prints in this queer guize. This difficulty wil pass away as the fashion of spelling changes.

If the reformer is a publisher, he fears the loss of sales; or if that be surmounted, there ar many vexations with the type-setters and the proofreaders, who bogl and protest, perhaps, at the unwunted labor.

In spite of all difficulties, however, the last ten years hav seen a great deal of amended spelling. In the Guvernment circular, No. 7, 1880, a bibliografy of spelling reform literature is givn, and it makes a respectabl show. In our Bulletin No. 16, is a gladsum recapitulation of the newspapers and periodicals which had then been printed in it. Even in so curt a summary as this I cannot forbear to mention the *Chicago Tribune* and the *Home Journal*. "On the second day of September, in the year of our Lord one thouzand eight hundred and seventy-nine, the great progressiv reprezentativ paper of the Northwest apeard in amended spelling thruout." The *Home Journal* of New York, the American jurnal of society, followd on the 17th of September. The *Utica Herald* should also be mentioned. Many papers amended a few words to apeaz their scolarly consciences. The *Princeton Review* printed "tho" and "altho," the *Library Journal* "catalog." "It is said [in 1880], that more than 200 jurnals and periodicals in this cuntry ar innovating more or less." Press asociations adopted resolutions in favor of the reform. A leag of the editors and publishers in its behalf was mooted. There was good promis of a new era. It is not eazy to say why this promis faild. But in fact the current of activ progress turnd in other directions, and we find ourselves now looking to less striking and less potent means of carrying the reform forward: increasing the membership of our asociation and "League," the circulation of an organ and other documents, preparing and introducing our vocabulary of amended words, and other hand-books and text-books, urging action by Congress, international action, and the like.

During the same period a similar reform has been set on foot in Germany, taken up by the Guvernment and put in force gradually in the scools, til it is an acomplisht fact. We lack compulsiv power. The utility of the reform is a mild motiv which is balanced in most persons by habit, and in sensitiv commonplace natures eazily outweighd by esthetic preference, exactly as with ladies' dress. It is of no use to talk to them about the cumfort, cheapness, or helthfulness of a strange, queer-looking dress. We hav no class whoze fortunes ar involved in pushing the reform. The impulse must cum from patriotizm or filanthropy. All the children who lern to read and write, waste from 18 months to three years in trying to master the spelling of our iregular words. There wer 5,658,144 persons of ten years old and over who reported themselvs iliterate at the census of 1870, 6,239,958 at the census of 1880. The "nearly iliterate" ar probably as many more. England is wurse off than we ar. But the other Protestant cuntries of Europe hav almost none. One of the cauzes of the excessiv iliteracy among the English-speaking people is the badness of the English spelling. But ignorance is blind and bad. Enthuziazm is wanted, fanaticizm would not be amiss, in behalf of this patriotic and filanthropic reform.

"Ten Years of Spelling Reform"! When this title of my adress was anounced, I thought that I might perhaps garnish the general history with sum personal experiences and reflections. But thoze I wil save up. I cannot, however, forbear to express my apreciation of the officers of the Association, who hav done the work from year to year,—Mr. Dewey, in reliance on whoze energy and executiv power I ventured to asume my title, Mr. Blackmer, Dr. Vickroy, and Mr. Scott. I thank them all most sincerely for their unfailing personal kindness. The Association is happy in being able stil to count on the activ service of Mr. Dewey and of Mr. Scott. The Association has plenty to do, and wel-digested plans of action. The great wind wil by and by swel the sails again.

Spelling and Progress

Wī hav ōlwēz had speling refōrmerz. Dhi mixstyur ov Anglo-Saxon and Nōrman, hwich grū intu yūs in dhi fōr sentyuriz foloing dhi Nōrman congcwest, woz at fūrst a despaizd and uncultivēted daialect, ōlmōst egzactli laik aur Pennsylvania Dutch. In dhōz long jenerēshunz ov tūrmoil and straif, everibodi tōkt acōrding tu hiz hwim, and ecsplēnd himself widh hiz sōrd. Az sūn az literatyur began tu bī prodiust in dhi niu spīch, dhi ōthorz began tu wuri at dhi scraibz for dhār bad speling.

> "Adam Scrivener," sez Chaucer, "if ever it thee befalle,
> Boece or Troilus for to write new,
> Under thy long locks thou most have the scalle,
> But after my making thou write more true."

Dhi mixstyur ov French and Anglo-Saxon wūrdz, ōlmōst ōl ov dhem manggld in dhi uterans, woz enuf tu giv eni scraib such disgust and contempt and distres, az nō pūr rīder ov dhi *Fonetic Niuz* ōr printer ov fonetic manyuscript can nauadēz fārli atēn tū. Hwen printing woz begun bai Caxton in 1474, it woz widh a fōrs ov Dutch printerz, hū set up the English manyuscripts az best dhē cud, after dhār Dutch fāshun, widh meni an objurgēshun ov aur gramarles tung. But in dhi grēt printing ofisez rūlz, ōr habits ecwivalent tu rūlz, sūn began tu grō up. Mōr ōr les sailent *e*'z mait bi yūzd tu spēs aut dhi lainz, but asaid from dhis wī seldum faind a wūrd spelt in mōr dhan faiv' ōr six diferent wēz in a wel-printed buk ov dhi taim ov Elizabeth, and dhi number ov vēriēshunz gradyuali diminisht. Sum edishunz ov dhi English baibl wer veri cārfuli spelt, and fainali Dr Johnson gēv dhi stamp of ōthoriti tu dhi prevalent habits ov dhi London printerz, and wī araivd at a standard orthografi. Not widhaut prōtest, hauever. Dr Johnson woz nō scolar and nō refōrmer, but a literari man, an extrīm conservativ and a vaiolent Tōri. Dhār wer meni atacs on him in England, but dhi printerz tuk hiz said sō fār az speling iz consurnd, and sins hiz dē buks ār not printed bai dhi speling ov dhi ōthor, but bai dhi speling ov dhi printing-ofis. Thingz went sumhwot diferentli in America. Dhi ōld Tōri'z nēm did not recomend hiz buk on dhis said ov dhi wōter. Aur ansestorz rejoist in Horne Tooke's expōzhur ov hiz ignorans, and sum ov dhem thōt wī had beter hav an American langgwej, az wī wer tu hav an American nēshun. Dr Franklin and Noah Webster ār dhi best-nōn promōterz ov dhis mūvment. Dhē fēvord thuro refōrm ov dhi langgwej on a fonetic bēsis. Dhis woz dhi dōn ov saientific comun sens in dhi relm ov langgwej; but dhi printerz prūvd tū strong fōr dhem.

"Spelling and Progress." *Spelling: A Magazine Devoted to the Simplification of English Orthography* 1.4 (December 1887): 171-73.

Webster'z dicshunari haz, indīd, in nēm, sūpersīded Jəhnson'z az a pəp-yular gaid, but ecsept in dhi endingz *-or* and *-ic*, dhi lēter edishunz əv Web-ster hav fərgətn, ər remember widh fēnt prēz, dhi refərmd spelingz bai hwich hī set such stōr. Ɑfter the revolūshunari ɑrdor past, dhi literari clas tūrnd widh reniud afecshun and delait tu dhi ōld cuntri, dhi ōld hōm. . Hapi wəz hī hū grū up in a haus hwār dhār wer cəpiz əv Shakespeare and Milton, əv Addison and Locke, Pope and Dryden, and Burke and Junius. An ōld fōlio əv Ben Jənson, Spenser, Chaucer, Piers Plowman, ōr wun əv Gervase Mark-ham's les stētli cwōrtoz, widh a grandfɑdher'z nēm ən it, mēd a man fīl az dhō hī had blū blud in hiz vēnz. Dhi veri pēper and bainding and dhi speling wer swīt and venerabl tu him. Bai and bai arōz Sir Walter Scott and Byron, Wordsworth and Coleridge, and ōl dhi hōst əv dhat wunderful jenerēshun. Dhi tōk əv an American langgwej past awē ōr retaird tu dhi bacwudz. And hwenever scīmz əv refōrmd speling wer brōcht, az dhē wer nau and dhen, dhi literari clas tuk dhem az a kaind əv pūrsonal insult, and ōverhwelmd dhi refōrmerz widh immezhurabl reprōch and inextinggwishabl lafter. . . . .

Widhin dhi last fifti yīrz, hauever, a cəmplīt revolūshun haz tēkn plēs in dhi aidīalz and pūrpusez əv dhi scəlarli clas. Dhi haiest wūrdz əv dhi ōld scəlarz wer "cultyur" and "biuti." Dhē sōt tu mōld dhemselvz intu biutiful caracterz. Dhē sōt tu dwel widh biutiful əbjects. Dhē wer fənd əv sēing dhat biuti iz its ōn exscius for biing, dhat a thing əv biuti iz a jəi fərever.

Dhi haiest wūrdz əv dhi niu scəlarz ɑr "prəgres" and "pauer." Niu trūth dhē wōnt, and niu frūt everi dē in dhi imprūvment əv dhi stēt ov man. Cultyur tūrnz frəm ficshun tu fact, frəm pōetri tu saiens. Linggwistic studi shārz dhi spirit əv dhi ēj. It haz tūrnd frəm drīming ōver ōld luv stōriz tu dhi studi əv nēshuns and əv man az recōrded in langgwej. Dhi filəlojist raivalz dhi jīəlojist in rīding dhi recərdz əv dhi rēs in dhi fəsilz əv langgwej. Hī iz a histōrian əv dhi taimz befōr histori. He givz us dhi pedigrī əv nēshunz hūz nēm and plēs nō mədern man cud ges. And he wishez tu dū sumthing fōr hiz feloz, tu bār hiz pɑrt in imprūving dhi cəndishun əv dhi rēs, and natyurali in imprūving langgwej. Dhi faundēshun əv dhi saiens əv langgwej iz lēd in dhi saiens əv vōcal saundz. Everi stiudent əv dhi mədern saiens studiz fonəloji. Dhi mīnz əv reprezenting saundz bai vizibl sainz ɑr ōlsō pɑrt əv hiz studi, and dhi speling əv dhi English langgwej amung udher things. And sō dhi speling əv dhi English langgwej haz becum dhi əprōbrium əv English scəlarz. Dhi grēt scəlarz wer natyurali dhi fūrst tu spīk aut bōldli. Dhi grētest jīnyus amung gramērianz, Jacob Grimm, but a fiu yīrz agō cəngratyulated dhi udher Europeans dhat dhi English had nət mēd dhi discuveri dhat a hwimzical anticwēted ərthəgrafi stud in dhi wē əv dhi yūniversal acseptans əv dhi langgwej. Nau wī cud fil a vəlyūm widh expozishun and əbjurgēshun əv dhi unaprōchabl badnes əv aur speling, frəm dhi penz əv eminent Englishmen and Americanz. . . .

Hwail dhis mūvment wəz gōing ən amung dhi scəlarz, anudher strīm əv influens tuk its raiz amung tīcherz. Fiu chēnjez əv dhi last sentyuri ār grēter dhan dhōz in dhi trītment əv children. Dhi methodz əv disiplin and əv tīching and dhi aparētus fōr dhem ār ōl chēnjd. Dhi mēn aparētus yūzd tu bī dhi rəd. And dhār wer hārdli eni buks speshali adapted tu dhi capasiti and nīdz əv dhi yung. Dhat ēbl men, grēt men, shud mēk a studi əv dhem, invent methodz əv instrucshun, rait buks, mēk ōl ārt and nētyur tribyutari tu dhār enjəiment and imprūvment, iz a hōlli mədern afār. Hapi ār dhi yūth əv dhi prezent jenerēshun; dhē hav dhi wūrld at dhār fīt. Dhat sum wē must bī faund əv tīching rīding widhaut tīrz wəz plēn.

Nōr iz tendernes fōr aur children ōl. Wī hav cum tu recəgnaiz dhi rait əv manhud, and sum ov us ov wumanhud, tu a vois in dhi guvernment. Wī trust aurselvz tu dhi masez. Dhen dhi masez must bī edyucēted. Dhē must lūrn tu rīd cwicli and īzili. Ignorans iz blaind and bad. . . . Dhi prəblem ov illiterasi haz ləng bin familyar tu Americanz az wun əv dhi mōst impōrtant əv sōshal saiens. It haz lētli cum up fresh and fīrful in England. And it iz fuli recəgnaizd dhat dhi trubl laiz in dhi irregyular and unrīzonabl speling əv English.

On Literature

March's foremost claim to posthumous fame was undoubtedly his then-revolutionary proposals for altering the teaching of literature at the college level. As noted in the Introduction, he was the first person to hold the title of professor of English and the first to teach a required Shakespeare course. His own education at Amherst College, in common with similar standards at other American colleges and universities of the day, had been typically classical in content and recitative in instruction. Professors of rhetoric and oratory (or of Classics) such as those under whom he had studied normally served merely to introduce their male students to choice passages from great poets as a means to create "gentlemen" who would know "intuitively" what the belletristic meanings in a work of literature happened to be (Graff and Warner 4). Philologists such as March, scientifically educated in the historical groundings and meanings of literature through their linguistic studies, necessarily used literary texts to illustrate linguistic changes.

As March noted in an essay entitled "Recollections of Language Teaching," the instruction he offered as a philologist worked with "Anglo-Saxon and English texts to read and understand them; not lectures about the languages, not lessons in descriptive or critical discourse about them, not a rhetorical but a linguistic study." He advocated those books for study that "contain weighty truths, important facts, close packed, expressed in musical simplicity, or with rhythmic distinction." In a move unprecedented in his time, March insisted that major English authors—Chaucer, Milton, and Shakespeare—and even then-contemporary writers warranted the same kind of study and analysis that Classical writers routinely received. His writings on now-canonical English writers form an important part of the history of literary criticism, and his more incidental comments on nineteenth-century writers, including Charles Lamb, William Morris, Robert Browning, and Walt Whitman remain of interest today. One should not expect modern methods of critical analysis in these writings. But for their day they were relatively revolutionary and suggest how seriously the country's first Professor of English took the study of English language and literature.

WORKS CITED

Graff, Gerald and Michael Warner, ed. *The Origins of Literary Studies in America*. New York: Routledge, 1989.

March, Francis A. "Recollections of Language Teaching." *PMLA* 8 (1893): xix-xxii; rept. *PMLA* 115 (2000): 1738-41.

Review of *The Ancient Classical Drama*, by Richard G. Moulton

Mr. Moulton's book on *The Ancient Classical Drama* is noteworthy for several reasons. One is that it is a product of his work as a lecturer in the Cambridge University Extension scheme, and givs some notion of the way that work is carried on. He is a Master of Arts and Scholar of Christ's College, Cambridge, and is sent out by the University to lecture on subjects that ar usually considerd very high and very remote from men's business and bosoms.

He has lectured since 1880 on the Ancient Drama. A course of lectures is givn, which is accompanied with regular exercises by such of the audience as wil take part—"always a considerabl percentage"; they ar tested at the end of the course in a formal examination. Mr. Moulton has conducted such courses in twenty-six different places, with audiences in which not one person in ten would know a word of Greek or Latin. His largest audiences wer at Newcastle-on-Tyne, where they reacht a weekly *average* of over seven hundred.

The book shows that this work is, in some respects, excellent for the University men who take part in it. A great deal of University literature—novels, or the like, in which University men figure—suggests a life without wil. The man is lost in heaps of books and lectures, his intellect floating among a thousand plausibl opinions and ten thousand fascinating criticisms, his active powers unused, paralyzed. Skeptic, agnostic, or pervert, he cannot make up his mind.

Mr. Moulton has come out of that state, if he ever was in it. It is easy to see how the necessity of interesting such audiences as he has, in the Greek drama, would compel him to make up his mind on hundreds of debated niceties. In our colleges omniscience is esteemd the special attribute of tutors, but ther is surely a plain final cause for its appearing also in the constitution of an Extension Lecturer. Mr. Moulton seems always to be telling things which ar clear and certain. His style is admirabl, neither hesitating nor pugnacious, but strong and simpl, in unaffected good English—with

---

Review of *The Ancient Classical Drama: A Study in Literary Evolution, Intended for Readers in English and in the Original*, by Richard G. Moulton. Oxford: Clarendon P; New York: Macmillan, 1890; *Independent* 42 (April 10, 1890): 16.

no borrowing from the Greeklings, nor from the slang with which some of the university men ar lately trying to make their books attractiv.

The substance of the book is also excellent for its purpose. Ther ar six lectures on tragedy—four treating the origin and development of tragedy in Greece, one on Roman tragedy, and one in which Shakespeare's *Macbeth* is arranged as an ancient tragedy. Ther ar six lectures on comedy—four of them on Greek, one on Roman, one on the modern Romantic Drama. And ther ar appendixes giving analyses of a number of ancient plays, tables illustrating the development of the drama, courses of reading to accompany this study and good indexes. Altogether it is a good solid body of useful matter to one who should wish to do work in this field, and exhibits the method of working fully and favorably.

This serious commendation might perhaps suffice, but special attention is drawn in the preface to the method of studying literature here exemplified, and the common methods ar deplored as spending too much time in examining the language of the great masterpieces. This is said to be study of grammar, of science, insted of literature.

The peculiarity of Mr. Moulton's method is that he studies literature as a development. He calls his book *A Study in Literary Evolution*. He begins with Ballad Dance, which he calls "a sort of literary protoplasm," an elementary form of all literature, including poetry, music, and gesture. Hence by augmentation and differentiation, come epic, lyric, and dramatic pieces. Hence lyric tragedy, whence dramatic tragedy, developing five structural parts—prolog, parode, episode, choral interlude, and exode, these again develop a structure of their own, material, metrical and other. A study in this literary evolution would consist of an arrangement of successive prologs, such as to lead from the simplest beginnings of Arion up to the last elaboration of Euripides by additions so slight, by differentiations so natural, that each prolog should seem to grow out of those before it as easily as any child from its parent. So with the parode, the episode and the other structural parts, and thus with tragedy as a whole.

This is clearly scientific study. It is a study of literature, to be sure, but not a literary study. It is like a lecture by Huxley or Marsh on the evolution of the horse, which makes an easy series from the orohippos, as big as a fox and with four toes, thru mesohippos with its three toes, and hipparion, up to the solid-footed equus. But a literary study would begin, perhaps, with the horse in Job, his neck clothed with thunder, crying, Ha, Ha, among the trumpets! and end for us with red Berold, or Roland, who brought the good news from Ghent to Aix.

Work in evolution is excellent when applied to organized structures. It makes an admirable preliminary arrangement of material phenomena.

But even in these spheres it is somewhat overdone. Scientists often think that all is done when phenomena ar stated in progressiv series, that no cause of the progress is to be sought. Serch for causes, for the intelligent energy which produces the augmentation of the successiv terms of the series, is not demanded; 2+2=5 is all right, if time enuf be givn. The Tenterden steepl passes for the fundamental law of logic. Reason in its higher functions is thus aborted by disuse with a considerabl number of our students.

Ther ar no fields in which the application of the progressiv series is less satisfactory than in the arts and in literature. We know wel what the intelligent energy is which makes the progress here. We know Watt and Edison. We know Æschylus, Euripides, Shakespeare. The presentation of *Macbeth* so that it shal not be thought of as the work of Shakespeare, but as the 975th term of a progressiv series of parodes, episodes, exodes and what not, is science. It is interesting, but its interest is scientific. It is profound, as handling natural laws; but not the profoundest. The profoundest exhibition to us of the divine energy is thru the personality, the wil of man.

Literature has its distinction in the works of the great geniuses. The student of literature seeks primarily and eminently to rethink the thoughts of these master minds, to repeat in himself their aspirations, hopes, loves, resolvs.

But in getting up the evolution business of Mr. Moulton, one is rethinking Mr. Moulton's thought. It might be done fairly wel with the slightest knowledge, and with no appreciation or enjoyment, of those thoughts which make the dramas masterpieces. In Mr. Moulton's book, indeed, the evolution proper is but skin deep, and the evolutionary method is by no means thuro. A large part of it consists of natural narrativ and description of the contents of one after another of the famous plays, with abundant explanation and reflection after the manner of a modern novel-writer, and with decorativ quotations of happy passages. He avails himself, as a good Extension Lecturer should, of all kinds of interest availabl with his audiences. They do not know Greek or Latin. Filological interest is therefore not availabl. He succeeds very wel without it. But he seems to be wrong in ruling it out of proper literary study. The central idea of primary literary study is to rethink the thoughts of the authors of the masterpieces. The primary work therefore is thuro study of their language line by line, word by word. We lern the full meaning of a word to the author by tracing it thru all his works, and then thru other works with which he was familiar, gathering up its associations of thought and music perhaps from many bold or beautiful passages, and thus we get all the author's pictures rightly drawn and shaded leisurely into our minds. Filological study is the natural means of clearing up, enriching and impressing the thoughts embodied in literature.

Mr. Moulton has been very successful in his literary courses without this kind of study. He is led to argue, in favor of carrying on the higher education even in the universities without much of it. He would read one book of Homer in the original, and the rest of it in English, to save time, and to study systems of evolution. His thought is, of course, that the rest of the books ar not to be thuroly masterd, the poet's thoughts not to be rethought; since if that wer to be done, it would take longer to do it with an English version than with the original. Skimming or skipping along, as we do in reading English, with some vague notion of the general meaning, some flashes of light here and there thru the vague, but no distinct knowledge of the precise meaning of half the words, is to be the method of studying literature. This is getting to be a popular view. Even those who insist on the study of Greek and Latin, many of them, talk incessantly about managing the study so as to read Greek as we do English, meaning such reading of English as was just characterized. It would be far better to talk of reading English as we do Greek, with minute and profound attention to every word.

Mr. Moulton thinks that the form of Shakespeare is almost out of intelligent reach of those who are ignorant of the Greek drama. A filosophic or scientific student would certainly wish to know these antecedents. But evolutionary explanations are seldom needed, except to account for some odd survivals—a scrap of chorus in *K. Henry V*, or something of that sort, which remains from a former age, like the buttons on the back of a gentleman's coat.

Mr. Moulton thinks that the ancient classics ar second only to Shakespeare and Goethe as an attractiv subject for lectures. It is true that they ar most admirabl material for evolutionary ingenuities, such as delight quick-witted intellects who do not much value moral or esthetic culture. But for the primary interest of literature, the great thoughts to rethink, they ar not so eminent. Mr. Moulton has done well with them, but in all his material from the tragedies ther is hardly a character to admire, a sentiment to cherish, an act to imitate, or even a wise saw to repeat. It would be idle to attempt to place English versions of them in our schools for popular study in place of the great masters in the modern languages whose thoughts ar the food and inspiration of modern life.

The Relation of English Literature to Æsthetics

How can the highest educational efficiency be secured for English in American colleges? This paper is to speak of the æsthetic influences of English, especially of English Literature. Æsthetic influences, to the teacher, are those influences which kindle in the student love of the beautiful and feed it and form it, which make his love of beauty intelligent, which prompt him to think beautiful thoughts, to utter beautiful words, to do beautiful acts, to become a beautiful person, to construct for himself a beautiful environment.

What is there in literature to exert such influences? Literature, in its eminent sense, is a picture of life painted by an artist under the influence of æsthetic feeling. Whatever objects are known to man which are capable of calling forth admiring love appear also in literature; in pictures, indeed, but with their beautiful traits made more attractive. The literary artist shapes the shows of things to the forms of the mind, shapes facts according to the laws of beauty, and gives them a gleam that never was on sea or land. So with beautiful thoughts, and beautiful acts, and ideal characters, and ideal environment—all that have been known, in fact, or imagined by genius are presented in literature in the most attractive form. All the influences of consecrated example and of sympathetic imitation are put in the hands of the teacher of literature.

Another source of æsthetic power in Literature is found in its peculiar sense material—sound. Language on one side, thought on the other side is sound. But sound is a more spiritual material for creations of beauty than even sight. Music has a beauty that rouses the roughest and thrills the toughest. The human voice is the natural bearer of emotion. Voice and thought are early identified in speech. From a series of separate signs of objects, disjunct, fragmentary, several, like the finger signs of deaf mutes, language, in which sound and sense have fused, runs and flows; it adds the powers of music to those of sensible signs and of the natural language of the emotions, and becomes capable of large combinations reflecting

"The Relation of English Literature to Æsthetics." *Proceedings of the College Association of the Middle States and Maryland*, 1892, 31–35.

and expressing with strange perfection and beauty the most complex states of mind and heart. It is worth observing further that a classic language is mainly the creation of literature.

Persons in the state of nature take their language by tradition from those about them. They catch up from their parents and their playmates the words and phrases they hear oftenest and need most. Their speech is the product of social necessities, acting under the common laws of association. Every tribe, every family, every person has natural peculiarities. Dialects, idioms are free, and in some sense there are as many dialects as persons. Language, at this stage, is well enough said to grow. Each person talks for himself, and knows no better speech than his own. A standard speech may appear through the influence of government or literature; it becomes a classic language through literature, under the shaping of the laws of beauty. Whenever deeds are done, or to be done, which exalt the faculties of large numbers of men, the creative power, genius, works in language. The poet, the orator rouses to heroic acts or recounts inspiriting achievements in worthy forms of speech. The happiest forms of the popular dialects which had grown by association are selected and combined into speech more perspicuous, more vigorous, and more musical than had been known before. Successful compositions of this kind are remembered and rehearsed; they make part of the education of the noble and cultured. They are imitated and accumulate from generation to generation till the time comes for Homeric poems and classic Greek, or for the Wyclif Bible and classic English. The part of a language which is standard in the eminent sense, or classic, is at first small, happy idioms of the Bible, the Ballads, Chaucer. Then for generations, there is slow increase, perhaps—one new idiom from this author, two or three from that, till Shakspere gathers them up by the hundred and adds his hundreds more. How many generations has it taken to incorporate the phrases of Milton into the speech, so that we use them without quotation or allusion, and his "Babylonish dialect" is standard English? In the struggle for life among the words and phrases of each generation many of the fittest survive. A classic speech is a kind of anthology, a record of the supreme moments of national life, the inspiration of new generations.

Another source of æsthetic power is thus seen to exist in the accumulation of moving associations upon the idioms of a classic language.

Striking expressions, happy and strange, used by Chaucer arrest the attention from their very strangeness. It fastens them in memory, makes them spring up with special promptness and kindness. "There is no excellent beauty," says Bacon, "that hath not some strangeness in the proportion." They pass on from Chaucer to Spenser, to Milton, to Tennyson, to Longfellow or Lowell, gathering new allusive charm from each new and beautiful passage in which they appear. They are nuclei of mysterious throngs of association, ganglions of nervous energy and expression, radiants of beauty, genius barks in idioms.

Another source of æsthetic influence is found in certain works of criticism.

The greatest authors invite and provoke criticism from other great authors, and they inspire their critics. Comments like those of Goethe, Coleridge, Lowell upon Shakspere, or of Child, Furness, Stedman are proper literature, works of beauty themselves as well as revealers of beauty in others.

This sketch of the sources of power in literature enables us to say with confidence that English Literature is eminent among literatures for its power as a means of æsthetic culture. Its galleries of beautiful pictures, thoughts, acts, its ideal characters, its music, its moving idiom, its hoards of allusion, its noble and beautiful criticism, are hardly equaled by any other literature. How can these influences be made efficient upon college students?

1. By getting them to read the passages which are to influence them, seeing the pictures of life, rethinking the thoughts, repeating the feelings, the ideals, the music. Courses of reading like *Winchester's Short Courses* may be prescribed, and they may be carried on by requiring written reports and holding examinations upon them, without occupying many recitation or lecture hours.

2. By lectures to point out, illustrate, illuminate, commend suitable selected authors, books, and passages.

3. By thorough study of a few representative books of representative authors. This includes going over representative passages in class with a professor word by word, using all the resources of philology and other sciences to bring out, clear up, enrich, and impress the thought and the style. It includes the attaining a clear conception of the unity of the whole book and the order and proportion of the parts, and grounding the whole in the character of the author and the age.

Such study implies, of course, rapid general reading of the author studied, since to learn the full meaning, and exact meaning of his words and phrases and figures in any passage, the first step is to find how he has used them in other passages. It implies also more or less study of æsthetics as a science, and of histories and theories of the development of literature.

This is the study which makes students rejoice in the masterpieces of literature and remember them forever. With it comes sound æsthetic culture, good in any language, but in the mother tongue of inestimable value to youth, providing them with the very words to guide their highest thought, and with forms of graceful speech, ever prompting them to easy utterances of courtesy, and affection, and devotion.

How many and what kind of college exercises should be given to English Literature?

The direction of reading, and lectures of Exposition and History of Literature, might be carried through the whole college course, using one recitation or lecture hour a week.

The thorough study ought to have four weeks for two terms in the Junior or Senior year required of all students; and electives equal in number to those of any other language for editors, preachers, teachers, lawyers, and amateurs.

These times are in addition to those of practical instruction in reading and writing correctly.

The professor's main reliance should be on his hours of thorough work, and he should aim to make it as hard as Greek. Those professors who proclaim it their purpose to make their department a realm of beauty, who rule out root-digging and gerund-grinding, philology, and the higher criticism, and make lectures of beautiful quoted passages, in which they add to the rhyme of the poet the beauty of their own voices, and deal with difficulties after the manner of the great singer who made it her rule to render any passage which she did not understand with special effusion—such professors do not retain rank among the great forces of their colleges; English under them does not rank as one of the important studies. The heavy-weights, the Scientists and the Grecians, occupy the earnest hours, and the English is left for the frills and outward flourishes, to fill up corners here and there.

It would be a branch of this subject to discuss the selection of books to read and study; a list of books and noble passages might be presented. But the time allows only a remark or two.

There seems to be something about harping on beauty which suggests trifling, weakness. This is certainly so with hard-headed young men. They will not listen to much beautiful talk from professors, and they reluct at tenderness and pathos. Shall a football champion weep over imaginary woes? Passages chosen for study should have solid importance, be the utterances of great minds speaking passionately and rhythmically of the very truths or experiences the inspiration of which has made them great.

American literature is eminently worthy of study. The great English literature of the formation period is religious throughout, as Professor Hunt tells us, and liberty-loving, and chaste. It grew up in the midst of struggles for religion, in the midst of the contests of freemen, in the midst of a people fond of nature and of home. The same people on a higher plane of culture and power, loving nature and home, religion and freedom as dearly as their ancestors, have here passed through similar struggles for religion and freedom, and have produced literature of the same high strain. A peculiarly depressing tone has for a long time been plain in the literature of England. The verses of Tennyson wail over the vanished life and heroes of the old time. There is a dying fall in the exquisite cadences of Morris. The *Earthly Paradise* is an Egyptian feast with a death's head by every flower. The lesser artists have the same pitch. But in America life is fresh and exultant. Bryant, Longfellow, Lowell, Webster give us lyrics and orations upon which to rear our youth, the product of higher poetic and rhetorical endowment, and more manly experience and culture, as well as full of strength and hope, and the old love of home, and freedom, and religion.

The World of *Beowulf*

The world of *Beowulf* is a strange world. Its characters ar strange; the action goes on in the midst of a strange nature. Some explanation of its strangeness was attempted by examining the manner in which its effects on the different senses ar presented. The words wer collected which show the effect of objects on the sight, then those which represent sounds, smel, taste, etc. The use of descriptivs of sight is very abundant. It is the habit to giv the color of objects. But upon collecting the words they ar found to describe degrees of light and shade, rather than different qualities of color. Objects ar described as bright, white, grey (beorht, blâc, blondon, brûn, scîr, torht, hâr, græg), or as dark, murky, swart, wan (deorc, myrce, sweart, wan), or the like. Of red, orange, yellow, green, blue, indigo, violet, yellow is the only one that figures in this erly world. Yellow is common. The ocean, the roads, the horses ar yellow. It is the great expanse of a white and dark world in the far north, a monochromatic sketch of a world not yet tinted. Into the midst of this nature, however, man brings some specks of color. These ar carefully described as fâh, variegated,— peculiarly colord. Furniture and arms wrought with gold ar golde-fâh, or with jewels, sinc-fâh; and we hav bân-fâh, brûn-fâh, stân-fâh—the roads ar stân-fâh—but oftenest of all ar objects blōd-fâh, dreor-fâh, swât-fâh, wael-fâh. The blithesome raven is black of course; and horses of the chiefs ar glistening, *blanc*; in one splendid gift which Beowulf makes to his lord there ar four horses of apple-yellow (æppel-fealuwe). In this pale land is found no breth of fragrance. There is but one mention of smel. A dragon is said to smel or follow the scent of his enemy's footprints. Nor ar the flavors of taste distinguisht. There ar great feasts celebrated, but no solid food is mentiond. Beer, ale, wine, mead, *lith* and *wered* flow freely, but their taste is not described. Water is abundant, but it starts no suggestion of drinking. Cold and hot, hard and soft, occur.

But, perhaps, the most impressiv fact relates to the descriptivs of sound. So far as objects of nature ar concernd, there ar no such descriptivs. The inanimate world utters no sounds. Men talk, laugh, two or three times; they weep, roar with pain or grief, sing, play the harp, sound the trumpet, rattle their armor, make a din. Three or four times objects associated with men ar raisd to animation and utterance. A wepon sings, the

"The World of *Beowulf*." *Proceedings of the American Philological Association* 13 (1882): xxi-xxiii.

ship and the funeral pile of Beowulf roar, the black raven, blithe of heart, announces the rising of the sun. But the great world surrounding man is silent,—a soundless as wel as a colorless world. In this world men, a few weak beings, liv their life, standing by each other, and fighting monsters. No man harms any other man in this story. Beowulf risks his life over and over to help others, and this is his simple nature; not a religion, not a duty even,—a simple matter of course. He has no ambition; does n't want to be a king, does n't seek adventures. He was neglected and overslaughd in his youth because he was not enterprising. He is good-natured thru and thru, and serenely wise; loyal above all to the king and his children, and to Hygd, the young queen. The later romances would hav been sure to make this Lancelot in love with this Guinevere. But Beowulf is not of that kind. He forms no ties. He is more like the lion of the romances who gards the Lady Una, and livs for nothing more than a tuch of her hand. This type of caracter that likes to lie in the sun, but rises to any emergency, is a favorit with all mankind. He is not, however, presented with any elaboration of caracter. The poet seems only interested in the story he is telling, not in the development of the caracter of his hero.

There ar some things in the poem which, in spite of its general rudeness and obscurity, suggest that the author had a cultured and even artificial love of the picturesk. The opening of the poem is one of the most picturesk incidents to be found among the tales of erly man. The obsequies of the hero Scyld, by embarking him in his boat with his tresures and trofies, and his flag flying above him, and sending him out to sea to return whence he had come an infant, the story of Hiawatha, of the *Kalewala*, of Arthur and the rest, is the same in its picturesk effect as that of Tennyson's Ulysses.

No one can say who receivd the load,
says the Beowulf.
It may be that he reacht the happy isles,
And saw the great Achilles.

This beginning, so striking in itself, has a certain artificial aspect, because it is not a part of the following story, but relates to the ancestor of the heroes of it. The conclusion is also in the same picturesk manner. A monument is wrought over Beowulf with striking ceremonies, on a hill high and broad, and seen afar by seafaring men. Ten days they built it, the best of funeral piles, that far-seeing men might find it most honorable and becoming. The same manner is shown in many particular descriptions, as in that of the region in which Grendel had his lair. Striking details ar here givn simply for picturesk effect. The author knew something of the Bible. He mentions God, the devil, hevn, and hel, very much as men do now. He puts the Bible monsters on the same footing as those of his own mythology, just as Milton does. But there is no Christ or any special Christian thought in the book. Several passages suggest an acquaintance with Homer or Virgil. But if the author had taste to decorate parts of his poem, he had not sustaind vigor of imagination to bring the whole of his material into an epic unity.

The Morte Darthur

Le Morte Darthur. By Syr Thomas Malory. Faithfully reprinted from the original edition (1485) of William Caxton. Edited by H. Oskar Sommer, Ph.D. Vol. I. Text. London: David Nutt.

The *Morte Darthur* is the most familiar by name of all early English books; perhaps the most familiar to the general reader of our time of all prose romances before those of Walter Scott. But it has been one of the rarest of well-known books. It is but a few years since it was not known at the New York libraries that there was a copy in America. Now, however, the one perfect copy of the original edition in the world is owned by Mrs. Abby E. Pope of Brooklyn, N.Y. Only one other copy, imperfect, is known. It is in the library of Earl Spencer, bought long ago for £320. This edition was printed by Caxton, who finished the printing, as he tells us, in the Abbey of Westminster on the last day of July, 1485. A new edition was printed by Wynkyn de Worde in 1498, and another in 1529. Only one copy of each is known to be in existence. There are other black-letter editions, four at least; the last, Stansby's, printed in 1634. All are rare. It was not printed again till 1816. In 1817 an edition appeared under Southey's name. A good edition in its way, by Thomas Wright (1856), and a later Globe edition made the old romance accessible to general readers who read for the story and the style. But for students who wish to be sure of the exact words, the spelling and punctuation, and all that, it has remained inaccessible. Here at last is the very thing that was wanting—a faithful reprint of the original of Caxton, page for page, line for line, word for word. It is printed with clear large types—Roman types, however, in place of the black letter. There are 861 pages on heavy white paper, with ample margins, and it makes a royal volume. The editing and printing give good promise of accuracy. It is from the Ballantyne Press, and edited by H. Oskar Sommer, Ph.D.

Dr. Sommer's special attention was drawn to this book in his Spenser studies. It is used very freely in the *Faerie Queene*. He found that a new and scholarly edition was needed, and made up his mind to undertake it. Now see how they do such things in Germany. He communicated his in-

"*The Morte Darthur*," Part 1. *Nation* 50 (January 2, 1890): 15-16; Part 2. *Nation* 51 (September 4, 1890): 196–97; Part 3. *Nation* 54 (January 21, 1892): 58.

tention to his Excellency the Royal Prussian Minister of Public Instruction, Herr Dr. von Gossler, and requested leave of absence for six months. This request was readily complied with, and a grant besides was made him from the public funds to enable him to prosecute his labors. Thus armed and equipped from the Prussian treasury, Dr. Sommer proceeded to the British Museum and set to work upon Earl Spencer's volume. He copied it with his own hands, and read the proofs and revises with the original. Twenty-one pages also had to be collated with Mrs. Pope's volume in Brooklyn. This work occupied the full time of his leave of absence, and we have the result of it in the noble volume now published by Mr. Nutt. A second volume is to contain the apparatus which German scholarship deems necessary for a critical edition of such a masterpiece—an Introduction, dealing with the language and the like, a Treatise on the Sources, Various Readings, an Index, etc. As a compliment and guerdon, perhaps, to English buyers, an essay on Malory's prose style by Andrew Lang is to be added.

This book is a sort of *Iliad* of Chivalry. The adventures in it had been separately told in ballads and metrical romances, and chanted in baronial halls, for two or three centuries. Coleridge said that he would engage to compile twelve books with characters as distinct and consistent as those in the *Iliad* from these metrical ballads and other chronicles about King Arthur and the Knights of the Round Table. It was safe to say. It had been done already by Sir Thomas Malory in the *Morte Darthur*. There is very much such a plot and unity in it as in the *Iliad*. Arthur grows up, the Round Table is fitted with knights who have glorious adventures of fighting and of love, then the sin of Launcelot and Guenever sets the knights against each other, and they perish in two bloody battles. The "passing of Arthur" after the battle is familiar to every one in Tennyson's versification of it. Every one who likes it there should read it in Malory. The Queen and Launcelot retire to houses of "religion" and die in the odor of sanctity. "So whan syr Bors & his felowes came to his bedde they founde hym starke dede & he laye as he had smyled & the swettest sauour aboute hym that euer they felte." Like the *Iliad*, the *Arabian Nights* and all great folk stories, the 'Morte Darthur' has its interest for persons at any age. A boy is ready for it when he is in the early foot-ball stage, reading the "Lay of the Last Minstrel," and *Ivanhoe*, and *Tom Brown*. There is rushing and tackling of the most vigorous kind at almost every turn. This is the way Sir Gareth and Sir Ironside go on:

> "And thus they foughte tyl it was past none and neuer wold stynte tyl att the laste they both lackt wynde, and thenne they stode wagging, staggering, panting, blowing, and bleeding, so that all that beheld them

for the most part wepte for pytie. So whan they had restyd them a whyle, they yede to battle againe, tracing, racing, and foyning as two bores. And at sometime they toke their renne as hit had ben two wild rammys, and hurtled to gyders that somtyme they felle to the erthe groveling; and their armour was so sore hewen that men might see their naked sydes."

Most of the jousts and encounters of adventure do no more damage than a university foot-ball game. Sir Launcelot in one of his adventures "had the better hand of five hundred knights, and yet," exults the chronicler, "there was none slain of them"; to be a murderer, to kill men in jousting, is the greatest shame that a knight may have. The knights can bear any amount of "smiting, racing, tracing, foyning," and the like. Sir Launcelot, for example, fights all day with a spear-head in his side, smites and pulls down more than thirty knights, and then rides off and gets well in a few days. The leeches are often women, and do wonderful cures. The attention of the young reader is held by a rapid succession of adventures, told in the briefest, simplest, and most realistic fashion. If there is any way in which a knight, or a knight and his horse, can be turned "up-so-down," or otherwise put *hors de combat,* which is not here described, it must be some later evolution. The variety of wounds can hardly be matched from Homer. There are some combats with monsters and giants, mostly in foreign countries. When Arthur was subduing the Romans, he met the giant Galapas: "He shorted hym and smote of bothe his legges by the knees, sayenge, Now arte thow better of a sise to dele with than thow were." And he does not leave him to fight upon his stumps like Witherington, in similar doleful dumps, in "Chevy Chase," but smites off his head forthwith; "and the body slew six Saracens in the falling downe," says Wright's edition, but that was not known to Caxton. Sir Servause is contemptuously described as one "that had neuer courage nor lust to doo batail ageynst no man, but yf it were ageynst gyants & ageynst dragons and wylde beestes." There are also a thousand and one love stories, and as many tricks of magic, and much mystic lore of religion, especially in the quest of the holy grail.

It must be confessed that to an unsympathetic reader there may be something monotonous in the succession of adventures, and the knights and their combats seem all alike, as babies do to bachelors. The shifting figures have something of the Punch and Judy aspect. All the world is a stage—no seasons, no weather, no nature; everybody is always in character, serious—no humor, no laughter, except now and then, when a knight is tumbled up-so-down in jousting, the "queene" or the "haute prince," perhaps, will laugh so sore that they may not stand. But if the old critic, or the philosophic student, is not fascinated by the stories, the book has other charms. It is a vivid picture of the ideals, the characters, the manners, the life of the age of chivalry. Courage, strength, size, activity are primary heroic qualities. "Sir Tristram was called the strongest and biggest knight of the world, for he was bigger than Sir Launcelot, but Sir Launcelot was better breathed." Meekness and gentleness are eminent moral qualities; Sir Launcelot was "the meekest man and the gentlest that ever eate in hall among ladies." Sir Galahad is "demure as a dove."

Truthfulness and hatred of treason are among the vows of knighthood and continually shown in remarkable ways. Every knight should be a lover. "Why," said La beale Isoud, "are yee a knight and bee yee no lover? It is a shame unto you." The knights are all fair riders. "What is a knight," says Sir Launcelot, "but when he is on horseback?" Sir Tristram is a "curious harper." They learn hawking, hunting, chess playing, carving. Surgery, medicine, magic, and music are common accomplishments of the ladies; they sometimes compound love potions, but they are wholly unversed in coquetry; they speak their love right out for the heroes who please them. Chastity is the crowning virtue of a knight. Sir Galahad needs to be a "pure maide" to win the holy grail. A gentle piety pervades the book, a contrast with "Piers Ploughman" or Chaucer. The men of "religion," often hermits or "white munks," are pious, good leeches, good confessors. The language of piety is simple and tender: "Faire, sweete Father, Jesu Christ," "Mild mother Mary," "Faire father God." Nice touches abound. Sir Gareth "knightly ate his meat and egerly"; he had "the fairest and the largest hands that ever man saw." "The King wept and dried his eyes with a handkercher." "These Britons brag as though they bare up all the world," says the Roman Emperor's cousin.

For the student of language no English book is more fascinating. It is packed with the most expressive words and idioms just strange enough to stimulate interest, piquant, picturesque, gentle, as well as queer combinations of words which offer grammatical problems as inviting as the particles of Homer. But to the discussion of such matters we shall be introduced by the apparatus of the second volume.

Le Morte Darthur. By Syr Thomas Malory, faithfully reprinted from the original edition (1485) of William Caxton. Edited by H. Oskar Sommer, Ph.D. Vol. II. Introduction. London: David Nutt.

The first volume of Dr. Sommer's reprint of Caxton's *Morte Darthur* was duly noticed by us and cordially welcomed. It is a faithful reprint of

Caxton's text, page for page, line for line, 861 pages, on heavy white paper, with sample margins—a royal volume. The apparatus of a complete critical edition was to have been given in a second volume; but Dr. Sommer found that it enlarged in the working up, and he has divided it for two volumes. The second volume, now published by David Nutt, contains the bibliographic and the linguistic apparatus; discussions of the sources and of the style are reserved for a third volume.

Many interesting facts are presented in the bibliographical part. Nothing is known about Sir Thomas Mallory except the mention of him in the *Morte Darthur*. Dr. Sommer cannot ground the later references to him as a Welshman, or the hypothesis that he was a priest. The single perfect copy of Caxton's edition, which had been in the library of the Earl of Jersey at Osterley Park, was sold in May, 1885, for £1,950. The British Museum bid £1,800. "It is very much to be regretted," says Dr. Sommer, "that the English nation lost this splendid specimen of Caxton's printing, containing, as it does, the traditional history of their King Arthur, a national epic." It became the property of Mrs. Abby E. Pope of Brooklyn, N.Y., who seems to have been just as ready to give Dr. Sommer access to it as Earl Spencer or the authorities of the British Museum would have been.

Dr. Sommer explains his title-page. Caxton followed the MSS., which had no title-pages. Wynkyn de Worde introduced them after the death of his master. Wynkyn de Worde's *Morte Darthur* of 1529 is the first text ever printed with illustrations throughout. "They are very coarsely executed woodcuts." This is the edition from which the later reprints have been derived, with two exceptions. The last of the black-letter editions, Stansby's (1634), which has been copied in most of the modern reprints, is from East (1585), which is from Wynkyn de Worde (1529). The preface of Stansby informs the reader that the phraseology of the volume is corrected in many places, where King Arthur or some of his knights "swear prophane, and use superstitious speeches, all (or the most part) of which is either mended or quite left out"; "so that, as it is now, it may passe for a famous piece of antiquity, revived almost from the gulph of oblivion, and rescued for the pleasure and benefit of the present and future times." Many a good round oath from the mint of Shakspere has been lost for ever by King James's prohibition of profanity, but one can find Mallory's oaths intact in Dr. Sommer's Caxton. Dr. Sommer gives a few early references to *Morte Darthur*; one, from Ascham's *Schoolemaster* (1570), presents a Puritanic view of it, as one of the books "made in Monasteries by idle Monkes or wanton Chanons," the whole pleasure of which standeth "in open mansslaughter and bold bawdrye."

And after specifying deeds of Sir Launcelot, Sir Tristram, and Sir Lameracke, the *Schoolemaster* goes on: "Thus is good stuffe for wise men to laughe at, or honest men to take pleasure at. Yet I know when God's Bible was banisht the Court, and *Morte Arthure* received into the Princes Chamber." One might pass this as *schulmeisterisch;* but if Dr. Sommer had made later collections, he would have given us very much the same tone from Ben Jonson. "He had no Arthurs," says Jonson of young Lord Beaufort,

"Abortives of the fabulous dark cloister,
Sent out to poison Courts, and infest manners;
But great Achilles', Agamemnon's acts,
Sage Nestor's counsels and Ulysses' sleights,
Tydides' fortitude, as Homer wrought them
In his immortal fancy, for examples
Of the heroic virtue."

And even Shakspere sets *Hotspur* railing about "the dreamer Merlin and his prophecies, . . . and such a deal of skimble-skamble stuff." But perhaps Milton's favorite, "our sage, serious Spenser, whom I dare be known to think a better teacher than Scotus or Aquinas," will outweigh the whole theatre; and he knows no happier source than these romances to point a moral or adorn a tale.

On page 28 begin the notes on the language of *Le Morte Darthur*. This book, compared in 1474, printed in 1485, belongs to the date of transition from Middle to Modern English. When examined by grammar rules drawn from Shakspere for Modern English, and Chaucer for Middle English, it seems to be very irregular and mixed. A grammar might be made from the *Morte Darthur*, and taken as a standard, which would make the language of Chaucer or Shakspere irregular; but Dr. Sommer does not attempt that. He gives brief notes of the most characteristic examples of the orthography, phraseology, and syntax of his volume. The orthography he attributes to Caxton and his printers, believing that they did not follow Mallory's manuscript. The new printers were without standard. The manuscripts had variant spellings. Mastery of orthography seems to have been an ability to recognize, remember, and use all these different spellings. The more ways a man could spell a word the better speller he was. The modern English *means* is spelt *menes, meane, moyne, moyan, moyane; realm* is spelt *reame, royame, reaume, royalme, realme, royaume;* and so they go. The proper names exhibit greater variety than the common names, so that readers generally do not recognize their identity, but multiply the characters, making the scene swarm with heroes as the sky with stars; and the best of the editors heretofore often duplicates or triplicates the real characters. The different spellings of Gromere Gumorson furnish Sir Edward Strachey, editor of the Globe edition, with three heroes for one, those of Gratian three more, those of Pertilope or Pertolepe two more, and so on.

There are nine pages of notes on the phraseology and syntax. A note refers us to a forthcoming work by Dr. L. Kellner, in which there is an elaborate study of Caxton's syntax, "a most valuable contribution to the study of the English tongue." A list of various readings between Caxton's edition and Wynkyn de Worde's of 1529 is given, about 10,000 in number. Then comes a list of names and places, "the first complete and critical Index to *Le Morte Darthur* ever compiled." There are nearly 1,000 names in the text. With each name references are given to the passages in which it occurs, and the gist of what is said in them, so that we have an authoritative biography of the person or facts about the places, very interesting and convenient for reference.

Next comes a glossary of 46 double-column pages, the first ever compiled to *Le Morte Darthur*. Dr. Sommer is preparing a Caxton Dictionary for all the works printed by Caxton, and he uses his general material pretty freely in this glossary, so that it is in effect a small etymological dictionary. He gives the different spellings that occur in the text, and precise references. There are very few words that are wholly unknown to the general reader, but the various spellings and novel shades of meaning are very often enlightening for the history of the word, and make the glossary a treasury of facts such as the student of language delights in.

The third volume, to contain Dr. Sommer's dicussion of the sources of Mallory's tale and a treatise on his style by Mr. Andrew Lang, is being actively pushed forward. It will be looked for with lively interest.

Le Morte Darthur. By Syr Thomas Malory. Faithfully reprinted from the original edition (1485) of William Caxton, edited by H. Oskar Sommer, Ph.D. Vol. III. Studies on the Sources. With an introductory essay by Andrew Lang, M.A. London: David Nutt. 1891. Pp. xxv., 338.

Dr. Sommer now presents to "the world of scholarship" the final volume of the work which he began to prepare for the press four years ago. The first volume contained the text of Caxton's *Le Morte Darthur*, a noble quarto of 861 pages; the second, 230 pages of introduction, including bibliography and essays on the various editions, collations, notes on the language, a complete and critical index of names and places, and a glossary; the final volume deals with the "Sources." It was well known that our Iliad of Chivalry was made from earlier romances. Caxton tells us in his preface that "Syr Thomas Malorye dyd take it oute of certeyn bookes of frensshe and reduced it into Englysshe." Malory, also, in the text itself, frequently reminds us that he tells the tale as the French book says. French books and English books telling similar adventures of the same heroes have been long familiar. Dr. Sommer has attempted to trace in detail the whole series of adventures, tell us where the original of each is found, and set the original before us by description and quotation, so that we can make out clearly what credit belongs to Malory. Thus he finds that the first seven chapters of book first run parallel with the *Merlin* of Robert de Boron. He therefore gives a *résumé* of this *Merlin*, with quotations of considerable passages, stopping at every turn to point out in what particulars, if any, Malory varies from the original. It is accompanied, of course, with much collateral information, such as the thorough student desiderates, about other texts, the bibliography, and the like, and makes a pretty long chapter—more than twice as long as the Malory.

The result of it, however, is to give a distinct picture of Malory's manner of working. In the first place, the De Boron story is more than five times as long as Malory's. The materials worked up in the whole *Morte Darthur* are ten times as long as the book. Then this brevity is not gained by dropping descriptive particulars, and reducing all to a thread of narrative, or an outline of adventures, but by modification of the series of events and persons, omitting such as do not suit the adapter. What he does tell he tells with minute realism, often adding fresh particulars. These Dr. Sommer sometimes finds in other versions, sometimes credits to Malory's invention. Changes are not infrequently made to adjust matters to different forms of the story which Malory has accepted in the later books. He is not merely collecting by whim a jumble of good stories. He has a plan. His diction also is seen to be his own. Sometimes he translates literally, sometimes not; but he never goes far without showing vital signs. So that, on the whole, Malory writing his *Morte Darthur* from De Boron, is quite like Shakspere writing a scene of *Julius Cæsar* from North's *Plutarch*.

With the eighth chapter Malory took up the "Ordinary Merlin," and at the eighteenth he changed to the "Suite de Merlin"; at book v. he took up the *Morte Arthur* in the version of the Scotch poet Huchown. Thus far Dr. Sommer goes on as in the first seven chapters, but afterwards he moves more rapidly. He goes through, however, the whole twenty-one books, and is able to give the originals of all except the seventh book and a few pages in the sixth, the twelfth, and the nineteenth. These last pages narrate Lancelot stories which are not found in any known sources. A study of them in connection with variations elsewhere from the known

Lancelots convinces Dr. Sommer that Malory has followed in the main a lost "Suite de Lancelot," which we may well hope may be found, or at least fragments sufficient to construct it with the help of Malory. The seventh book is the adventures of Gareth and Lynette, with which Tennyson begins his Round Table series. Dr. Sommer can trace no part of this book, nor can he find anywhere the slightest reference to Gareth's exploits on this adventure, or to the Lady Lyonesse, her sister Lynet, her brother Gryngamor, or the five brothers whom Gareth fought and overcame. He suggests that it is a story not belonging to the Arthurian cycle, but adapted to it by Malory, or by some unknown author whose version has been lost. Malory speaks of his "frensshe book" as usual in this narrative, but the style is perfect Malory—Malory delighted with the unwonted humors of his personages. He evidently relished the later lively fabliaux; possibly this may be one of his own making. To the general reader it is like one of Shakspere's comic scenes in a tragedy: it gives a delightful laugh; and now that Tennyson has repeated it we may safely say that its introduction shows high art in Malory. Tennyson closes:

"And he that told the tale in older times
Says that Sir Gareth wedded Lyonors,
But he that told it later, says Lynette."

So far as appears in Dr. Sommer's "Sources," all the old books say "Lyonors," that is, "Lyonesse." It is Tennyson who says "Lynette," that is, "Lynet."

So far as the statistical setting forth of the immediate antecedents of Malory's book is concerned, Dr. Sommer's volume is of great value. He has completed a work of immense labor. It is pleasant to learn that he means to continue his investigations. There is opportunity, one sees, for hundreds of papers of research and criticism upon the exact relations of different versions, MSS., and editions to particular passages of Malory. On the other side the more inviting question of the origin and development of these romances waits for solution. Much has been written on it, and by great scholars. Dr. Sommer gives us some bibliography. By and by, perhaps, he may give us a volume.

Mr. Lang's introductory essay brings Malory into pleasant relations with Homer and Tennyson, and gives him much gracious praise for the enjoyable elements of his work, "the noble and renowned acts of humanity, gentleness, and chivalry" which he likes to tell, and the simplicity and picturesqueness of his style.

The Fluency of Shakespeare

Fluency of speech at the lowest, vocal fluency, implies promptly working nerv connection between the concepts of vocal sounds and the muscular movements necessary to produce the sounds; and, also, promptly working connection between the vocal concepts of words, so that a stream of words may flow freely without attention to the meaning. Children of lerned households often hav this fluency erly, and, if deficient in intellect, exhibit it painfully thru life. But it is a great gift for the student of languages, in original reserches in etymology, for exampl, and for the orator and the poet. Shakespeare's possession of it attracts attention in his playing with words euphuistically, in his puns, and in nonsense-talk like that of Pistol or Dogberry. It is closely connected also with his command of musical expression in prose or rime.

Intelligent fluency implies further promptly working nerv connection between the concept of each vocal sound and the thought concepts of which it is the sign. This thought concept may be an image of sum object which the word denotes, or of sum quality which it connotes; more often it is an indefinit group of qualities, and relations, and feelings not strictly connotativ or denoted. The fluent man may need to hav the sound concept rize and the muscular utterance follow upon any one of these qualities or relations.

The power of Shakespeare's utterancy has often been thought to be here, and to consist in a peculiarly close connection between words as sounds and particular natural objects which the words denote, in the identification, it is said, of the word and the object, so that his speech is without effort the presentation of pictures, or lively group of concrete thoughts and facts. It is plain that there is truth in this, but how the peculiar Shakespearian charm is connected with it, and how far it reaches, needs to be studied in the particular facts. To find what there is new in Shakespeare's speech I hav caused an examination to be made of the words in A in Murray's *Dictionary* to see how many of these words appear for the first time in Shakespeare, and in how many meanings any appear for the first time.

The date of the play is first givn, then an abbreviation for the name of it, followd by an alfabetic list of the words having meanings which

"The Fluency of Shakespeare." *Transactions of the American Philological Association* 26 (1895): 147-54.

appear for the first time in the play. Words which appear for the first time ar stard.

1588, *L.L.L.*, 25—abate, abbreviated, abrogate, academe*, accidentally*, acute, adjunct*, affected, ajax*, ambassy, animal, anon (2), antic (2), apathaton*, apology, apostrophe, art, athwart, attack, attainder, attending*, audaciously*.

1588, *Tit. Andr.*, 7—abjectly*, aged, aim, alphabet, anchorage, appoint, architect.

1590, *Com. Err.*, 8—abet, acquaint, adjudged, alluring, anatomy, apparel, aspect, assembly.

1590, *Mds. N.D.*, 18—abridgment, acheron*, acorn, adamant, after-supper*, age, air, airy, along, amazedly*, and, apprehension, apt, arm, ass, at, aunt, austerity.

1591, *Two Gent.*, 10—about, advise, after, allicholly*, anthem, applaud, at, attend, augury.

1591, *Rom. and Jul.*, 15—abused, addle, ahighlone*, alack, along; ambling, ambuscado*, amerce, anatomy, and arbitrate, aside, atomy, attending, awakening*.

1592, *Ven. and Ad.*, 3—Adon*, amaze, ashy.

1593, *1 Hen. VI.*, 11—abrupt, accomplice, across, add, against, arbitrator, assembled*, atilt, attorneyship*, audacious, await.

1593, *2 Hen. VI.*, 10—abortive, abrook*, accuse*, again, aidance*, anend, approach, arouse*, at, await.

1593, *3 Hen. VI.*, 8—a, abode*, abodement*, abuse, answer (2), artificial, assail.

1593, *Rich. II.*, 10—accused*, administer, amazing*, antic, appellant*, army, ascend, ask, atone*, awful.

1593, *Lucre.*, 3—acquit, answer, attempt.

1594, *Rich. III.*, 14—accessary, adore, aerie, after, afternoon, air, all, all (in combs), anchor, answer, apology, attainder, attorney*, aweless.

1595, *John*, 7—absey, accent, adjunct*, adulterate*, affect, almost, amazement.

1596, *M. of Ven.*, 10—a, above, acceptance, accoutred*, act, agitation, air, along, appropriation, attribute.

1596, *Taming of Sh.*, 6—aglet, agreed, amends, anything, appendix, artillery.

1596, *I Hen. IV.*, 11—advised, air, alien, all-hallow, amble, anchovy*, answerable*, applaud, armed, athwart, attribution.

1597, *2 Hen. IV.*, 19—aboard, about, absolutely, accite, accommodate, aconite, active, agate, aid, alarum-bell, among, ancient, answer, antiquity, appearing, apple-john*, appliance, atomy, avoirdupois.

1598, *Merry W.*, 16—about, accoutrement, adhere, admirable, admittance (2), adoption, affecting, affliction, allicholly, anthropophaginian*, arched*, armiger*, arras, arrest, article.
1599, *Hen. V.*, 11—abreast*, abutting*, accomplishment, action, advised, answer, arbitrament, argument, arrive, attaint, attest.
1599, *Much Ado*, 9—accordant, accordingly, ache*, action, answer, apprehend, approved, assault, attired.
1600, *As Y. L.*, 7—accent, all, allottery, animal, assembly, atone, attend.
1600, *Lover's Comp.*, 3—acture, annexion, act.
1600, *Sonnets*, 3—alchemy, art, assail.
1601, *Jul. C.*, 6—acting*, afoot, airless*, ambitious, apparition, apprehensive.
1601, *Twel. N.*, 5—adoration, ahungry, air, attract, author.
1601, *All's Well*, 9—acquire, acutely*, admiringly*, adoptions*, aid, appliance*, application, arm, auspicious.
1602, *Hamlet*, 16—abhorred*, actively, alley, amazement, ambition, annexment*, apoplex*, argal*, arouse, aslant, assay, assign, assume, attractive, attribute, avouch.
1603, *M. for M.*, 23—about, absolute, actor, adoptedly*, advantaged*, advertising*, after, akin, allied, ambassador, answer, appear, apprehend, apprehension, approbation, arch-villain, arrest, athwart, attempt (2), avail, ave, awaken.
1604, *Oth.*, 13—ability (2), abuse, accommodation, action, addiction, adopt, advocation, aerial, affrighted*, antre*, arrivance*.
1605, *Lear*, 9—abhorred, able, address, affect, aheight*, alarmed*, allow, anchoring*, attask.
1605, *Macb.*, 13—adhere, air, alarm, all-hail (2), anticipate, applaud, arbitrate, armed, aroint*, assailable*, assassination*, attempt.
1606, *Tr. and Cr.*, 23—abruption*, acquired*, added*, addition, affectionately, affront, allayment*, amazement*, antiquary*, appalled, appertainment*, apprehend, arch, asinego, aspiration, assumption, at, attachment, attend, attest*, attributive*, awkward.
1607, *Coriol.*, 12—achieve, adopt, adversely*, after, agreed*, aidless, allying*, anhungry*, appear, arithmetic, as, ascent.
1607, *Timon*, 4—apperil*, applauding*, attempt, attraction.
1608, *Pericles*, 3—anear*, appearer*, attraction.
1610, *Temp.*, 9—abstemious, act, advantage, advantageous*, ahold*, answer, arch, aspersion, auspicious.
1610, *Cymb.*, 14—accessible*, acorned, act, adorer, affirmation, affront, air (2), allayment, arm, assault, attempt, attemptable, aver.
1611, *Wint. T.*, 4—admiration, aired, altering*, attorney*.

1613, Hen. VIII., 8—acquire, act, agreed (2), alleged*, allegiant*, appliance, attempt.

It appears that there ar 95 words appearing for the first time, and 317 having meanings which appear for the first time; and that enuf words with more than one new meaning appear, to make the hole number of new meanings 420. The hole number of words in A in Schmidt's *Shakespeare-Lexicon* is 1066, so that more than one word in three has a new meaning. If the proportions ar the same thru the alfabet, there ar about 1900 new words and about 8400 new meanings due to Shakespeare. From Milton ar recorded in A in Murray 42 new words, 120 new meanings (his prose and poetry giving numbers nearly equal), from Tennyson four new words and eighteen meanings.

The number of new words and meanings in a play is not much affected by Shakespeare's age, so far as the table enables one to judge; they depend upon the subjects talkt about. The three plays in which the number is greatest (25–23) *Love's Labor Lost* (1588), *Measure for Measure* (1603), *Troilus and Cressida* (1606), ar nearly of the same dates with *Titus Andronicus* with 7 words; *Julius Cæsar*, 6, and *Twelfth Night*, 5; *Antony and Cleopatra*, 5. The sonnets, *Venus and Adonis* and *Lucrece*, hav each three new meanings and no new words, except *Adon*. The familiar Roman plays hav few new words.

A large part of the new words ar to be clast with the once-uzed words which wer discust in a paper at Cornell (*Proceedings* for 1886, p. xxx.). They ar not striking poetic compounds like many of Tennyson's. They ar largely familiar stems with living affixes, *accidentally, audaciously, abjectly,* etc.; *attending, awakening,* etc.; unfamiliar Anglicizing of foren words, *academe, ambuscado, Adon, apathaton* (epithet). The new meanings ar also largely exactly such unuzual variations as we commonly call blunders, as in *epithet* uzed for *expression* or *frase* in general. Ben Jonson would willingly hav playd the professor to them and corrected them by the hundred. Perhaps Shakespeare would hav "blotted a thousand" if he had prepared his plays for the press. But a large part of the new meanings hav been accepted, and many hav displaced the erlier meanings.

A considerabl number ar characteristically Shakespearian, characteristic utterances of that profound, sweet, tender spirit who has charmd the world, whom we all rejoice in being akin to. They all flow easily in Shakespeare's lines, and their number and their kind strongly suggest that his fluency is not the unprompted, unguided flow of establisht association, but the movement of intelligent wil.

I hav caused an examination to be made of the characteristic words most frequently uzed, bringing the passages of their use together from the *Concordance*, to examin, among other things, whether they fall into stereotyped frases like the kennings of erly poetry, in Homer, *Beowulf*, and the like, elements of a mechanical or instinctiv fluency.

They do not take such forms. We find

	Shakespeare.	Milton.	Tennyson.	
gentle	393	36	12	
gentleman	445	0	7	
sweet	865	90	80	{Tennyson's
love	2602	144	634	most frequent word.
heaven	856	517	143	
heart	1083	103	388	
God	1149	446	191	
come	2592	247	586	

But except *gentleman,* which might be taken as a compacted kenning, we find none to mention. The happy passages seem to be beamings and breathings of a free spirit. See further, *Proceedings of Am. Phil. Ass.*, XXI, xxxi.

Literary fluency, a fluency grateful to luvers of literature, implies an easy flow of words in the familiar idioms of literary English. Fluent prose has its musical cadences, and Shakespeare's fluency is the more acceptabl in his erly works for running often in the current forms of Marlowe, Lily, Lodge, and Spenser.

Poetic fluency implies a connection of words by their sound with the ideal cadences of certain establisht meters.

Poetry has its life in harmony, in the accords of two musical series of sounds, the regular melody of the typical verse, and the varying melody of the poet's words. There must be establisht connection of concepts by which the poet's words flow into the familiar meters. An examination of the different metrical combinations of syllabls, feet, and hemistichs, found in Shakespeare, shows him to hav the freest use of the harmonic combinations in English iambic verse. Professor Price enumerates twenty-seven types of perfect verse in *Othello.*

In the erly plays the typical melody of the verse is often dominant; it sounds constantly. Its equal cadences lead on the music of the words, making verse more fluent than prose, and when feeling moves with it, making music of the simplest utterances, as when Lear says:

> Her voice was ever soft,
> Gentle, and low, an excellent thing in woman,—

or:

> Pray you, undo this button: thank you, sir,—

In the late plays the music of the thought and words is dominant; when the speech is without poetic thought or feeling it is often hardly distinguishabl from prose.

Sumtimes besides the typical melody of the stanza a poet has a strain of music proper by which he builds his rime. Sum of Shakespeare's songs so sing themselves as to persuade us that he had prior tunes to which he composed them.

The laws of suggestion which describe the connection between objects of thought ar givn in psychologies as resemblance, contrast, contiguity in time and place, and cause and effect. These may all be applied in Shakespeare, as elsewhere. But poetic fluency, freely working imagination, implies inner connection between feeling and the vocal concepts. We ar familiar with it when pain produces groans, or tickling laughter. With the poet, with Shakespeare eminently, fainter feelings hav quick connections with musical tones and with the sounds of articulate speech. The instruments of all orchestras ar redy in that fonograf, the brain. An esthetic longing wil set the horns of elf-land faintly blowing. The hole orchestra sounds with the passion of Lear. These vocal sounds bring with them concepts of objects they ar signs of, and hense the similes and metafors which giv to airy nothing a local habitation and a name.

Shakespeare had glad periods, had melancholy years; and the plays ar glad or sad accordingly.

Shakespeare's fluency is not always in perfect exercise. There is effort, struggle, evident now and then, even when what is said has markt Shakespearian quality. Prior to all these fluencies, vocal, intelligent, literary, poetic, musical, there is the living power which flows, with its charm of personal qualities which ar Shakespearian. This power flows forth most freely, Shakespeare utters himself most easily, when speaking thru a second person.

In one of the great plays of Shakespeare the primary creation is a being, a person, a person begotten by Shakespeare, life of his life.

Then follow the particular facts and acts which exhibit the newly created character, especially the language. All talk Shakespearian, as in an opera all sing. At the sheepshearing in *Winter's Tale,* Florizel, Perdita, and Polixenes all talk far above singing. In the forest of Arden under the shade of melancholy boughs, wise saws of true Shakespearian quality flow freely from girls and fools and philosophers. These ar all prior phenomena of Shakespeare's world. The personality, the environment, the language, ar all so beautiful, because all ar the creative utterancy of the man Shakespeare, a character delightful, luvabl, charming with all charms.

The facts we hav observed about his language seem to show that his plays and poems ar not a mechanical or instinctiv flow of thoughts and words, but his conscious creation as a free self livelily selecting from a copious instinctive supply of materials, and seeming to act so easily and perfectly, because he has such wonderfully comprehensiv and rapid self activity.

A Confession about Othello

The scenes in which Iago moves Othello to jelousy seem to me unnatural. I hav tried since my boyhood to make them seem natural, but I hav not succeeded,—that is my confession.

If we compare the jelousy of Leontes we find it natural though utterly groundless. It springs from temperament and mood in Leontes. But in *Othello* the attempt is made to show us a man, not jelous in himself, convinced by testimony and reasons that he has cause for jelousy.

His own view of his wife presents her to him in perfect purity. We ar to believ him overpowerd by reasons. There is great elaboration of the steps of Iago's procedure to convince him. We ar led therefore to scrutinize them, and we must see they amount to nothing. How could any man like Othello be moved by such tricks and trifles? It is possibl, to be sure, that a man should hav such perfect confidence in another as to accept his views without good reasons. If we ar to recognize such a friendship between Othello and Iago, grounds for it should be shown in the character of Iago in the earlier part of the play. But he is exhibited as a rascal, and a gross one, form the first. It is hard to think of such shallow rascality, so obtrusively set forth at every turn, as deceiving any one. Was there some actor of Shakespeare's time who had a natural expression of superhuman trustworthiness, some unimaginabl "confidence man," looking on whom the theater coud believ that any Othello must trust him in everything? Or has Shakespeare for once lowerd his genius to giv the actors an opportunity to show off their power of depicting changes of mood and passion too artificial for nature?

"A Confession about Othello." *Proceedings of the American Philological Association* 11 (1880): 31.

Review of Furness's *Variorum* Editions of Shakespeare

FURNESS'S VARIORUM *HAMLET*

A New Variorum Edition of Shakespeare. Edited by Horace Howard Furness, Honorary Member of the "Deutsche Shakespear-gesellschaft of Weimar." Vol. III, IV. *Hamlet*. Philadelphia: J. B. Lippincott & Co. 1877.

The *New Variorum Edition of Shakespeare* now includes *Hamle*t. The readers of the *Nation* have been acquainted with the plan of the work and its general merits in notices of the earlier volumes, which, they will remember, are devoted to *Romeo and Juliet* and to *Macbeth*. *Hamlet* is in bulk double either of these, and is doubtless the outcome of tenfold the labor. A variorum edition of it, harvesting and gleaning, as Mr. Furness does, the literature not only of England, but of Germany and France, and storing all away in two volumes of this size, might be the work of a lifetime. Mr. Furness did well to address himself to it at once, as soon as he had fixed his method and fairly settled down to his work.

The difficulties begin with the text. The editor has to determine the relations of three different versions to each other, and to the old lost play which was on the boards in Shakspere's youth. No one of the three is the complete text as it finally left the hands of Shakspere. Are they all variations of the same text, or do they represent texts composed at different times? Can any one be accepted as a standard, and the readings of the others noted as variations? Mr. Furness inclines to the view that Shakspere made two revisions of the old play. He began by working over the first part of it mainly. This proved a great success, and was pirated and printed in the first quarto. Then he revised it and finished it up. The other quartos and the folio are acting copies somewhat differently abridged from this same final revision.

At any rate, Mr. Furness has found it necessary to construct a text for himself by collation and comparison of the others. He has done it with

Review of four volumes in the *New Variorum Edition of Shakespeare*, ed. H. H. Furness. *Nation* 25 (November 1, 1877): 272-73; 31 (November 4, 1880): 327–28; 52 (March 5, 1891): 202–03; 55 (August 11, 1892): 112–13.

admirable judgment and care, and given a good, conservative text in modern spelling and printing. Perhaps he makes a little too free with the punctuation-marks; modern punctuation may be freely used to bring out more clearly a meaning with which the old punctuation agrees, though even then it is not best to make much effort to bring out nice distinctions or decide mooted questions of shades of meaning left undecided in the original. But when the meaning is changed it is a different matter; careless and blundering as the pointing of the old editions is, a change of it often constitutes a less probable emendation than the change of a word. In Act. V., sc. ii., 210, the quarto reads:

"The readines is all, since no man of what he leaues,
knowes what ist to leaue betimes, let be."

This Mr. Furness gives:

"The readiness is all. Since no man, of aught he leaves,
knows, what is't to leave betimes? Let be."

It is much simpler to take *ist* for *it's* or *'tis,* and leave the passage in its plain meaning according to the old pointing: "Readiness (for death) is all our part, since no man knows in respect to aught he leaves, what is the best time to leave it."

Along with the preparation of the text there is the gathering and arranging of the various readings suggested by editors, and critics, and everybody—a vast labor even with the aid of the Cambridge collections. Then come notes grammatical and explanatory. These are presented with admirable brevity and clearness, and are occasionally enlivened and enlightened by pithy remarks of the editor, all too few. The effort at compression, which is made evident in many ways, keeps a critic on the watch for matter which might be omitted. There are some grammatical notes which are, perhaps, of this kind. It is hard to draw the line between general grammar and usages so Shaksperian that they ought to have a place in such a commentary. Obsolete constructions and forms need explanation even when common in Shakspere's time; but the study of the old forms of the language is becoming so general that it is no longer necessary to enlarge on such forms by giving their history and use in other authors. This remark was suggested by the note on *its,* Act i., sc. ii., 216, a good grammatical discussion, which tells about the Anglo-Saxon declension of *he,* and the uses of the Bible, Bacon and Milton, as well as some other matters, all which are interesting, and ten years ago might, perhaps, have claimed a place in such a *Variorum*, but which are now among the commonplaces of English grammar in all our good schools. This note is, however, exceptional; the general habit of Mr. Furness is just right. The fact is stated as briefly as possible, and a reference made to Abbott, or Maetzner, or some other historical grammar. If in one or two cases (Act i., sc. ii., 151 and 221) a reference to a grammar is given without explanation, they are rare exceptions. The references of this kind to former volumes of the series are, however, numerous.

The explanatory and critical remarks also go to an extreme of compression. It gives a comic cast sometimes to the æsthetic criticism to use abbreviations for the names of the characters, making Mr. Lowell, for example, say Ham. and Oph. It is a more substantial shortcoming that Mr. Furness has not given more notes to explain and apply his own views. Thus, he tells us in his general remarks that "Hamlet is neither mad nor pretends to be so," without expanding or explaining. The student will almost certainly turn to passages where *Hamlet* himself seems to contradict that view, as, for example, Act v., sc. ii., 215:

"What I have done,
That might your nature, honor, and exception
Roughly awake, I here proclaim was madness.
Was't Hamlet wrong'd Laertes? Never Hamlet;
. . . Who does it, then? His madness."

Here we find nothing in the commentary to indicate what modification of the apparent meaning of the text or of his theory Mr. Furness would have us make.

The text and notes which have now been referred to make a volume of 473 pages, including an index of 15 pages. It is pleasant to find that, so far as verbal criticism is concerned, there are almost no difficulties in *Hamlet* left without a fair solution. There is hardly a passage of which the general sense is doubtful, very few which eluded the wit of all the early English commentators. Thus, the famous nonsense passage in Act i., sc. iv., 35, which Mr. Furness leaves untouched in his text:

"The dram of eale
Doth all the noble substance of a doubt
To his own scandal,"

is obviously the enforcement of what Hamlet has just said, that the noblest character may "take corruption" from a single defect; and its general meaning must be conveyed by the early correction:

"The dram of base
Doth all the noble substance oft corrupt
To his own scandal."

But this is not good enough for the commentators. They are haunted by the cases in which some exquisite Shaksperian expression has been found lurking in the printer's nonsense, like that of Falstaff's death, "for his nose was as sharp as a pen *and a' babbled of green fields,*" which was disguised under "*a table of green fields,*" or "*on a table of green frieze,*" as Mr. Collier's Commentator read it. So the new conjectures grow more numerous from generation to generation. There are six great pages on the passage just quoted from *Hamlet*; *eale* may be for *evil,* or *vile,* or *ill,* or many other things as well as *base,* and *of a doubt* may have been *oft debase,* or *infect,* or *adopt,* or *adapt,* or *dout* (do out), or a hundred other things. One of the later commentators does let a gleam of Shakspere upon the passage by reading "*oft subdue* to his own scandal," reminding one of the famous lines in Sonnet cxi.:

"And almost thence my nature is subdued
To that it works in, like the dyer's hand."

Here, by the way, Mr. Furness's reference is to Sonnett iii., where the word is not found.

The second volume, under the name of an appendix, presents the student with a collection of documents and critical discussions too extended to be placed in immediate connection with the text. The most important are an essay on the date and text; reprints of the first quarto and of the prose *Hystorie of Hamblet*; a translation of an old German play, *Der bestrafte Brudermord* (*Fratricide Punished, or Prince Hamlet of Denmark*), with an interesting note upon the acting of English plays in Germany at the beginning of the seventeenth century by companies of traveling English actors, "a curious and almost inexplicable fact," which the Germans have lately studied up. Then there are selections from British and American essays of criticism, and translations from German and French—about 50 Germans are represented—and last, not least, a bibliography of *Hamlet* literature. Most students would have been glad to see this volume larger, but all will recognize the excellent judgment with which the selections have been made and the fidelity and art of the translations. Beyond all question, the work furnishes important facilities for the study of this great poem. Mr. Furness says that he does not flatter himself that this is an *enjoyable* edition of Shakspere; he regards it rather as a necessary evil. It is doubtless true that most of the textual criticism is only preliminary to the real study of the poem, that explaining the obsolete expressions has little or nothing to do with the mastery of Shakspere's poetic art. But there are few fields of thought more interesting or more fruitful than the æsthetic crticism of *Hamlet*. This youngest of Shakspere's tragedies has been hardly less by its defects than by its wit the source of wit in others. The essays of Goethe, Coleridge, Lowell, and the rest form a body of literature comparable to *Hamlet* itself. Nor are the six pages on the *dram of eale* without their interest to the student of human nature. In these days, when two swarms of insects cannot fight without bringing upon them the microscope and the pen of the reporter, the battles of the commentators are worth their record. Are they not vertebrate animals?

FURNESS'S *KING LEAR*

A New Variorum Edition of Shakespeare. Edited by Horace Howard Furness, Ph.D., LL.D., Honorary Member of the "Deutsche Shakespeare-Gesellschaft of Weimar." Vol. V., *King Lear*. Philadelphia: J. B. Lippincott & Co. 1880.

We have now an admirable hand-book for the thorough study of *King Lear*. Mr. Furness gives us the substance of a hundred volumes in one. It contains a critical text, with all the various readings and interpretations and explanatory notes from the beginning to the present time, with the criticisms and comments of all kinds, lexical, grammatical, æsthetical, and the rest. Mr. Furness works with more ease and expresses his own opinions more freely than in his former volumes, and this is a gain. In an appendix there are discussions of the date of composition, the sources of the plot, the actors, the costume; extended passages of English, German, and French criticism; a good bibliography, and an index. In all there are 503 close-packed pages, and it is a piece of work which Mr. Furness and his collaborators may well be glad to have done. There is no book to be compared with it; it is indispensable to every student of Shakspere.

An examination of it shows that this, sometimes reckoned the greatest of Shakspere's works, is still imperfectly comprehended. After all the study of it a great many difficulties remain unsolved both in the text and the interpretation. In *Hamlet* the verbal difficulties seldom or never extend to the throwing of doubt on the meaning of a sentence; the coherence and familiarity of the matter enable us to follow the sense with confidence. But in the broken and exalted utterances of this play the sense of whole clauses is often doubtful. Mr. Furness's greatest labor must have been with his text. The printed originals are abridgments, and they are so different as to suggest that the copy from which the folio was abridged had been rewritten after the quarto was abridged. Mr. Furness follows the folio, but with many corrections; perhaps too many. It would be simpler and more satisfactory to most students to have the folio always, if it makes sense and metre, even though some other reading seems to be more perspicuous, or poetical, or Shaksperian. Shakspere is not always at his best, nor are we; we may see the dark passage in a new light to-morrow. Thus in I. i, 226, when France suggests that Cordelia must have done something monstrous and unnatural to make her father so curse her, she beseeches him to make known that

"It is no vicious blot, murder, or foulness."

For this Mr. Furness reads:

"It is no vicious blot or other foulness."

It must be admitted that the new reading is at best rather an improvement than a necessity. Indeed, if "murder" is something too monstrous for Cordelia, the other is too tame for Lear's curses and charges. Mr. Furness might have taken warning from Mr. Richard Grant White, who at first accepted the new reading, but at last rejects it. The example may stand for one class of objectionable corrections; reading *burdocks* for *hardokes* (IV. iv. 4), because the botanists cannot identify *hardokes,* is an example of another class.

Mr. Furness is more and more disposed to adhere to the exact forms of words used by Shakspere. "Why should Shakespeare's text be modernized?" he says; "we do not so treat Spenser. Is Shakespeare's text less sacred?" So he has retained *it* for *its, moe* for *more, vilde* for *vile,* and the like; and he regrets that he has not printed the "then" of the folio for "than." On this hint Mr. Furnivall is about to publish a cheap reprint in the old spelling throughout, and it will be a useful book. It is perhaps better in an edition like this to take the mean between a literal reprint and the usual modernized page. Mr. Furness might, however, carry his adhesion to the folio much farther than he does in the direction of significant and reasonable spelling. In the first scene we find that he has changed *weigh'd, craz'd, lov'd,* and the like to *weighed, crazed, loved; banisht, voucht,* and the like to *banished, vouched; interest* to *interess'd; honor, honor'd* to *honour, honour'd.* It would be a little quaint but not offensive to have retained *bountie, libertie, shadowie, dutie;* the good old ending *-ie* should not have yielded to the penman's fondness for final *y*. So *bin* for *been* might well stand to testify for our American pronunciation. And why should such a truthful word as *horson* have its etymology and pronunciation disguised by heading and padding it with *w* and *e?*

Mr. Furness has noticed that particles sometimes wholly disappear through absorption into adjacent words, and he keeps a sharp lookout for them, and indicates them by an apostrophe. Thus, in I. i. 275 he reads

> "Prescribe not' us our duty,"

because he thinks a *to* has been absorbed by the *t* of *not;* and in II. ii. 116 he reads

> "Such a deal of man
> That' worthied him,"

because an *it* is absorbed in *That*. But in neither passage is there any such absorption as he supposes.

In the critical study of *Lear* a great difficulty arises from the point of view. We easily accept the view in *Romeo and Juliet*, where everything appears as it does to the eye of youth; Juliet, thirteen years old, is old enough. In *Hamlet*, too, we see the world as it appears to one just entering the battle of life. The father of our Ophelia is still a superfluous old Polonius. But, as Shakspere grows older, he passes beyond the experience of great numbers of his readers. In *Macbeth* and *Othello* the point of view is that of middle age, and in *King Lear* the world is seen as it appears to an infirm old man. We must take the truthfulness of the presentment with a large measure of faith. We never have been old men; we do not know how they feel; we never have had thankless daughters; we never have been insane; we do not even know by observation how the insane act and talk. The difficulty of bringing us to this point of view is increased by the story, which turns upon the doings of the young married couples who have to entertain in their families the old king and his hundred knights. It is very easy to take the point of view of the young folks when they say:

> "—all-licensed fool,
> And other of your insolent retinue,
> Do hourly carp and quarrel;
> Our court grows like a riotous inn.
> Fifty of these followers are surely enough."

Change the sex of Lear. Literature has hardly a point of view more familiar or more easily taken than the married man's view of the worrying mother-in-law. Shakspere does not disguise the facts. He shows us the king in his unreason, his passion, his worrying, his domineering. How, then, does he bring us to accept his point of view?

The most obvious source of this power is the perfect utterancy of the king, the ease and copiousness with which he gives intense expression to his feelings. He is regal withal, every inch a king; and in the first scene, as we hear him dispensing kingdoms and curses so grandly and so strangely, we give the reins to imagination and bid farewell to the regions of common sense, as though we were listening to the heroes or gods of Æschylus. The difficulty of keeping us in sympathy with the old king afterwards is partly met by showing the young folk committing crimes against each other abhorrent to human nature, so that no one thinks of questioning the justice of their father's reproaches and curses. At the crisis of the play, at the tempest, the whirlwind of his passion, when conversation with other men must needs be pitiful or laughable, the powers of nature—night, and storm, and darkness—fill the stage; rain, wind, thunder become the old king's interlocutors in place of thankless daughters. We see the heavens taking part against us, and the gods killing men for sport as wanton boys kill flies. It is a matter of course that he who could carry us with the king to such heights of frantic passion at the wounds offered to his imagination and kingly pride, should be able to keep us with him in his truly human woe at the death of the daughter he loves. The tears shed over Cordelia need no explanation. But Lear's perfect utterancy in gentleness is as noticeable as that in passion.

Perhaps no other character in fiction or history has been set forth with such minuteness and eloquent elaboration, on the hint of so few recorded traits, as Cordelia. But the commentators treat her mainly as she appears in the final scenes. With her tears and smiles for her poor father, and her immortal voice—ever soft, gentle, and low—she seems the incarnation of filial piety. When her father appeals to her in the first scene to say how much she loves him, she might be expected, if she could not speak, at least to look her love, and tenderly deplore her want of utterancy. But she defends herself sharply in her silence, and commends her want as a virtue. She also roundly declares that she expects to love her husband, if she shall have one, and that she will not pretend to be wholly devoted to her father. Some of the critics expound these passages as showing that Cordelia had a spice of her father's temper. It does not seem to have occurred to any that she has already looked with love on one of her suitors; but that would explain much on better grounds than temper.

Francis A. March

FURNESS'S *AS YOU LIKE IT*

As You Like It. [*A New Variorum Edition of Shakespeare*, edited by Horace Howard Furness. Vol. VIII.] Philadelphia: J. B. Lippincott Co. 1890. Pp. ix, 452.

A preface is generally the part of a book written last, and read last, or not at all. But when a new volume of the *Variorum Shakespeare* appears, the old student of Shakspere is apt to choose the preface for first reading. Mr. Furness has a way of laying by good things for his preface, and making it an appetizer for the banquet. He begins with an essay on the value and interest of variorum notes over and above verbal explanation and antiquarian information—the penetrating and enlightening thoughts of keen intellects. Reading him here, it seems impossible not to agree with him. Shakspere is not only witty himself, but the cause of wit in others. A Shakspere symposium of Johnson, Coleridge, Hazlitt, Campbell, Christopher North, Mrs. Jameson, Lamb, Mrs. Kemble, Lady Martin, Goethe, Schlegel, George Sand, is "a feast of the gods." One, indeed, to whom literature is a by-play, who turns to Shakspere as to a comic opera to dream away an idle hour, may find all he wishes in rapid and sympathetic reading, or merely receptive hearing and seeing a play of Shakspere, and Mr. Furness says truly that we all have such moods. But this is only an introduction to Shakespeare. Even in this vacant mood, pictures sink into the memory which rise again a wonder and a wild delight; expressions which cannot be forgotten suggest new thoughts, new views of life, provoke, startle, baffle us, lead us on to earnest study of the text and the context and everything that has been said about them, and of everything that Shakspere has written and everything that he was.

It is a surprise to find Mr. Furness objecting to the study in the plays of the personal history of Shakspere. That is another of the topics of the preface. He does not believe that either Shakspere's outer or his inner life is to any discoverable degree reflected in his plays. The smallest dash of the author's self would mar the characters. The whole subject of the time and circumstances under which one of the plays was written is one which with him "has absolutely no relations whatsoever to the play itself or the enjoyment thereof." But it is certain that every thought uttered in these dramas was a thought of Shakspere. Of the myriad facts and judgments which are the elements of the speeches there is no one but was drawn from Shakspere's knowledge or opinions. The words the characters used are Shakspere's; one idiom he brought up from Stratford, another he picked up in London; he caught one from Marlowe, another from Jonson; he made a third. What is a man's inner life? Are a dreamer's dreams no part of it? If one could meet Shakspere, as Jonson did at the Mermaid, and hear him talk till midnight, till morning, in his happiest vein, would that open his inner life? Did the sonnets unlock his heart? Most men's talk is a phonotype of their morning newspaper and evening magazines. The inner self is not spoken out in any phrases, facts are fables agreed upon. And yet the students of character ask triumphantly, How can a man be concealed? Phenomena which are nothings one by one, become data for the reason to apprehend, to compare, to interpret, to comprehend; we can study out the sense of cuneiform inscriptions, of hieroglyphics; no cipher can keep it secret.

It is possible, indeed, to conceive a poet who gets up baffling poems, who, when old, says to himself, Now I will write as a youth, or who stores up his experiences, as Goethe did, till time gives them poetic glamour. But Shakspere was not of this type. He uttered himself freely. Mr. Furness says: "For my part I believe that Shakespeare wrote his plays, like the conscientious player that he was, to fill the theatre and make money for his fellow actors and for himself." But it seems probable that the peculiar Shaksperian qualities were the main attraction of his plays; that he knew that the best play to fill the theatre was the play in which his genius was most manifest, in which he could work most freely and happily, in which his felicities flow through every line. Life is not shown in Shakspere as in a plain mirror. No person ever talked in the rhythm of Hamlet, or Jacques, or Rosalind, any more than in the strains of an opera. There is a miracle of preëstablished harmony between these dreams of beauty and music and the natural world, and there is a mounting spirit in us which proclaims these dreams more real than nature, more true than fact. To dwell content in single plays, as scenes of real life, and care nothing for the laws which govern them, the laws of the Shaksperian world, which are traits of the character of Shakspere, seems exactly parallel to the study of nature as described by Bacon: "While the Minde of Man looketh upon Second Causes Scattered, it may sometimes rest in them and goe no further. But when it beholdeth the Chaine of them Confederate and Linked together, it must needs file to *Providence,* and *Deitie.*" A single speech of Hamlet may please us for a time as a gem of thought; reflecting on all his speeches, we frame a character of Hamlet; an induction from all the speeches of all the characters in all the plays leads to the inner life of the poet.

Mr. Furness says further, that if we are to infer the experiences of Shakspere from the tone of his dramas, it would be an error to infer that a sad life prompted sad writing. He would surely retreat to an inner world of his own creation where all was fair and serene. And so Mr. Furness suggests that it was possibly from a life over which sorrow and depression brooded that there sprang the jocund comedy of *As You Like It*. That *As You Like It* sprang from a sad heart seems true, but no such paradox as Mr. Furness pleases himself with, is need to explain it. The life is led "under the shade of melancholy boughs," and one does not need Jacques's power to suck melancholy out of a song as a weasel sucks eggs, to find it plain in all the merriment.

> "Blow, blow, thou winter winde,
> Thou art not so unkinde as man's ingratitude."

We feel the winter wind from the first, and there is not a flower in the forest; there are sermons in the stones. The play is a companion piece to *A Midsummer Night's Dream*—a November day dream. We give ourselves up to the enchanter, and encounter the most surprising matters and things without surprise, as we do in our dreams. The old Shaksperian lion is here, as much at home as the deer; here are palm trees, oaks, olive trees. Time and space adjust and readjust themselves to the story, and so do the characters. Orlando looks in the eyes of Rosalind and talks love, and does not know her. The villains of the play are as good as girls. When we wake from our dream, we recognize that the magician who creates it is the same who created the dream in the wood near Athens, but that he is sadder now and older, and has a commonplace book crammed with thousands of wise saws which flow freely from all his mouthpieces, from Jacques, Touchstone, Rosalind, from philosophers, and fools, and girls.

FURNESS'S *THE TEMPEST*

The Tempest. A New Variorum Edition of Shakespeare. Edited by Horace Howard Furness. Vol. IX. Philadelphia: J.B. Lippincott Co. 1892. Pp. xi, 465.

Mr. Furness gives us, in his preface to the *Variorum Edition* of the *Tempest*, an appetizer, as usual, for the feast of the commentators. It is an exposition of "the human and poetical side of Caliban's character." The central point is, that he had a soul imparted to him by Miranda as she taught him language. He never heard language from other lips than those of Miranda and Prospero. Mr. Furness sketches a lovely picture of summer night on the Enchanted Island from the glimpse which Shakspere gives when Caliban says that his mistress showed him the man in the moon with his dog and bush. With such a teacher, at such hours, it would be impossible to resist the atmosphere of poetry whose charm pervades the Enchanted Island. He always speaks in rhythm. It is he who gives the descriptions of the island which make it the "one magic isle of our imaginations."

One of the striking features of the volume is the number of beautiful passages from the commentators. The study of the play seems to have an effect on the students similar to that which Miranda and the island had on Caliban. Hazlitt, Hugo, Mrs. Kemble, Lowell, Ruskin, Dowden, Furnivall, Coleridge, Schlegel, and others of great name and fame rival each other in an eloquent admiration and happy exposition which takes a tone from the play itself. Allegorical interpretation is another striking feature of the commentaries. Shakspere is Prospero, Miranda is Art, Ferdinand is Fletcher; or may be Prospero is King James, and the teaching political; or it is a polemic against witchcraft, or a drama of reconciliation. Some of these speculators talk of the love tale as an episode, and complain of the Miranda and Ferdinand scenes as too long. Dry old heads these are. To simple youth all the rest is only a frame for these scenes.

There is a copious collection of discussions of the date of composition of the *Tempest*—thirty-four great fine-print pages. It would seem impossible to believe that it was one of the early plays, but that is argued at great length. Such argument belongs to the period before development ruled men's thought, when genius was regarded as something miraculous, a wonder-working power; the stranger the product attributed to it, the more readily it was believed—*credo quia impossibile*. A youth could write a book embodying the experiences of age, just as a world full of series of fossils could be made in an instant. One now can hardly help seeing that the author of *Romeo and Juliet* looks at Juliet and her father, and the author of *Hamlet* looks at Ophelia and old Polonius, from a very different point of view from that from which the author of the *Tempest* looks at Miranda and Prospero. They are young eyes which see old Capulet and Polonius as superannuated old bores. Those are grave old eyes which give to Prospero a gleam that never was, on sea or land. He does not seem to be very wise in wordly wisdom, does not utter maxims like Polonius. He has traits of the weakness of age; he keeps calling attention to what he is saying, as though he fears he is not listened to; he scolds with harsh language, but feebly, without discrimination—Ariel as harshly as Caliban, and even Ferdinand; but he has a halo around him. The two or three passages which are so universally thought of as expressions of Shakspere in his proper person, bidding farewell to the stage, and which are so sad and grand, give a pathetic grandeur to Prospero.

"We are such stuffe
As dreames are made on: and our little life
Is rounded with a sleepe"

this Shakspere has passed through the distressed questionings of the *Hamlet* period; he worries no longer. But his thought is like that of the heathen councillor in Beda who compares life to the flight of a sparrow through the banqueting hall, from darkness into darkness.

The text of the *Tempest* is one of the very best of the First Folio, and yet the commentary is very copious. The few passages which are obscure have been endlessly discussed. Mr. Furness suggests that it may be because this play is first in the Folio and other old editions, and the critics come to it with unspent zeal. Mr. Furness usually gives a satisfactory decision very briefly. In the longest collection of all, that on the passage where Ferdinand, dreaming of Miranda as he piles logs, says:

"I forget:
But these sweet thoughts doe euen refresh my labours,
Most busie lest, when I doe it."

Mr. Furness thinks Ferdinand is apologetic, excusing himself for stopping and dreaming, on the ground that it will refresh him for more work. That seems rather a feeble lover, a Hamlet. He may be simply rejoicing in his thoughts, and encouraging himself to go on briskly by remembering that they refresh his labor even when he works most busily (most busiliest). Any meaning which makes "lest"emphatic makes woful metre. The criticisms of the Shakspere Society of Philadelphia, 1864–'5, are strikingly good. This Mr. Furness thinks is the oldest Shakspere Society in existence, having had continuous life from 1851 to the present day.

Dryden's version of the *Tempest* is here reprinted, with very slight omissions, and *The Fair Sidea* in English translation. Some Germans, with eyes such as Mr. Weller desiderated—double million magnifying gas microscopes of extra power—see in this play the source of Shakspere's. The appendix on the sources is very full and interesting, forty-five pages. There are discussions of the duration of the action, the music, costume, and many other matters; among the rest, a good deal of etymology and other philology.

F.A. March, c.1860s (*photograph by R. Knecht, Easton*)

Jan. 1858
Easton Penn^a^

Miss. Mildred S. Conway
My dear friend;
I hope this Cyclopaedia of American Literature may reach you on your birth-day, as you are thinking over the friends of your girlhood. Perhaps it is not the fittest book for a gift. One often becomes attached to the separate works of a favorite author with a personal regard, as if the book were the man. But, if this is not likely to attract any special enthusiasm, it has something in it suited to almost every mood; and I hope it may prove a pleasant companion for many happy years.
Your sincere friend,
heartily & always.
Francis A. March

Letter from March to Mildred Stone Conway, who became Mrs. F.A. March in 1860.

F.A. and Mildred March on the porch of their home in Easton, 1909.

March in his Lafayette classroom.

Sent 30/7/87

Lafayette College.
Easton, Pa.
June 21, 1887

Dear Dr. Murray:

I hav just sent my last copy of your List VI, Special Quotations wanted, to Dr. J. Hammond Trumbull, Hartford, Conn., who is the best scholar we have in the antiquities and curiosities of speech in early America. He finds, looking thru Part III, that he might hav sent you some things from his pile, as he should have been glad to do, he says, only he felt sure they were not needed.

I hav exhorted him.

Wil you kindly send me a half a dozen copies of the List. There is great and growing appreciation of your work here. You ar happy in having such a life work in hand.

Yours Ever,
F. A. March

Prof March
Greatest Eng. scholar of
America

Draft of a March letter to James M. Murray, editor of the *Oxford English Dictionary*, for which March was director of American readers.

F.A. March, c.1890s? (*photograph by Kreidler and Crider, Easton*)

March beside the March Field grandstand. March Field, Lafayette College's athletic field from 1894 to 1926, was named for F.A. March's son Francis A. March, Jr., also professor of English at Lafayette College.

March reading the Lafayette student newspaper in his classroom, c.1890s?

On "Beauty and the Beast," by Charles Lamb

The readers of *The Independent* wil not grudge the space it givs to "Beauty and the Beast." They wil be glad to see it, pictures, music and all, as a literary curiosity, even tho they may not find it thrilling, or particularly characteristic of Charles Lamb.

As a matter of fact, no stranger to Lamb wil get a glimpse in these verses of his quaint and pathetic playfulness. An old acquaintance, if assured that he wrote them, can hardly help feeling that he is playing parson. Imagin Lamb stammering such verses as these by way of instruction for an ardent lover:

He "sat humble, or submissive stood,
Or, audience crav'd, respectful spoke;
Nor aim'd at wit, or ribald joke."

But if there is no display of Lamb's peculiar humor, perhaps there is of his insight, his supreme good taste. He saw, let us say, that the story is not one to be decorated with quips and cranks. Virtue is best plain set: "Beauty and the Beast," when unadorned, is adornd the most. The tale had never before been told so simply. Our story tellers, who make authorship a trade, work their stories up with beautiful descriptions and elaborate analysis. These do not make us like their heroes or heroines better, or enjoy their adventures more; they may make us admire the author and his art, as when we hear a speech and say, What a splendid orator! "A very excellent piece of work, madam lady, would 'twere done." That suits us old readers of a critical age, but each generation begins at the beginning, and imaginative youth of ten and upwards always belong to the primaeval world and like their stories plain.

"Beauty and the Beast" is made up of adventures of several wel known types. there is the Cinderella, or Aschenputtel story, in which two bad sisters abuse a younger beauty, and suffer while she comes to happiness. Then there is the Alcestis or Andromeda story, in which the heroin offers herself to a monster in behalf of one she loves. Then the

"Beauty and the Beast." *Independent* 37 (November 26, 1885): 4.

Prince Marcassin story—a prince transformd to a beast who must win the love of a beauty to regain his proper shape. Then the Psyche and Cupid story, in which the heroin lozes her lover by some wrong she does him, and wins him again by her pains and love. Stories of each of these types are numerous and wide spred. "Beauty and the Beast" is, perhaps, the happiest combination of them to be found in any fairy tale. It was first published under the name of "La Belle et La Bete," by Madam Villeneuve, in 1740. It ought to be mentioned in the vocabulary of noted names of fiction in *Webster's Dictionary*, and in the index of Dunlop's *History of Fiction*. But one can get upon the track of anything now by using Poole's *Index of Periodicals*. Conway tells us in his *Demonology* that Emerson finds in the fondness of the English for this national legend a sign of the Englishman's own nature. "He is a bear with a soft place in his heart." It found a place, he adds, in the heart of Theodore Parker, also, who loved to call his dearest friend "Bear." Everybody knows Miss Alcott's Bear.

In all these references, the Bear is taken as the central figure of the story, and the main adventure is his wooing. It is a love story, and this is a natural interpretation of the common version. But in this rimed version, Beauty is brought into greater prominence, and her filial affection and domestic virtues ar shown at greater length. The erly home narrativ has many details not in the version familiar to me, and Beauty's Song. The distinct love-making of the common version, the daily "Wil yu marry me?" is entirely omitted. The welfare of the household fils the scene rather than a love affair. The Prince, with his Persian name and magical surroundings, seems rather forein to the rest, as tho he wer brought in by Santa Claus, fresh caught in the relm of good Haroun Alraschid. The good girl must, of course, be rewarded with a grand husband.

In the real old folk tales there is something different from this deliberate bestowal of rewards and punishment. Winds blow and waters roll blessedness for the beautiful and good. If virtue is feebl Heaven itself wil stoop to her. And a divine instinct moves in the heart which draws it toward the true prince in whatever disguise.

Shakespeare, young Shakespeare, ventured to play with, and parody the devout myth in the adventure of Titania and Nick Bottom. But it is a fairy and no woman who can be thus enamored. The gentle Shakespeare coud not make Miranda subject to such charms, more than Milton the Lady in *Comus*. It was reserved for Pope to parody the myth in favor of Vice:

"Vice is a monster of no frightful mien,
As to be hated, needs but to be seen:
Yet seen too oft, familiar with her face,
We first endure, then pity, then embrace."

And some realistic commentator has declared his belief that Miranda would hav fallen in love with Caliban if—, and if—. There our story touches the lowest ultimate.

Walt Whitman's *Leaves of Grass* Redivivus

Much of this book is a loud and longwinded replication of Emerson's egoistic pantheism:

"I am owner of the sphere,
Of the seven stars and the solar year,
Of Cæsar's hand and Plato's brain,
Of Lord Christ's heart and Shakespeare's strain."

So Whitman claims to be everything, and fills up page upon page with mention of the particular things which are—apparently, everything he can think of. It is in substance intolerably dull, and when it was first printed, a quarter of a century ago, it was unspeakably commonplace to the readers of Emerson, Goethe, and the like. Emerson, in admiring Whitman, had fallen in love with his own shadow, if, indeed, we are not mistaken as to the extent of Emerson's admiration, which, according to this latest biographer, George Willis Cooke, was very limited indeed; so much so that he was annoyed by the use made of something he had written as to the poems now in consideration and would have been glad to recall it.

As to form, it was worse, if anything can be worse, than dullness. Those were days of great delight over the dactyls of "Evangeline" and the "Bothie of Toberna-Vuolich," the time of the popular catching up of Tupper's rhythms. Hence the form of the *Blades* [sic] *of Grass*. The lines begin with capital letters and a fair suggestion often of dactylic rhythm. We fall into the movement; but when it should round to its close it sinks to a driblet or breaks into an incongruous gush of prose. It gives a shock as of lameness or impotence in every line.

The diction is repulsive. It is the strained speech of an uneducated man, who lugs in all the big words he knows—Spanish (apparently bad Spanish), queer French, scraps of Latin and Greek, and what not.

Besides all this, the author is a literary "crank" of a most desperate kind. He is a prophet of the nude. He scouts all modesty.

"Walt Whitman's *Leaves of Grass* Redivivus." *Independent* 33 (December 29, 1881): 10.

"Walt Whitman, a Kosmos, of Manhattan the son.
Turbulent, fleshy, sensual, eating, drinking, and breeding."

If the book were illustrated with cuts of the objects, the organs freely named in it, it would rival the fullest of those medical works which the doctors lock away from the laity. If it were illustrated with pictures of the groups of persons described in it, committing the acts as described, lively painted in manner and form as described, it is hard to believe that any obscene book which the police hunt down would equal this in boldness and copiousness of illegality. It is said that Whitman has an irresistible impulse to print this stuff, in spite of remonstrances, in spite of his own reason. He looks for glory to the future; but, if the thousand years of English literature show anything, they show that the red blood of the Anglo-Saxon always has its pudency, and the redder the rosier.

It is sheer madness to believe that such dreams as these will ever be counted objects of art by the general voice of the sane. The handful of critics who are busy applauding him in England as the American poet are his fit audience, fit and few.

Whitman changed with the war. He ceased to chant the phallus; "Drum-taps" and the like came on. His rhythms drew nearer to poetry, to the common movement of blank verse, and to rhyme; but, in preparing the new edition of his poems, he has preserved the old leaves and strown them all through the book. Shame on the publisher who is sending them with his imprint to unsuspecting American homes.

Robert Browning

It was somewhere about 1840 that Browning's "Paracelsus" became known to the college students of New England. That was a glorious time. They were repeating "The Psalm of Life" and "Excelsior," reading Emerson's earliest and most inspiring words, and Carlyle's and Tennyson's. Webster was making his wonderful speeches, dilating the imagination with the greatness of our country and of man. There was to be no more war. There was to be a federation of the world. We were to have a new literature of a higher strain than ever rang from Grecian or Roman lyre, or any other.

So far as English literature is concerned, that dawning was followed by an Indian summer, an aftermath to the great period of Scott, Byron, Wordsworth, Goethe, Schiller. Of all the British poets of the time, Browning has best kept his early promise, the promise of his "Paracelsus." There was no worm i' the bud with him, no halo hovering round decay. He does not wail over the vanished life and heroes of the old time; he is no idle singer of an empty day.

His veins are full of red blood; he rejoices in hearty food and drink, in choice fruits and odors, in pure air and light, in a fiery horse, in a proper man or woman, and in music. He is, at the center, a powerful personality, full of vigor, and rejoicing in it, of tireless energy, and bold as a lion.

He deals with a great theme, centrally, eminently, that of Paul, the tragedy of man's natural life and the birth of the soul to new nobleness by union with the divine life.

This theme naturally develops into a treatment of the influence of each finite personality upon those with whom it is brought in relation. A series of dramas is thus produced, illustrating those profoundest experiences of life. The dramatic form is obviously an excellent one to bring out the secrets of these experiences. The dramatic monolog, especially, enables the poet to utter the innermost movement of the soul, so far as language can do it. It follows the example of Paul. But to read such dramas with ease one must have had similar experiences, or great familiarity with this kind of writing. It requires considerable effort in a reader to make out the action and story of a common play. There are many readers who cannot easily make them out even in Shakespeare. It is

---

"Robert Browning." *Independent* 42 (January 2, 1890): 1.

vastly more difficult with Browning, who seems possessed with his feeling and thought and only anxious to be delivered of it: and his throes are protracted. Emerson, a serene soul, with the blue blood of Puritan ancestry, finds inspiration from the over-soul as easy as breathing or sleep. But Browning is so full of will, so strong a personality, that to let the divine personality, or any other personality flow freely into his thoughts and acts is a struggle. Then he is copious and bold, with little fear of critics and none at all of grammarians. Instead of reshaping and retouching imperfect expressions, he dashes out into new ones; he interjects, explains, questions, accumulates new figures, new analyses. He does not show the temperance that gives all smoothness. He is more of a prophet than an artist, tho he is a great artist and preacher to artists. He does not study perspicuity nor gracious formality, nor distinction of style. He is often very obscure.

There are, however, a considerable number of choice spirits, ingenious and highly cultured persons of devout temper, who find in Browning perpetual stimulus and elevation. To these his obscurity is a wonderful source of influence and charm: it has infinite possibilities. But most even of those who appreciate the power of Browning and sympathize with his purposes and the development of his thought, find something strange and remote about his great works on account of the nationality of his characters and their foreign surroundings. Particulars of many kinds—plants, flowers, fruits, animals, or architecture, furniture, dress, habits, traits, functions—are accumulated as abundantly as psychologic analyses. They are almost never English; the characters have strange names and outlandish ways and singular experiences; the touches of Nature which make the whole world kin are comparatively rare. The intense earnestness and vivid diction of the author fix our attention and bear us breathless through the soul's tragedy; but no homelike interest in the characters or their story is produced. Some striking thoughts and turns of expression remain in the memory, the rest passes into shadow with the drama of India and China, or the miracle plays of the Middle Ages. It will very likely prove true of Browning, as it has of so many other great men, that the works upon which he labored most will be forgotten, and his memory be preserved by those he produced as by play. Browning's brief romances and lyrics are readable and memorable and musical. The same Browning appears in them as in the longer works.

He is never wholly without earnestness. He is full of life and hope, but it is a hope based on the certainty that badness will be thoroughly punished, with no pretense of loving all the rascals:

> "There may be Heaven. There must be Hell."

He has not the Shakespearean tenderness any more than the Shakespearean humor. But floods of tears have been wept over the lady who loved Mertoun, more than over Cordelia. Spenser's cry is not too bitter for her:

> "I feel my heart perst with so great agony,
> that all for pitie I could die."

Each of the simpler poems has its originality of the Browning type, some subtle moral, some explanatory psychology, some unexpected analysis, some breathless effort, something intellectual to give it body: then its own music, singing sometimes—and there are many tunes; talk sometimes, far above singing.

There are enough of these poems in number and bulk for a fair volume, an immortal volume.

On Education and Philosophy

The nineteenth century was a time of dramatic expansion in higher education. As Christopher J. Lucas points out, at the time of the Revolutionary War there were a mere nine colleges in the U.S.; by 1802 there were nineteen; and by the time of the Civil War there were 250. Hence conversations about pedagogy were legion, as were expressions of dissatisfaction on the part of students (who complained of spartan living conditions and their colleges' isolated rural locales), administrators (who wanted more paternalistic control over students' behavior), and professors (who wanted to be treated as professionals). March's long professorial tenure enabled him to see the range of issues confronting higher education in his time—and to anticipate the direction that education should be taking.

March's own experience was at two liberal arts colleges: Amherst, where he studied for four years, and Lafayette, where he taught for 51 years. In one of his essays, he distinguishes between the kind of personal educational experience a student receives at a small liberal arts college and that offered by a large university. At Lafayette, March says, it is "thought best to have every morsel of truth lubricated well with good professorial palaver": students' educations should include the opportunity to interact with their professors. March also defended elective courses as part of a student's course of study, even as he dismissed erroneous ideas of what the term "electives" might mean to the uninitiated.

Lafayette provided the venue and occasion for speeches that yield considerable information on the scope and practice of education in the 1880s. In his dedicatory remarks about Pardee Hall, for example, he used the building layout to survey the college curriculum: in the East and West Wings were sciences and engineering; in the center were "the library, collections of art and antiquities, lecture-rooms for history, social science and language, the society halls, and the great Auditorium." In a post-prandial (after-dinner) address, he offered other reflections on education, including the importance of compulsory chapel attendance, as well as the "gentlemanly" playing of college athletics. Though both speeches reveal March as a man of his time, so also do they deserve an important niche in the history of higher education.

March's most influential comments, though, were on the teaching of English. In the selection of essays in this section, he forcefully defends what we now call "close" reading of a text, as well as early instruction in reading, to be proffered through a phonics approach. In an early version of today's "writing-across-the-curriculum" initiative, he proposes that instruction in writing extend to all departments in a college, not merely to English; the use of writing should be abundant: "Handing in a written analysis makes sure that [a text] is studied." Indeed, March's contributions to the history of composition are seminal: as Donahue and Falbo point out, the narrative of composition generally holds that the teaching of composition began at Harvard; but it had several earlier points of origin, including in March's classroom at Lafayette.

The contents page of his *Method of Philological Study* provides a précis of his approach to the study of literature, which he characterizes as progressive. It begins with questions on syntax, grammatical equivalents, rhetorical forms, and historical elements, applied to Bunyan's *The Pilgrim's Progress*; continues with punctuation, poetical forms, and epic art, with Milton's *Paradise Lost*; moves to etymology of pronouns, pronominal elements, instinctive forms, dramatic art, and creative power in language, with Shakespeare's *Julius Cæsar*; continues with questions about derivation, romance of chivalry, and Spenserian stanza in Spenser's *The Faerie Queene*; and, finally, looks at phonetic, orthographic, and historical elements, as well as "criticism of uncertain Text," in Chaucer's *The Canterbury Tales*.

The technique that March used is illustrated in his analysis of the opening scene of *Julius Cæsar*. He begins with a long series of historical questions about the author and the text, followed by a close linguistic analysis and larger questions about structure and meaning:

> Where was [Shakespeare] born? What kind of place is Stratford geographically? What kind of place was it botanically? . . . What literary opportunities? . . . When was *Julius Caesar* written? . . . What lesson is it intended to teach? What conspiracies in England during the life of Shakespeare? On the Continent? . . . What in his relations to Elizabeth and James would add interest to the matter? . . . What is the first clause? . . . What kind of clause—declarative, interrogative, imperative, exclamatory, or optative? . . . What is the verb? . . . What does *hence* combine with? Kind of combination? . . . Does it complete or extend the predicate? . . . Is it an adjunct of time, place, mode, or cause? What language is it from? . . . Next clause? . . . Scan the first verse! What kind of a foot is the first? . . . Where is the cæsura? . . . Scan the second! Cæsura where? Fourth foot was kind? Scan the third! Cæsura where? Third foot what kind? Scan the fifth verse! Cæsura where? . . . Is this a good scene to open

with? Why? What is there to attract attention—show, bustle, fun eloquence? . . . What variety in this scene among the characters? . . . What variety in the action? . . . What variety in the sentiments? . . . What variety in the language? . . . What unity between the tribunes?. . . Is there any unity between the comic and serious parts? . . . What is the main idea of the play? How does this scene contribute to its development? . . . How is the genius of Shakespeare shown in this scene?

And so on.

March's interrogation was nothing if not rigorous. His publications on pedagogy suggest how seriously the first Professor of English took the study of English language and literature.

WORKS CITED

Donahue, Patricia and Bianca Falbo, "A Story of Reading and Writing: The Example of Francis A. March, Lafayette College," in *Local Histories*, ed. Patricia Donahue and Gretchen Moon, forthcoming.

Lucas, Christopher J. *American Higher Education: A History* (New York: St. Martin's, 1994).

March, Francis A. *Method of Philological Study of the English Language* (New York: Harper & Brothers, 1865), esp. 37-73.

The Scholar of To-Day

Under the old philosophy the highest word was CULTURE; under the new philosophy the highest word is PROGRESS. The scholar of the old philosophy sought, by self-development and self-government, to educate himself to his highest worthiness. The Baconian devoted himself to the discovery of truth and to the progress of the race.

The scholar of the old time—the man of perfect culture, trained to all feats of mental activity, ready in all branches of knowledge, always under control, strong, alert and graceful, the delight of all men, and women—has often been held up to our admiration. Let us celebrate to-day the scholar of to-day, the servant of truth, the interpreter of nature.

It is a central fact with the scholar of to-day, that he is a working member of a great brotherhood laboring together for the advancement of knowledge. Lord Bacon set forth his ideal of an organization of scholars in his *House of Solomon* in his romance of the *New Atlantis;* but all the splendors of his prophetic imagination pale before the facts of to-day. The same general ends and means are, it is true, before us. We still seek "the knowledge of causes and the enlarging of the bounds of human empire to the effecting of all things possible." We still use observation and experiment. But the instruments and operations of Solomon's House are child's toys and child's play compared with the wonderful enginery with which we vex and scrutinize earth, air and sea; mind and matter; the present and the far off; and quicken the past and the future.

Nor is the fraternity of workers less wonderful. No close corporation now embraces the conquerors of nature. The army of explorers overruns the whole world. The mightiest nations are privates in its ranks. The Czar of all the Russias keeps step with the imperial democracy of America. He uses his whole empire as a cabinet and laboratory. He takes note of every drop of water that falls or lurks in the air, of every breeze that blows, every sunbeam that tints or warms, every tree and animal that knows the soil. His imperial government records the physical facts and the history of all its tribes of men, catches every form of speech that drops from living lips or lingers on old monuments, and sends out all in

"The Scholar of To-Day: An Address before the Phi Beta Kappa Society at Amherst College, Commencement, July, 1868." *American Presbyterian Review* n.s. 1 (January 1869): 76-95; also published separately as a pamphlet (Springfield [Mass.]: Samuel Bowles, 1869).

fair type for the great fraternity of scholars. It experiments on new forms of social organization, abolishes old penalties, institutes new rewards, new tenures, new schemes of education, new fashions of dress, and food, and manners.

The American scholar has the same work before him. We are lawyers, doctors, preachers, editors, engineers, or teachers. We are also scholars.

> "With that clause
> We make drudgery divine."

Not a plant is so thoroughly known that the ablest botanist can write its biography. The lazy-limbed lad with live eyes may yet lie by the old wall around the College Campus, and watch the lichens with his microscope, and see facts as good as Robert Brown ever saw. New metals wait their finder, new coals, new secrets of growth in the soils, and all the unimaginable marvels which chemistry deals out with such a lavish band from her infinite store. In these departments the value of organized labor is fully recognized. We have associations of science, which every scholar can help, and where the chiefs of each department are ready to receive the smallest contributions of fact or thought, and where no lover of science fails to obtain sympathy and honor.

Coöperation and progress should be just as familiar to those who work in books and language. A perfect edition of Shakespeare, or Chaucer, or Homer, or the Bible; or a complete dictionary of our language, would be as helpful to the race as a perfect flora or fauna of North America. But such a work must accumulate the observations of a thousand scholars for a thousand years. What scholar has not passages in his favorite authors which he understands better than all the commentators? Who has not noted strange words, or meanings of words, unknown to Worcester or Webster; or has not hit an etymology which has baffled the learned, or an illustrative sentence which opens the soul of a word with a new completeness? We should have a common hive for all these gatherings. Meantime, the Philological Society's *Dictionary* is waiting for just these facts and truths, and the press is always at our service.

Scholars should reverence the powers of the press and use them. They too often sneer at what it is their sacred duty to serve. A knot of professional men will have their daily gibes at the crude columns of their local newspaper. Why not send the broken meats from their tables and feast the rustics?

But no duty has more peculiar claims on the American scholar than observation and experiment on man and his institutions, with a view to improve our social organization and government, and to establish sciences of mind, of ethnology and history, on their proper foundations.

We already have organizations for the advance of social science, and our scholars are making valuable contributions to the doctrines of general education; the treatment of the insane, the idiotic and the criminal; of the causes of disease and crime; the laws of population; the adjustment of labor and capital. They are familiar with the fact that such problems may be investigated without mingling in party politics.

But the same spirit may be carried into many questions of governmental organization and policy. Each New England town is a working model of the state, in which experiments may be tried with little danger. The American scholar has no excuse for being an *idiōtēs*. Many new questions are before us.

Our government is a representative democracy. We call it a government of the people, it is really a government of the majority. In our day *tyranny* of the majority is worse than the tyranny of one man or a few men, because it has no restraint. Conscious weakness makes the few cautious. The King of England has not dared a veto for generations. The majority vaunts its voice to be the voice of God. Where this form of atheism prevails, and minorities are regarded as opposers of manifest destiny—the majority God—and contemned as wicked instead of being heard and conciliated as equals, tyranny of the majority impends. The liberal leaders of European thought suppose that this danger may be averted by organizing all representative assemblies, so that the governing bodies shall have the same proportion of parts which exists among the people themselves. Then all minorities would have weight in proportion to their actual strength, all opinions held by able men would have able advocates in authority, and all able men would have their chance for a public career without bidding for the vote of a party. There are doubts and difficulties connected with the practical working of such a scheme, which can best be resolved by trying it, on a smaller scale, in our voluntary associations, our private corporations, and the directories of towns. Here our professional men and scholars might promote the trial, and study, and report the results.

It is a question, again, how far it is desirable to introduce a new moral element into the balance of power by giving the vote to women.

Other questions are connected with executive patronage. Year by year the host who live by their connection with political Rings, grows rapidly in numbers, power and shamelessness. No party can now safely defy them. No politician can safely refuse to recognize their leaders as his peers. They are fast coming to control the state. They make our political life a perpetual scramble for spoils. All scholars know how vividly this state of things was depicted and predicted by Alexander Hamilton. It is now upon us, and it is a matter of life and death. Our statesmen are proposing means of relief. Shall the tenure of office be changed to good behavior? Shall the appointing power be held by Congress?[1] Shall it be vested in Boards of Examiners? As long as it is massed in a few hands, it will pay for organized corruption. But it might be diffused among the people. Each local officer might be chosen by the people of his locality. The power of removal, that right hand of the executive, would then give him dignity and authority without exposure to corruption. A trial of this system might be set on foot, if our professional men would refuse to sign papers recommending local officers, and urge their nomination by a vote of the precinct. Such nominations would be respected at Washington, and the plan grow in favor in proportion to its merits.

Such are illustrations of the manner in which the American scholar may work for the republic and for man. I have dwelt on them the more because distaste for politics so much affects us. It is often urged that scholars should take up politics to purify them. What has been said would suggest that we should seek to withdraw as many questions of statesmanship and social science as we can from the sphere of party politics, and hand them over to the investigation and experiments of our scholars. Then our laws may answer to Bacon's noble description of those of Henry VII: "His laws, whoso marks them well, were deep and not vulgar, not made on the spur of a particular occasion for the present, but out of providence for the future; that he might make the estate of his people more and more happy, after the manner of legislators in the ancient and heroical times."

It is to such scholarship as this, that the lovers of the race turn for that influence which shall make it possible to have a parliament of man, a federation of the world; and such scholars will be the peers in that parliament, the representatives of the general reason of mankind in the good time coming.

If the essential characteristic of the scholar of to-day be his fellowship with the brotherhood of workers for progress; if devotion to the conquest of nature, the discovery of truth and the welfare of the race, be the root of true scholarliness, we may go on to develop several branches of the scholar's character.

---

[1]Such a combination of the legislative and executive functions would overthrow our system of government, and set up an oligarchy, too numerous for responsibility, too few to be out of the reach of Rings.

And first: The scholar of to-day should devote himself to some particular branch of study. To accomplish most we must use division of labor, and this most of all in discovery and invention. It is not the poet alone who is born. Newton, Faraday, Alexander Hamilton, Chief Justice Marshall, Bopp, Grimm, every successful observer, and every creative genius, has his special fitness for his special field of truth. And though Machiavelli divides mankind into those who see of themselves, those who see what is shown them by others, and those who neither see of themselves nor what is shown them by others, it is doubtful whether any pair of eyes was ever made that was not well worth looking through. The short-sighted see what is invisible to others. The observer must find the proper focus of his own eyes. And to all men the new comes most as suggestion from the familiar, the long brooded over; whose every aspect comes to mind without effort; yea, in spite of effort; which haunts the thought by day and the dreams by night; which possesses one like a passion. He who would truly advance the empire of man must concentrate his sphere of thought. The scholar, armed at all points with glittering generalities, ready to bear his part brilliantly in a discussion of everything knowable and talkable, ashamed not to know when everybody lived and died, and all about the old battles—of the kites and crows, as Milton says; and talking

"Frensch ful faire and fetysly
Aftur the scole of Stratford atte Bowe,"

and other languages to match, is not the scholar we celebrate. Such a scholar is simple, not bound to shine, eager to hear, more eager to see for himself, glad to tell you what he has seen for himself, and well aware how little he has seen, as he has walked by the beach of the infinite ocean of truth.

It is a further development of the same thought, that the student should be wedded early to particular truths. He will not spend his life in general devotion to truth, without cultivating any one truth; celebrating and worshiping truth as a goddess, wooing and winning none of her daughters. It is well enough in the teens, this general laudation of truth, the open mind flushing at every suggestion from man, or running brooks, or stones, or anything; but the old scholars, who, having linked their names with no science or art, revive their old flames for our benefit in essays and orations, have the lack-a-daisical air of the old bachelor who proclaims himself the devoted admirer of the ladies. The lover of truth should fall in love betimes with some particular truth, should woo like a man with his whole heart, marry early, and be faithful as to a spouse for generation, fruit and comfort.

It should seem, in the third place, that our scholar will seek to learn facts and laws rather than to practice mental gymnastics. It is a current thought, that the growth of the mind is analogous to that of the body, that education is a gymnastics. Discipline, not truth, is said to be the object of study. The search for truth is said to be better than the possession of it. There is something in this view peculiarly fascinating to the young and strong. What college senior has not held his breath, as he has read Sir William Hamilton's absorbing citations of the exultant utterances of the heroes of literature.

"Did the Almighty," says Lessing, "holding in his right hand *Truth,* and in his left hand *Search for Truth,* deign to tender me the one I might prefer, in all humility, but without hesitation, I should request *Search for Truth.*" We do not always remember that these exulting pinions droop at last, and that a philosophy of nescience is the end of this search. Good hunting and no game taken is a sorry jest. The savor of the venison is needed to stir us to repeat the chase. The joy of capture is needed, that we may return with ardor to the pursuit.

There is, moreover, in all worthy growth, as in all magnanimity, an emotional and moral element. A notable gymnastic cultivation of the attention, memory, judgment, generalization, inventive combination, and other intellectual faculties, may be made by chess puzzles. But the judgments of wisdom are the fruit of attention kindled by love, and directed by conscience; and all imagination, properly so called, proclaims the activity of the æsthetic emotions. The delight of the possession of truth is needed to warm the soil from which new thoughts are to spring. The time comes, when old books, old friends, old truths, the dear delights of our youth, come to be thrice dear as the recognized root of all the growth of our manhood. There is, indeed, a plain analogy between the training of the special senses and gymnastics. The young scholar should be practised to see, as he is to walk. Particular mental processes which need to be often repeated, such as the application of the ground-rules of arithmetic, or of the rules of grammar, have an analogy with gymnastics, in so far that practice enables us to perform them more rapidly, easily, gracefully, and accurately. The mind needs to be run in the right ruts. But the growth of the mind, the incubation and development by which it passes from imitation to creation, from one stage of power to another, learns to see one truth after another, has very little analogy with the operations of the body.

Those who have studied man in history, especially those who work on his very soul as it is preserved in its progress by language, can not help feeling how completely inadequate are all the phrases commonly used to express this progress, how completely unlike gymnastics is the conversion of an infant into a ripe scholar of to-day. The ablest savage left to train his own powers, is ages behind the dullest head that learns to use an Indo-European tongue. Some naturalists say that the human embryo passes through its stages of likeness to a plant, and to each lower order of animals up to man, completing in its due months the development of a million of millions of years. So the mind, by the aid of language and the mysterious leaven of truth, completes in its score of years the proper growth of ages. We are struck with wonder at the operations of genius. We tax our language to express the novelty and splendor of the changes it works in the world. We call it inspiration rather than gymnastics. But by the wonderful power of language and truth, we may repeat in ourselves these same marvels of perception and power.

An attempt to analyze this process, leads only to profounder deeps of wonder. Plato was carried back by it to infinite ages of pre-existent life. He thought these new ideas were only reminiscences; and the philosophic poets have chanted the noblest responses to the thought, as they have celebrated

> "Those shadowy recollections
> Which, be they what they may,
> Are yet the fountain light of all our day,
> Are yet a master light of all our seeing."

But if we do not receive these thoughts of Plato, the word *education* does not express this process. The genius inspires us, magnetizes us. A magnet does not *educate* a piece of iron or steel. The wonderful thing is not a *drawing out* of power, but some mysterious flowing in of power. Savage warriors imagine that the strength of those they conquer passes into them. The old Hebrew figures, too, are good. The mind is soil for seed. The germs of thought once dropped in the mind, grow while we sleep. We wake surprised at the greatness of the thought we took in over night, and it spreads its branches day by day, and year by year; nor do we always suspect what kind of seed is planted. The amaranth springs among the tares in the soul of a tinker's apprentice, "a weed of glorious feature."

So man is a tree for graft, so he has his new births. We go from grub to chrysalis, from chrysalis to butterfly. The history of the scholar's mind is not graphically given by any words which imply that it is a gymnastics, or solitary development. Even the nations do not often have an indigenous civilization; but are raised by the efforts of foreign races. The individual is lifted and expanded by communion with higher intelligences, mainly by the power of higher minds acting through speech, and by the inspiration of objective facts and laws. It is not the working of the mind, considered as gymnastics, which expands it when truth is gained, so much as the possession of truth itself. The effort swallows the leaven; the leaven leavens the whole man. The soul crawls in getting a truth into the mind; when it has it, it may flutter and soar in the play of its creative energy. There is work in getting a truth into the mind, there may be play in its possession. The latter is the true progress, the greatness and the glory of the soul.

It would seem, then, that language is the scholar's true foster-mother. She takes the infant, and introduces him to nature by name. The senses give only indefinite apparitions, or intuitions. These become knowledge, *information,* when particular objects, qualities, or acts are singled out and examined. What shall be so singled out is determined almost wholly by language. The learner follows the names which his elders so eagerly teach him. Language in this way prompts and directs his classifications; she leads him on to reasoning, supplies him with instruments, and suggests the arguments. She is the interpreter between the scholar and the great discoverers of all time. Shapen into literature under the direction of the æsthetic faculty, language moulds his passions and sentiments to sympathy with the great hearts and souls whose words of fire she loves to repeat, lifts him from his feet with the great voice of eloquence, raises his religious feelings to supernatural elevation by her utterance of the revealed word, and prompts him to graceful and noble utterancy, which may win all men to the truths he loves.

Language is the nurse of science historically. The philosophy of Greece appears before us in the Socratic discussions as a child of language still in leading strings. Its questions and its argumentation do not distinguish thought as thought, from the use of language. It was not till the development of geometry, that coherent thinking was known, independent of the thoughts embodied in popular speech. And though the sciences of to-day have their own language, the true scholar never so weans himself from this foster-mother of sciences and scholars, that he does not desire to confide his thoughts to her—does not run to her with delight at each new discovery.

It would seem, further, that the pursuit of truth in nature is analogous to the study of language. The great *stone-book* is the geologist's name for the earth. Says the botanist, Bernard Jussieu, "The perfect book is open to all; it is only necessary to learn to read it." "There is a certain character, or *style,*" says Dugald Stewart on the hint of Sir Isaac Newton, "in the operations of the Divine Wisdom, . . . in the perception of which *philosophical sagacity and genius* seem chiefly to consist." He who has interpreted one fact, learns to interpret another and another; gazing on one truth, we learn how to recognize its sister truths; having learned to read the handwriting on one page, we may turn to another and read with ease. An eminent educator has enforced his doctrine of "power-culture," by saying that Napoleon might have summoned all the force of his mighty mind, and struck out at a blow a new system of Mental Philosophy! But such blows are never struck. Truth is not conquered; it is read. It comes to earnest, humble seekers. The mighty mother unveils her face to the child. He who is smitten with love for that face, into whose soul those divine traits are burned, seeks them forever, and traces them through all veils.

It would seem, further, that our reader of nature, our lover of truth and progress, is least of all men pugnacious. It has ceased to be the scholar's fitting eulogy that he is a war-horse, even against error.

In the first place, the history of errors shows that they are not quelled by fighting them. Witchcraft and like delusions show brave fight for centuries, then die, because men are lifted to a higher plane of thought by the power of new truths. The scholar, as he labors for the progress of the race, will seek to use the expulsive power of new truth, rather than arm himself and ride forth to give battle to monsters and chimeras. Such is the method which Lord Bacon inculcates. Such is the method of Christian progress.

So, in a subjective point of view, it would seem that struggles and skepticism are by no means a desirable *propædeutic* for the scholar. There is a masterly pugnacity in man which makes us exult in battle and conquest. It is hardly weaker now than it was before Christ. Two thousand years of lip-assent to his teachings have hardly dimmed the warrior's glory. Our generation, indeed, begins to hear its heroes announce, "The empire is peace:" "Let us have peace:" and this is great gain. But the old Berserker blood still runs duly in our Puritan veins. The historian says: "It was ever the fashion of Cromwell's pikemen to rejoice greatly when they beheld the enemy," and the reverberation of that shout of stern exultation has not yet died in our Southern savannas. The same blood shows itself in our intellectual efforts. Our very peace societies are pugnacious in putting down other people's wars, as well as in defending our own. It is characteristic of New England college culture to pride itself on its struggles. We go to our recitations with hearts of controversy. We enter the lists of debate in our society halls, as the knights came forth at the sound of the trumpet. We talk of these halls as arenas, where we may "drink delight of battle with our peers," and be fitted for the great battle of life. This temper has its honors. It is better than sensuality. It is better than stagnation. I confess to the relish of these delights.

"Better fifty years of Europe than a cycle of Cathay." It is most truly a preparation for the battle of life. But the young Puritan no more needs a kindling of the spirit of battle than the young tiger needs to lap blood. And from the point of view which has been taken to-day, it may be seen that we are apt to overrate the influence of disputatious adroitness. Shakespeare's fools are the "smartest" men in his plays. Great men of action are seldom disputants, great men of thought perhaps still less so. The great thinker answers other men's arguments by stating the truth as he sees it. When we have been years out of college, we find that it is not the struggles of the recitation room, or the society hall, perhaps, that make epochs; but the summer evenings on the chapel steps, the simmering of thought and heart at the hearth of a friend, from which sprang the thoughts which made us free of the realms of beauty and truth.

But whatever may be the thought of the fight against error in other respects, its association with skepticism is surely unscholarly. The scholar in these times should believe all he can. He must not stand of set purpose in a skeptical attitude. Yet our young men often feel as though they are only half-educated, if they have not doubted everything their elders believe. The bright-minded college student has his attack of skepticism as surely as the boy has his measles and whooping cough. He doubts the existence of matter, of mind. The sciences in succession are shaken from their moorings. Mental philosophy, logic, political economy, history, religion, drift into the shadow of doubt. The seeds of truth, just germinating in his mind when he enters college, he pulls up for examination as recklessly as children take up the seeds in their garden beds. But fruitful truths, never to be doubted, should possess the mind of youth, and, by their proper growth, fill it and expand it from month to month, expelling errors as simply as day drives away darkness.

It may be further remarked, that a scholarship of self-forgetfulness, of an objective direction and employment of the faculties, will show itself in literature. Instead of general flourishes about the pursuit of the true, the beautiful and the good—the dumb-bells and vocal gymnastics of our culture, which our authors never will lay down—the scholar of to-day will set to work on some science of plants, like Goethe, or at making a dictionary, like Jean Paul and Milton, or at ichthyology, or entomology, or social science—any way to learn the handling of the keys which unlock the secrets of nature, any way to find the charm to open the heart-gates to the entrance of angels. New spheres of positive thought will thus be brought under the shaping power of the æsthetic faculty, and expressed in harmonious utterance whose cadences have been caught afresh from nature. A new and greater *Iliad, Kalewala* and *Beowulf* will be possible,—simple, grand, natural, as the old folk songs of heroes, but of a higher strain than the ages of kings and carnage ever knew. Our critics, too, will know the traits of nature, and never mistake the watching and recording of sensuality, which now threatens us with a new era in literature; never mistake these long-drawn eunuch dallyings of Swinburne or Whitman for the throes of virility, or a mountainous consciousness for manhood.

Much might be said of the relation of these views to education. We have made a distinction between studies of gymnastic, and studies of incubation and development. A college course must be in great part gymnastic: that is to say, it must be occupied in training students to working habits in the use of the laws of language and the simpler mathematics, and in actual manipulation in the natural sciences. This gymnastic training should be on such subjects, and within such limits, as will most aid future progress.

In Language, it would seem wrong to spend a long time in learning to talk a little bad Latin, or French, or German, so as to be ready if we ever should make a three weeks' tour of the continents. Learning to talk requires a wholly different gymnastic from other mastery of speech.

The Mathematics, in addition to their much commended virtues, are, I believe, the best intellectual safeguard against college pyrrhonism. I have known more than one who held by that anchor, when heaven and earth seemed to mix.

The Natural Sciences do not always deserve their reputation as bread-and-butter sciences. Professors of Natural History expound the structure of the useless plants and animals. The great Jussieu cautions his collectors against varieties produced by cultivation. These should be left, he says, to the amateurs. Rumford may found a mechanical institute for real workers, but as soon as the lords and ladies begin to come to the lectures, the scheme changes. But the uses of manipulation can not be overstated. Chemistry, the idlest of all textbook or lecture studies, is the best for the gymnastic of manipulation; Botany next. These make a new man of the obtusest and clumsiest. Precision, purity, dexterity, grace, of hand, eye and mind, are their gift.

To the more common gymnastic studies should be added the English Language and Constitutional Law. Latin and Greek are an admirable introduction to the freer and higher forms of speech which the advancing nations have since shaped for themselves. Representative passages of the representative works of the representative authors of the great epochs of modern thought should be studied in the light of modern philology, line by line, and word by word. And we should add scholarly judgment to the instinct with which we speak our mother English, the growth of all the ages. Every college student should know the Constitution of the United States better than the rules for syntax, by rote and by heart.

The method to be used in the studies of incubation and development is different from that in studies of gymnastic. The last begin with the simplest processes, and with tireless repetition lead on to the more powerful, rapid, and complex. The others almost reverse the process. The intellect and emotions must be roused at once. When the artist would awaken the perception of beauty, he takes us first to St. Peter's.[2] The grand half-outlined thoughts of geology, exultant, all-embracing systems of the cosmos, the reconstruction of the primeval and the unwritten history of man from language, the records of old heroism looming large through the mists of antiquity, the thoughts of old thinkers interpreted by new thinkers, the strange beauty of old languages, anticipations of new truths hovering round the lips and eyes of genius, visions of the future,—these have power to kindle the enthusiasm and quicken the intellect of youth. Nor should it be forgotten how far the greatness of New England is due to the quickening of her common mind by the truths of theology. A Westminster Catechism is a battery that gives a rousing shock.

It would fall in well with such views, if a considerable part of the college course should present a number of elective studies, in which each student might follow his own bent, in the pursuit of particular sciences or branches of learning, in connection with professors who are themselves rejoicing in investigations of their own.

Thus far I have spoken as though culture and devotion to the progress of science and the race did not go together. It is often said that the individual withers as the race is more and more. It is said that devotion to objective results in some particular branch of knowledge changes man to a mere tool, a one-sided monster, a blacksmith's arm, a weaver's thumb, developed in but one direction, and hence not developed at all as man, a sacrifice to nature and material ends.

If this were so, two of the highest principles in man would be in conflict; for surely love of a beautiful manhood is a passion hardly less strong and noble than love of truth. No Amherst student of our day was not moved to admiration and longing by the vivid picture so masterly painted by our Professor of Greek, of Socrates the son of Sophroniscus,

---

[2]Corinne iv. 3

the statuary, as he takes his thought from the shaping of the marble figures around him, and resolves to mould his own character to the model of ideal beauty. It is said that happiness is not to be reached by direct pursuit, but is a bounty bestowed on him who works hard for worthy ends. May it not be so with culture? What is a beautiful character? What is a well-developed manhood? Is their beauty independent of all relations? Would Apollo's arm be beautiful wielding the blacksmith's hammer?

Great men are not great in all things. In all works of art there is orderly subordination, a variety brought to unity by relations to something central and supreme. Every beautiful growth has its center or axis of growth. So in men of admirable character there is some heroic trait, some axis of growth. Some supreme power shows itself, and the others work to heighten its effect. Nor are all men alike in their type of beauty. They are various as the departments of thought and life. A sincere devotion to some special sphere of labor, is the best means of harmonious development. As the advancing mind rises to higher relations of the special pursuit, the view widens, new powers are called forth, and brought into harmonious working with the old. Such is the harmony between the world and the soul that the leadings of nature may be trusted to the end.

> "Unless above himself he can
> Erect himself, how poor a thing is man."

Even the intuitions need exercise on nature for their full development. How does space expand to the astronomer, time to the geologist, right to the student of God in history!

Nor will it befit this presence to pass over the more secret reason why truth and material nature so inspire and develop. What is truth, but fact seen as the embodiment of law, which is the will of God? And this complex of facts which we call nature, what is it but a material expression of the character of God? As the student of the tribes of nature seeks to rise from the history of individuals to a scientific knowledge of species, to conceive the types of genera and families, he is not abstracting and combining by whim; these types were present to the mind of God before they were in nature. The attempt to find them, is an attempt to rethink the thoughts of God. And as in thinking the thoughts of the wise and great we enter into their life, so in reading the book of nature, we may be raised to communion with God, and rise above ourselves, height above height.

This view of the sacredness of nature, plain to the ancient Hebrews, not unseen by Plato, lost by reaction from Grecian and Roman nature-worship, has been regained to our literature from the grandest of unchristian modern thinkers, the Jew of Jews, "God-intoxicated Spinoza." The true scholar will not fail to recognize, as its necessary complement, the central thought of the philosophy of Paul, the mystical union of man with Christ, by which the inmost fountain of the human will itself may be filled with the divine life, as the branch with the life of the vine.

And if it be true in the intellect, that self-renunciation, devotion to man and science, the objective direction and employment of the faculties, is more favorable to the harmonious and orderly development of man, than any deliberate gymnastics, it can hardly be less so in morals and manners.

God forbid that the grand old name of gentleman should ever be dissociated from the name of scholar. There are other types of the *kalòs kagathós* than the princes of the last generation who were the first gentlemen of Europe. He who does many things gracefully from a sense of his own worthiness, may yet fall short of the perfection of him who forgets himself in others, in truth, in God.

There is no need in this presence to search history for illustrations. As I have been tracing these traits of the scholar of to-day, how often have my thoughts reverted to the Christian scholar who presided over this institution during our college days.[3]

Always most earnest in his recognition of the great brotherhood of scholars, he was one of the first to suggest, as he was the first to preside over, the American Association of Science. Wedded in youth to geology, he loved most that aspect of it which

> "seeks in golden chains to bind
> Science with reverence, liberty with law."

Constant through life, giving his whole heart to truth, he rose from one stage of intimacy to another with the secrets of nature which are the revelation of God. Losing self wholly in the contemplation of His ends, winning always to the good rather than worrying at the bad, shrinking always from conflict and controversy, regretting the loss of a day of doubt, believing everything he could, a soft, meek, patient, humble, tranquil spirit,[4] he was also a man to stand before princes, a man who could pledge noblemen at their own tables in his cup of cold water with a simple grace more beautiful than the color of their choicest wine.

---

[3]Edward Hitchcock.

[4] "The best of men
That e'er wore earth about him, was a sufferer;
A soft, meek, patient, humble, tranquil spirit;
The *first true gentleman* that ever breathed."—*Thos. Dekker.*

Few students of Amherst, while he was here, can have read Hawthorne's story of the *Great Stone Face,* without thought that its hero was with us. As he came in hours of sickness or trouble; or as, in his lectures, he kindled to the height of his great argument; or as, in the college chapel, when one read from the grand poem of Moses those scenes of creation so vivid to him, and the evening or the morning light saw that benign face instinctively turning upward, radiant with the gleam that never was on sea or land, the consecration of truth and goodness, who of us failed to remember those inspired utterances, dearest to every true scholar:

"The pure in heart shall see God."
"The beauty of the Lord our God be upon us."

An Address at the Reopening of Pardee Hall, Lafayette College, November 30, 1880

We meet to-day as friends of education, and, therein, lovers of our country and of our race, to celebrate the completion of this Hall of Science—PARDEE HALL—and to honor its founder.

Addresses of welcome and of thanks have been made; addresses of congratulation are to follow. This address is to set forth in a summary manner the uses of the hall, the nature of its equipment and apparatus, and the part they play in education. And such is the magnitude of the building and the extent and variety of its apparatus that a discourse upon them is really a discourse upon the general topic, "The buildings and apparatus of the modern college."

If we explore the EAST WINGS OF PARDEE HALL, we shall find them full of the apparatus of manipulation. Work-rooms for the department of mechanics and physical laboratories are the main features of the first and second floors. The third and fourth floors are occupied by the department of civil engineering. They are stored with instruments for work in the field, and fitted up for industrial drawing and office-work. In another part of the building there are rooms for other kinds of drawing, and laboratories for work in botany and natural history. A separate building is devoted to the laboratories of chemistry, and another to the astronomical observatory.

All good teachers now-a-days try to have the study of books accompanied with continual exercises of practice. It is not enough for the student of mechanics to read and compute; he must put together, handle, and run real machines. The student of engineering must shoulder his instruments and use them in the field. It is little for the students of chemistry to read and remember that water is a compound of oxygen and hydrogen. Each one for himself must take the water apart and manipulate the oxygen and hydrogen with his own hands. The student of botany must pick the petals from real flowers with his own fingers. The mathematician is always

---

"An Address at the Reopening of Pardee Hall, Lafayette College, November 30, 1880." Easton, PA: Lafayette College, 1881.

doing sums. The study of language goes on to the accompaniment of tongue or pen, and grammar-work for beginners consists for the most part in preparing papers of problems illustrating the laws of speech.

The necessity for this continual manipulation is plain from the nature of language. Words are artificial signs, and do not in themselves give knowledge of objects. We are made aware of this when we hear words in a strange tongue, or fall among the sesquipedalian monsters with which our modern books of science swarm. But it is just as true of the simplest words of the mother-tongue. The child hears the words *papa, water, laugh, kiss,* repeated in connection with those objects and acts until the sound of the word makes it think of the object or act. The sounds convey no knowledge, but only suggest the knowledge it had before. Words are signs of complex ideas. A person to whom only a single element of an idea is known may yet use the word for it with popular correctness, and understand a little of what is meant by a sentence in which it occurs. Words and sentences are therefore what we make them to ourselves. They are nothing, or full of great meanings, according to the furnishing of our own minds. The school-boy who repeats a passage from Webster or Bacon does not necessarily repeat in his own mind the thoughts of Webster or Bacon. One of Bacon's essays has been read by a school-boy as a composition of his own. The lad did not see anything in it which he could not have written himself.

It should be further remarked of the nature of language that it lags far behind the progress of thought. The innumerable judgments on which sagacity depends are comparatively few of them ever expressed in the formal speech of artificial signs. The old furnace-man tells from the look of the bubbles that the charge of steel is becoming ready, but he has no name for that look. The engineer puts down breaks at a peculiar noise in the engine as instinctively as his eyelids close when a fly approaches, but he has no name for the noise. All processes of reasoning need signs, but original thinking and practical sagacity demand the use of primary signs in place of the secondary signs of language. The book-boy who early soars in words, the shadows of the thoughts of others, when he comes to an age to produce for himself and act for himself cannot find his proper sphere in the actual world; he fades from sight. He was more than a boy at ten; he is less than a man at thirty. Manipulation is necessary to arrest this sublimation of the mind, and to make up the short-comings of speech.

Its most general use is to keep the mind awake and alert. Lectures are apt to go in one ear and out the other. The printed page passes before the eye like a shadow. We set ourselves to think, but we brood. The current of the mind often turns a stagnant pool. The thought returns on itself and passes in smother, as Lord Bacon says. To study without pen in hands is to dream. In manipulation thought passes into act, we use our hands and eyes; we are kept busy adjusting and controlling material objects.

The manipulator stores his mind with conceptions of the senses, with information from the eyes, ears, nose, the fingertips, the muscles, and the meters of science, those magnified senses. Without these firm roots men are poor sapless things.

Manipulation trains the organs of perception and practice, the eye of Herschel, the thumb of Phidias. Chemistry, botany, mechanics, drawing, afford most effectual gymnastic of manipulation. They make a new man of the clumsiest. Precision, purity, dexterity, grace, are their gift. The flout which George Herbert transmits to us, that "the German's wit is in his fingers," might well be turned to a plaudit. Sir Gareth is a goodly figure in the *Morte d'Arthure,* in that he has "the fairest and largest hand that ever man saw;" and some one has characterized the Anglo-Saxon as the race with more nerves in their hands than there are in the heads of another race.

It gives clear and distinct ideas. The complex ideas of modern science to which the technical terms must guide us are the result, for the most part, of wide generalizations. They are obscure and indefinite to every man until he has often applied them to real objects. The exact meaning of the botanical terms which denote the shape of leaves—and there is nothing simpler—cannot readily be told except by actually seeing numbers of leaves. Motion in a completed curve needs to be produced and exhibited to the eye. There must also be a clear conception of every element of the object and processes. In reading or exposition we dwell on important points and neglect minor matters, which are yet essential. In manipulating, every detail must be attended to. To select the objects named in a formula, and put them in the relations named so as to produce the proper results, clears up the meaning of every term of the formula, since error is a failure.

This process of minute attention and verification strengthens the memory. Once worked out is faster in mind than ten times learned. The affections of the senses redouble the inner memory. The recurrent force of muscular and nervous habits is added. A long verbal description often in fact belongs to a movement that is comprehended in a single stroke of the eye, or other brief experience, which the memory holds without effort.

The memory is lively also as well as strong in bringing up matters which have been manipulated. The will seems to attach itself specially to them and give them something of its own activity and freedom. They spring promptly to mind when needed. The difference between just knowing a thing so that you can think it up if you are questioned and have time, and knowing it so that it will come itself without effort, clear and bright, is like the difference between drudgery and genius.

But a greater advantage of manipulation is that it trains the judgment. The reduction of theory to practice cannot be an exercise of mere memory. There is judgment in determining the real object and facts to which the theory will apply; and then there are the hundred unformulated little matters which must be decided in each particular case—problems and difficulties connected with the material, its conditions, its relations to heat, friction, and other unnamed disturbances. All these compel the intelligent manipulator to extricate himself from the meshes of popular speech and the traditions of the books, and lead him to examine facts at first hand, and to be at one with the powers he uses.

And finally, the manipulator is in training to become an inventor and a discoverer. We cannot probe that vital point where the infinite and finite meet in the personality of the man of creative genius, but there are two sayings about its mode of manifestation which are specially worthy of remembrance. The first is the old Greek proverb, "Genius is the daughter of memory;" the other, the hint of Newton that there is certain *style* in the operations of the Divine Wisdom, in the perception of which *philosophical sagacity* and *genius* seem chiefly to consist. A mind well stored with the powers and forms of the world, which has caught the style in which these powers work and these forms combine, is likely to create according to Nature—to invent, to discover. But the manipulator has this well-stored mind, and since he continually watches the trains which real forces move in and the combinations which they actually make, it would seem that his ideas would be prone to move in accordant order, and that he, if any one, would catch the style whose last secret no one may comprehend.

These remarks suggest the usefulness of apparatus of manipulation to students of all branches of science and art, but perhaps it is most useful to those who are intending to become doctors of medicine or engineers. Every lover of the race must rejoice over any well-considered attempt to supply the means of uniting theory and practice in the education of our physicians and engineers, that they may give us more health and wealth, and kill and beggar us as little as may be. The Johns Hopkins endowment of a medical school in Baltimore, whose essential feature is a general hospital in which all the students are to have actual practice before they receive their diplomas, is the carrying out of a similar thought to that which guides the earlier study of chemistry and toxicology and physiology in our laboratories.

But it would seem that the engineers most of all demand special, long-continued preparatory practice. The objects with which they deal are peculiar. Large numbers of persons grow up without ever having had sight of a machine of any complexity, except, perhaps, a glimpse of a locomotive, and without ever having examined the make and action of any. They cannot follow the transfer of power from wheel to wheel of the commonest machines, and in a great shop their heads clatter and buzz and their eyes swim, and it takes longer to learn to walk safely among the belts and cogs than to keep out of the way of the omnibuses in New York. But a good engineer ought to take up a shop into his consciousness as simply and completely as a shepherd does his staff or Sir Lancelot his horse and arms. The inexorable conditions of economy make it necessary that the engineer should know all working machines and their products. The costliness and perfection of existing machinery make it a primary question for every new work or tool, How can it be put together from the best and cheapest products of the old machines? The great inventors work for the most part from ideas stored in early youth. Their materials must come to the mind without effort, haunt it in spite of effort, as do the lively impressions of youth. So young Shakespeare stored his fancy with the skies and earth and waters of Stratford; so Bunyan his, with the sloughs and meadows of Bedford. Nor was it less necessary that Newton should watch the millwheels and clocks and dials of Grantham, and that his young brain should teem with the constructions of geometry and the series of universal arithmetic. As the liveliness of youth passes away, the senses cease to store new objects, the forms of the imagination are fixed, the judgment begins to run in ruts. The morrow ceases to bring fresh woods and pastures new. It is of no use to try to work in strange beats. It would seem, then, that the best education of an engineer must include early and continual familiarity with machinery and its working.

It is said, however, that this working in laboratories, this perpetual manipulation, this study of particular facts or of second causes scattered, narrows the mind, makes men good perhaps for their own alley, but incapable of comprehensive plans or the wider views of science—that it makes the men of whom Bacon says, "A little philosophy inclineth men's minds to atheism."

That there is some truth in this view has long been recognized by the physicians and engineers. And as these professions year by year come to the consciousness of their own importance and dignity, their more eminent members are more and more earnestly advising aspiring young men to take a course of liberal learning in addition to the courses of a professional school. But many difficulties arise. The time and cost block the way. The long interruption by a course of pure culture may be a bad break. It has been attempted here to combine the courses. The technical studies are begun at once, but they are pursued in connection with other branches, and the students are made regular members of the college classes and societies, and share in the general cultivation and learned habits and associations of college life.

But we have dwelt long enough among the laboratories. Let us pass over to the WESTERN WINGS of the Hall. Here we find the apparatus of the classificatory sciences—mineralogy, botany, natural history, geology. Room beyond room, here are marshaled cabinets and collections of minerals, plants, and animals. Here the student is to learn the uses of all natural objects, and those relations of each to all others which tell us where to find them. He learns where to look for gold, where for pyrites, and where for coal and iron; what plants grow in what places, and what animals with them; what interdependences are to be found among all the creatures. He may here learn to frame schemes of production or traffic which include the world.

We have seen that manipulation, laboratory-work, gives acuteness and penetration. Studies of classification give subtlety and comprehension. The reason is awakened to its most vigorous exercise. As it constructs the types of species and genera and compares them with natural individuals, it learns that there are real kinds in nature, and that thinking out the truth in classification is rethinking the thoughts of God. And in certain rare spirits, brooding over these collections of facts and feeling the joy of translating fact into truth, the love of truth for its own sake arises, and once and for ever takes possession of the soul.

It is true there are persons familiar with these natural objects and groups who say that there is nothing but matter in the universe. It is plain, however, that man and other animals act upon experience and purpose. But matter has no memory nor purposes. The brain of every creature returns to dust as it was, and it cannot be told of any atom of carbon to-day whether it has gone through all the motions in the bodies of all the animals, from protoplasm to the brains of Newton, or has been lying in a coal-bed through all the ages. Experience and purpose belong to mind.

The production of organized structures is also seen to be a working upon experience. The natural series of species is like a series of inventions. Even those curious facts which most obtrude the material relations between them are first fully interpreted when referred to mind. Just as the buttons behind a gentleman's coat show that its pattern came from one who was familiar with coats on which the buttons were needed to support a sword, so rudimentary organs in natural structures show that their framer was familiar with similar structures in which the organ has use.

But they say that our senses give nothing but matter, that science knows nothing of causes, except as sensible antecedents, and that atoms of matter come to be matter *plus* mind by development.

John Stuart Mill once suggested that there might be worlds in which it should be regarded as an axiom that two and two are five. I have often pleased myself with imagining myself in such a world, putting pairs of twos together and always finding five. And I have wondered whether it would be impossible to convince the inhabitants of such a world that two and two are not five, but that two and two are four, and the fifth one is thrown in. However it might be with them, it is hard to believe that in our world any system of thinking can long prevail which uses as its first law of induction, "Two and two are five (if you give them time enough)," and which accepts the Tenterden steeple as a fundamental law of logic. On the contrary, we may still repeat with all confidence the familiar words of the prophet of inductive science, of which we were reminded in the laboratories: "A little philosophy inclineth man's mind to atheism, but depth in philosophy bringeth men's minds about to religion; for while the mind of man looketh upon second causes scattered, it may sometimes rest in them and go no further; but when it beholdeth the chain of them confederate and linked together, it must needs fly to Providence and Deity."

We pass on to the CENTRE of the building. Here, as of right, are the library, collections of art and antiquities, lecture-rooms for history, social science and language, the society halls, and the great Auditorium. With these should be counted in other buildings, other lecture-rooms for languages, the Greek room, and all the rest; and the Reading-Room, dear to all students of Lafayette.

These may be called apparatus for the study of man and for training for the mastery of men. Here are laboratories of mind. Here are cabinets of thought. And these must always be the main part of the apparatus of education. The study of other things, of plants and animals and minerals and machines, will vary with the varying needs and fashions of each generation and each country. Man is the one object which is always the study of man.

Knowledge of men, and power to control them, are the most universally useful knowledge and power. Training in penetrating the thoughts of others, and in presenting thought so as to rule the minds of others, is the most universally useful training. Language is the chief scholastic apparatus for this training, and the study of languages in books is the natural preliminary, accompaniment, and supplement to all other studies.

The interpretation of a difficult passage in a foreign language makes the nature of this training plain. We recall or look up the general meanings of the words, and analyze them for special meanings which will fit together. We beat every bush to start every possible meaning. The judgment is summoned to detect the wrong meanings and verify the right. We apply the rules of construction. We discriminate every particle and form, and every synonym. We grasp and hold large ranges of context. We run over and over the general train of thought. We peer into every corner for clues. We seek to examine every passage of our author, or of other authors, in which any of the words or thoughts recur. We collect and invent various readings. We resort to the library, and, if need be, to the cabinets and laboratories. We get up the whole subject-matter, the central persons and facts, and the whole environment. We scrutinize them in the light of psychology and of all science. Whatever of observation, imaginative reproduction, invention, acuteness, subtlety, and comprehension we are capable of, is called into lively exercise. This is the training most needed by the learned professions, and it is never amiss to any man. Eminent specialists who study nature and not language are often more happy in elaborating their own views than in catching the views of others. Two persons converse, and they think they understand each other, but there is nothing in which there is a greater difference between a trained and an untrained man. You spend an hour trying to expound your thought to an untrained man, and at the end he only knows, or thinks he knows, that you agree or do not agree with him; but talk half that time to an old lawyer, or priest, or professor of Greek, and he knows you better than you know yourself.

Nor is it to be forgotten, in estimating the value of the study of language or in approving methods for its study, that mastering it is of the highest value as a mastering of valuable thought. The ability to enter into the thoughts of great thinkers makes the advantage of an American over a Zulu. Books are the best tools of every workman. The youth who might of himself have nothing better to do than to watch the birds and beasts to snare or kill them, is able by means of our English language to enter into the thoughts of the great and wise of all ages.

In the history of man is also to be found material for the study of Providence. He who in the laboratories and cabinets has recognized an intelligent order in the world may here find evidence of a moral purpose, and in the later and better days in which Christianity has been the great power of history, evidence that love and justice are at one. Bibles and catechisms are a goodly part of the college apparatus.

Year by year these studies grow in proportional importance. Investigations in archæology and philology are pushing the history of man farther and farther back continually. Man is continually pushing forward. The librarians are the arsenals of the army of progress. Here are the trophies of its past victories. Here are the weapons for future conquests. We have just been having an era of inventions of labor-saving machinery, of which the most remarkable result is the improvement of means of communication. Steam-motors and telegraphs bring all men near together. We are entering, with little observation, upon a revolution of social organizations almost certain to be greater than the world has known before. Private corporations, whether for wealth or for power or friendship, stretch their arms around the world, and thousands of men distributed all over the earth are moved as easily as a corporal's guard. The irresistible power of organization is fully recognized in commercial projects. It is just as plain in politics. Out of this confused appearance of struggling corporations and associations and parties which our modern life presents, one portentous fact is emerging. Every organization must have a head, and the larger the organization the more absolute the necessity. Our largest organizations must have one head—and a good one and a permanent one—for the proper running of their machinery. The present state of matters in this respect is so new that language does not yet furnish us with words to designate these persons and things with courteous recognition, but the instinct of the people has found them out, and the masses have become as familiar with *bosses* and *rings* and *the machine* as with anything else in our great cities. Our good people are still hoping that all these unnamables will vanish. We ought really to be training youth to be the right sort of heads or organizations; it is high time for our corporations to develop souls. Science is now embracing man within its scope and studying the laws of his action and organization. Already many important branches of social and political science are developed, and the extent of the apparatus used in investigating and illustrating them, and the number of the professors required to teach them, are so great as to call for a national university.

To a national university must also be remitted the adequate apparatus for historic study of the fine arts.

The society halls are a most important part of the apparatus of a college. Here the students unfold their thoughts to each other and sharpen their wits in friendly combats. Thus they prepare themselves for the battle of life.

And here in the Auditorium is given the opportunity for the expression of their best thoughts, in sympathy with the great masters of English speech, under the glow of public declamation, the supreme effort of the life of a college student.

What are to be the products of the college apparatus? Men, of course, but what kind of men? The scholar of the old time, the man of perfect culture, trained to all feats of mental activity, ready in all branches of knowledge, always under control, strong, alert, and graceful, the delight of all men and women,—some specimens of this kind may perhaps be produced.

The scholar of to-day, eager for progress, devoting himself to some specialty, and therein enlarging the bounds of human knowledge and power,—this apparatus might be used for him. That would be a poor college which should not number such among its children. But knowledge is now built so high that special powers as well as the devotion of a life are needed to make advances. It would be hardly right to organize the studies and direct the methods of college-work to the development of men of genius or the instruction of incipient professors in archæological learning. The great purpose must be to prepare our youth to discharge the duties of good citizens in those professions or occupations requiring special preparation—to make good preachers, lawyers, doctors, chemists, teachers, journalists, engineers, merchants, master-workmen in every good work, and heads of every good organization in Church and State.

One thing more: manhood is good in itself and everywhere. Students are, first of all, living souls. On a college campus all paths lead to the college chapel. To pray well is to study well. It has always been the pride of colleges and universities that they give their scholars a professional spirit, a recognition of a brotherhood of scholars, who have learned to look on the possession of truth, the welfare of man and other intelligences, and the harmony of the world, as higher objects than any selfish pleasures or any private good. This character has been developed for the most part by religious teaching and by instruction in literature, the records of noble thoughts and acts which poets and orators have expressed in noble language—the grand old masters of Greece, and Rome, and Palestine, whose immortal voices echo through the corridors of time, and not less the nearer and dearer and greater masters of our own blood and language, utterers of that noble modern thought which makes noble modern men. Familiarity with these thoughts and acts, and with these inspiring forms of speech, kindles like thoughts in the minds of youth. And it must be remembered that each generation begins at the beginning in character as well as knowledge, and has to learn high ideals for itself. Machinery has material existence, and the knowledge and use of it live, but culture, nobleness, dies with each generation. A nation may lapse into moral idiocy in the midst of material greatness. A perfect course of training for professional workers, which should take them young to their own special fields, would yet not wholly engross them there, but would give them time and room for daily converse with the noble and the beautiful in history and art, and for the enjoyment and mastery of language and literature, to the end that they may become noble men as well as great powers.

The general structure of a modern college building is characteristic. It suits well with the ample gymnasium near it, and grounds prepared for athletic exercises, and rows of students' homes. The halls of the universities of Europe have been the theme of many an eloquent description. Too often they are enchanted palaces of the poets, fabrics of beauty only to the fancy—really, a hive of cells, cold, damp, dark, stifling, deadly to live in. This Pardee Hall is a fair and stately structure. Its rooms are large and lightsome. By arts unknown of yore, and at a cost that would have staggered princes, floods of fresh air warm and grateful pour up perpetually all though it to meet the bountiful expanses of windows and fill it full of sweetness and light.

It is one of the felicities of architecture that its works are adopted by Nature. This beautiful hall is henceforth of one family with the hills around us; not naked and alone, but robed and garlanded with these green slopes, this glorious sky, and all the wondrous beauties of earth in the midst of which it stands.

And it is a still higher felicity that it may receive a consecration, a light that never was on sea or land, from association with high thoughts and noble deeds. One such association is alive to-day in all our thoughts, and will live as long as these walls stand. It is put on record for all the generations of Lafayette in the following action of the Faculty:

WHEREAS, It has been held seemly to honor intelligent munificence, and for Christian scholars to tenderly preserve the memory of promoters of science and learning, and for learned foundations to have set times to honor their founder and cherish his grateful remembrance; and

WHEREAS, The celebration of such deeds of munificence is a powerful means of inciting youth to imitate them, and of training them up to all those liberal acts and thoughts which are the fruit of the highest culture; therefore—

Resolved, That to-morrow, the 21st day of October, being the first anniversary of the formal opening and dedication of Pardee Hall, the usual lectures and recitations be suspended, and the day marked by appropriate exercises; and that hereafter the Wednesday following the 21st day of October in each year be recognized as the anniversary of the founding and gift of Pardee Hall, and that it be set apart forever by Lafayette College, its Faculty and students, under the name of Founder's Day, as a day of commemoration of the founder, Ario Pardee.

The Growth of Lafayette: A Post-Prandial Address

There are no dreams of youth which every college student is more certain to dream than visions of the growth and greatness of his alma mater. And there are no college graduates who have more reason to cherish these dreams than the old alumni of Lafayette.

And that shall be the subject of my talk to-night, "the growth of Lafayette," or, to put it in more imposing form and in the latest fashionable phrase,—"the development of a modern college."

We Lafayette boys do not believe in developments and evolutions that develop or evolve themselves—that go it blind. We want an intelligence to start with. A wise and good power was needed for the development of the world; for the development of a college, a wise and good heart and head; for the development of Lafayette, Dr. Cattell.

It was in the year of our Lord one thousand eight hundred and sixty-three that the Reverend William Cassiday Cattell became president of Lafayette. His face was bright with a thousand hopes, but the most significant effluence of the new power was the waking of the whole college to new religious life,—God's blessing breathed upon old Lafayette,—Christ's stamp, to boot, upon the new president.

Troops of friends gathered around him, Mr. Pardee and Mr. Adamson in the van. No other college has, or ever has had, such a Board of Trustees. Students thronged in. The college developed.

In the first place, the courses of study were multiplied and differentiated.

The old college curriculum was intended for students who were expecting to be ministers, lawyers, or doctors. Work enough for four years before coming of age had been agreed upon by educators as the best preparation for professional study. Some of it is of practical use to professional men. The mathematics are needed by the lawyer to sum up his bills of costs, and by the preacher to see how he can make his salary go round, after he has paid his life insurance, and his interest at the bank, and his share of the million of dollars endowment of his church. The languages are necessary tools in original research. Doctors use the natural

"The Growth of Lafayette: A Post-Prandial Address." Philadelphia: Philadelphia Alumni Association of Lafayette College, 1888.

sciences. Others of the studies are good for mental discipline. All had come to be conventional accomplishments without which no one could pass current among scholars.

Lafayette was strongest in the studies for ministers. It had been established for pious students who could not encounter the costs and the temptations of the great cities and colleges. The first president, Dr. George Junkin, was a great man, a man of genius. He attracted other men of genius. Has any other college without endowment ever had among the professors associated with its first president such a roll of eminences as Samuel D. Gross, James M. Porter, Traill Green, Charles F. McCay, Washington McCartney, James C. Moffatt, William Henry Green, James H. Coffin, Isidor Loewenthal?

This type of teacher had been propagated. The college never had been common place. But in the period preceding 1863 half of the graduates studied for the ministry.

A new class of students now presented themselves, students intending to be miners, civil engineers, mechanics, chemists. Here are new learned professions. They grow rapidly in importance and dignity, and their most eminent members are more and more earnestly advising aspiring young men to take a course of liberal learning in addition to the courses of a professional school. New courses have been arranged at Lafayette to meet the wants of these new professions. They contain modern languages, especially English, natural sciences, technical studies, political economy, and history,—the keys and tools of modern man. This is our development by multiplication. It gives rise to a four-fold multiplication of courses to meet the demands of four kinds of learned professions.

A later duplication of this kind is just now demanded, mainly by teachers and scientists who have already graduated, but who seek for eminent positions, professorships in colleges or the like, and find it of use to take post-graduate courses for the degree of Doctor of Philosophy. These students now number nearly as many as our senior undergraduates.

Many of our sister colleges have developed courses for women. I do not know that any woman has ever made application for admission to the undergraduate courses of Lafayette. I have often wondered why. We have hosts of bright girls in Easton and thereabouts who carry off the honors in our high schools, and who afterwards combine into Chatauqua circles and literature classes. It may be they are afraid of Dr. Knox, now; but they could not have been afraid of Dr. Cattell.

Differentiation, to use a technicality of the evolutionists, gives rise to elective studies. When there are plenty of professors such studies are natural. There are often several different authors equally suited to the capacity of a class, but one having one kind of interest, another another kind. If there are half a dozen teachers of Greek, it is a pleasant arrangement that each give a course in a different author. Then a student who is thinking of studying law and likes legal oratory, can go into Desmosthenes, a preacher of the same college class into Chrysostom, a doctor into Aristotle, a literary man into Æschylus, if he is for tragedy, or Aristophanes, if for fun; or at certain grades a choice may be given between different kinds of study of similar difficulty, as between organic analysis and analytical geometry, between Blackstone and bridge building, or Hebrew and Homer, or *Beowulf* and Goethe.

In these ways the old Lafayette course of 2070 recitations and lectures has developed into 9263.

The electives at the other old colleges, at Harvard even, are for the most part like those at Lafayette, developments of the old college course. Innocent persons think from the newspaper talk, that they can go to Harvard and do what they please; walk into the laboratories and handle all the gases and blow up the buildings the first day, or into Professor Goodwin's Greek and Professor Child's *Beowulf* at their pleasure. But they would find that in order to take this study they must first have taken that; and before that, the other. There is a progressive system and they must begin at the beginning. It is a development of the old four-years course.

There is, I am told, a development of the old field school in some of our newer American universities. They undertake to get together a body of permanent instructors in every thing, to whom anybody can go, and hear somebody lecture on anything he pleases.

I dare say the friends of Lafayette would not very strenuously object to the establishment of well-endowed professorships there of minute or remote branches of learning, of thorough bass, for example, or Japanese; but a distinction should be made between a college and a university proper. The college work is the education of youth. Provision for professorial assistance to men in the labors of their middle life must be mainly relegated to government universities. A Bureau of references to heads of workshops of the right sort might be better even there than a permanent salaried body of professors in waiting.

The attempt to provide a great number of elective studies for college youth, not as parts of useful courses, but to please the fancy of the idle, or kindle the fires of incipient genius has not been necessary at Lafayette. The great mass of our youth are still pressing on hard to active life. Ninety-nine in the hundred are in haste to begin the work of some profession, and go to college to be fitted for it. This determines what is best for them to study. Our engineers do not gambol about in protoplasm or

Sanskrit. Our chemists do not spend their days and nights in Hebrew or quaternions. Shall our ministers that-are-to-be study Latin and Greek? That is not an open question for them. They must study them. They cannot get a license to preach without them. So must our lawyers study Latin or they cannot gain admittance to the bar.

There are, to be sure, a few persons now in our country who do not intend to practice any profession, or mingle with professional men, who mean to lead a life of luxury and pleasure, who abhor Latin, Greek and mathematics, but who fancy certain semi-intellectual occupations, some descriptive science perhaps, Shakespeare and the musical glasses, or athletics, and so prefer to hang about a college during their minority.

I very seriously recognize that it is most desirable that youth of this class should have the best influences of college life. Perhaps it is desirable that some modification of college rigor should be made for them. But that is rather for a university to make. Their numbers are small. I believe Harvard alone might provide for all this class of matriculates, and that there is no call whatever for the old colleges to attempt this sort of equipment, except the call which fashion makes.

With the development of our courses of study there was a corresponding development of our diploma. The student of law of medicine or theology wants a diploma to secure him his registration which shows that he has studied Latin and Greek. So does the teacher who applies for a class in classics in the High School. The teacher of science, on the other hand, wants a diploma which shows that he has studied the sciences; the engineer one that shows he has studied engineering. Harvard, which boasts its many courses, still gives but a single degree. That seems to be a case of arrested development. The Harvard graduate who wishes to enter as a law student in our courts, or to enter the graduate courses at Lafayette has to bring a set of papers supplementary to his diploma, or try to pass the Lafayette examinations. To be sure, if a graduate is going to do nothing in particular, it may suit him to pose with a degree that declares him to be nothing in particular.

At the same time with this development of the courses of study there has been a development of the methods of teaching. The early college had little apparatus of illustration or manipulation, and its work was mostly a gymnastic of the intellect.

The traditional picture of the student represents him in dressing gown and slippers, recumbent, his book fastened open before him, and needing nothing to help him study but the hydraulic pressure on the brain which he gets from his legs high propt on chair or table, desk or mantel.

But all study now is accompanied by exercises of practice or research. Munificent friends of learning and Lafayette have bestowed their hundreds of thousands of dollars in buildings and equipment for it. Our student of to-day would be best caricatured blowing himself up in the chemical laboratory, or caught in the wheels of machines, or making furtive sketches in the drawing-rooms, or upsetting a theodolite, or lugging armloads of books of reference.

All the best colleges use these methods in the study of the material sciences. A similar principle has been freely used at Lafayette in the linguistic and philosophic and historical studies. In these it has been common in our universities to give up the old text book study for lectures by the home professors. It is thought best to have every morsel of truth lubricated well with professional palaver. At Lafayette study of a good elementary text book has been retained, and inculcated; but it has been accompanied by continual exercises of original research. The students are made to write their own lectures, we say.

Suitable specific topics for research suggested by the text book are given out every week and every student is required to hand in every week a written discourse embodying the results of his research for the week. A number of these papers are read in class and the whole topic is handled in a general discussion.

This is a capital college training of American growth similar in principle to the German *Seminarium* work, which is just now being introduced into our most advanced universities.

In connection with it a handling of our libraries has grown up which is perhaps worth mentioning. The works of general reference, cyclopædias, dictionaries and the like, and also the works of special reference upon each of these topics of research are collected and left in open cases for free use by all the students in the Reading-room, and to be taken out at night by such students as are making researches in them. The actual use of these books is ten times what it would be if each book had to be drawn from the librarians. They are often in conditions to shock our model librarians, volumes out of place, bottom up, battered and all that, and worn out, many of them, every year. But what are books made for, Mr. Librarian? The main reading of the college is of these books, and of the periodical literature which is kept under the same regulations.

Novel reading has not much developed, Scott's novels are read more than all the rest together. And Miss Austen's *Pride and Prejudice* keeps from year to year in front of all books but reference books.

Our athletics must also be counted in our development. A professor of Physical Culture was elected in 1865, one of Dr. Cattell's earliest professors, as the new gymnasium was one of his latest endowments. Regular exercises in class are required of all the students, the same as in literary and scientific studies, and athletics are a most important addition to the old college training.

Whether it is due to the bracing air of Easton, or Presbyterian backbone, our college teams take the lead among those of undergraduate collegians. And we have little of the unfortunate effects most deplored in our largest universities. None of our students give themselves up to athletics; we cannot get our champions to practice enough. Nor do we have professional trainers. Foot ball was rather unsatisfactory two or three years ago. Our big brothers took to disabling the players rather than carrying the ball to the goal, and told us that it was the first principle of foot ball to throw away all thought of being gentlemanlike; and the city mobs began to jeer at games in which bloody noses and cracked crowns were not current. But the new rules with two good referees have changed all that, and we have never had better exhibitions of manly strength, endurance, and skill, and of knightly spirit upon our campus than the last year's games with Haverford, Swarthmore and Lehigh.

With all these added cultures of mind and body there has been a notable mellowing of social habits. There are handsomer rooms, more costly board. The college fraternities have grown in strength, and with their old memories and far-reaching associations are able to develop a more genial manhood.

I am not sure but we make college too good a place. Two persons may pass through the very same series of circumstances, and one find it all happiness and the other all misery. One begins a millionaire and keeps losing and losing till he reaches poverty. The other begins with poverty and works up to his million rejoicing all the way. An early life of hardness, a setting yourself at zero in youth has its advantages. I fear sometimes that our preachers may find their college life with its morning naps for beauty sleep, its studies as they please, its daily use of costly athletic equipments, its baths, its banquets, its music, its friendships, its spacious halls full of light and tempered air, an untimely life as a prelude to a struggle with sin and bad air, poverty, deacons and church choirs.

At Lafayette we are pretty nearly right; we are still for plain living and high thinking. When it comes to students having thousand-dollar rooms, and body servants, and horses, real horses to ride to recitation, and dogs, and canes all round, that is going too far.

An eminent professor of one of our greatest western universities, returning from a visit to a private mansion on the grounds of another university, described it to me as a palace of stone carved in figures and full inside of statuary, paintings, and what not. And he exploded with indignation that such an ideal of private life should be set before the unsophisticated American youth of the university. I was surprised at first by his heat; but I plainly see that the professors' houses at Lafayette are far better suited to their salaries. When we have a professor who is disposed to spend a million in building, and has the million, I most sincerely hope that he will put it in a public building like that of Mr. Pardee. I should be sorry to know that any of our students' room were so splendidly upholstered and garnished, that strangers were taken to them as a more imposing sight than our public buildings. It is very undesirable that the habits of social life at a college should be so expensive that a professor cannot live on his salary. That makes it necessary to seek oftenest for professors, either rich men's sons, or husbands of rich men's daughters, or elderly gentlemen who have accumulated wealth. These are very desirable ornaments of any institution, but better suit, I think, the great American universities than hard working colleges like Lafayette.

We see that all these developments of college studies, college manual training, athletics, social life, are in the direction of freedom, of more powerful personality, a richer individual character, a higher life.

The central source from which these movements flow is religion, more of that divine life which is the life of that vine into whom the true man is grafted. Lafayette was founded in prayer, and has been kept alive in prayer. It always has been a religious college. But there has been of late years an immense increase of religious life. It does not resemble at all the revivals of fifty years ago. It is not a revival of revivals, but a revival of religion. There is little of the old law work. Confession of sin gives place to profession of faith and love. Our youths seem easily to attain a consciousness of the divine life in them, and this not for enjoyment as with the mystics, but for action. They make a business of religion. They organize, equip themselves for service, and go out working in every direction. They are ready to go to the ends of the earth.

These feelings are common to all the old religious colleges, and yet we find a falling off in the number of college prayers, and other religious services of the whole institution.

"Dr. Luther," said his wife, "why is it that we pray less frequently now than we used to under the Pope?"

If I knew Luther's answer, perhaps I could explain the decline in college prayers.

No doubt many of our earnest Sauls, who are to be Pauls, are aware that their own prayers are more eloquent than those of the college authorites. But in some quarters loud objection is made to compulsory religion.

Compulsory attendance on prayers and preaching is a special object of attack. But it is almost a misnomer to call the college discipline compulsion. It is nothing like so strong as the obligations of professional life, or the tyranny of fashion, or social habits, or home influence. A college student is about the freest man there is. The compulsion to prayers, what is it? If a student is absent twenty times without excuse, word is sent to his father. But if he were at home and absent from home prayers his father would know it the first morning. When Adonis visits at the home of Edith, does the sweet compulsion to family prayers make the gracious words of the Bible less dear to him?

Much of the talk against college prayers is a survival from old times when they really had painful accompaniments. We used to get up at Amherst in winter while it was black night, struggle through the snow waist deep sometimes, and hear prayers in a chapel without fire with the thermometer twenty degrees below zero, more or less, and then have a Greek recitation by the light of little oil lamps, before we went to breakfast before sun rise.

At Lafayette it used to be the custom to hold these early prayers without any following recitation, so that the students who had tumbled up and taken prayers, for the most part tumbled into bed again.

But we have changed all that. It is certainly a pleasant sight to see our college now, bathed and breakfasted and ready for recitations, gathering at morning prayers. Our beautiful hill bright in the early sun, the valley lying in rosy mist with the rivers glinting through, the quiet mountains looking up as though they liked the looks, the white smokes curling upward from hearths of homes that may be temples, the spired fingers of the churches pointing heavenward, the college campus with its hundred paths all leading to the college chapel, the hundreds of young men rejoicing in their strength, and rejoicing in the morning and in the nature around them, which is in itself a liberal education, and gathering to offer a morning tribute of thanks and praise to the giver of all good, and ask him for stout hearts and clear heads for the labors of the day, and for the scholar's blessing, the pure heart that shall see God,—is a sight worth seeing. It is impossible to believe that it can be a burden to any.

I have seen many generations of college students grow up and pass through life. I have known hundreds of them well, and I am fully satisfied that the habit of attendance on religious exercises in college has been a most powerful influence for good.

I believe in it still. I trust it still. When I meet a Lafayette man, whether in the pulpit, or at the bar, a doctor, a teacher, a jounalist, an engineer, I hope to find him a leader among men. I hope to find that he wears still some grace won from the humanities, the fair humanities of Greece and Rome and the golden days of Queen Elizabeth. But I expect, I trust, that

I shall find him to be a better man for going regularly to prayers and church.

And that, after all, is the proper work of a college, to make Christian men of sound culture. It is not so much to develop genius; genius in the teens is either omnivorous or stupid, and either way considers professors a bore; nor is it to make incipient professors write up huge note books of statistics and bibliography. It is to prepare our youth to discharge the duties of good citizens in those professions requiring special preparation, to make good preachers, lawyers, doctors, chemists, teachers, journalists, engineers, farmers, merchants, master workmen in every good work, heads of every good organization in Church and State.

In this great career so auspiciously begun by Dr. Junkin and carried forward by Dr. Cattell, all friends of Christian education may rejoice with us that under Dr. Knox, clear sighted, upright and downright, and devout, and true hearted, Lafayette still marches on.

The Study of Anglo-Saxon

It is strange that there should have been no more study of Anglo-Saxon, the mother of our mother tongue. There is talk enough about it. From the way our orators and critics dilate upon the glories of the Anglo-Saxon tongue, and the beauty and power of an Anglo-Saxon style, one would suppose that everybody studies it. But it is only within the last ten years that it has had any place in our common American college course. Latin and Greek were thought to be the proper languages to study, and there was no time found even for English. The course has now been widened, and there are many things to be said in favor of admitting the grand-mother tongue.

THE CHARACTER OF THE LANGUAGE.

Anglo-Saxon is to be classed with inflected languages like Latin and Greek, rather than with analytic languages like French and English. It is, in fact, a sister speech with Latin and Greek, and shares with them the general constitution and family traits of the Parent Speech of the Indo-European languages. The noun has five cases, with four declensions growing out of the different stems; the adjective is declined in three genders and two numbers like the Latin, and also in a definite and an indefinite declension like the German; the personal pronouns have three numbers. The verb has six conjugations. The syntax is that of a highly inflected language. Some verbs govern the accusative case, others the genitive, the dative, the instrumental, or the accusative and dative, or accusative and genitive, or other combination. The uses of the modes and tenses are nicely distinguished; the subjunctive mode has its set of rules rivalling those of the Latin or Greek as apparatus for mental gymnastics. The order of the words is that of a Germanic inflected language, and needs to be changed in English. The rhythm of the poerty is measured by accents and alliteration. The sounds of the letters are carefully represented, and the relation between them and the sounds of analogous words in Latin and Greek and German is subject to definite rules. The Anglo-Saxons had popular poetry before their conversion to Christianity. Every one learned to sing their ballads. The harp passed round at feasts and

Report of the Commissioner of Education. Washington, D.C.: U.S. Bureau of Education, 1876, pp. 475-79.

each sang in turn. Most of what would have been their original literature was lost by coming under ban of the church and the contempt of the Normans; but we still have one heathen poem, *Beowulf*, and a number of Christian poems in the ballad epic style. There is a large body of prose, but most of it is translation or imitation of Latin works, and its interest is therefore mainly philological. There are many charters and other legal documents of much interest.

THE USES OF THIS STUDY.

Languages are studied for discipline, as a key to their books, as tools for further investigation, and as models or other aids in our own talking and writing.

The study of Anglo-Saxon will plainly give the same kind of discipline as that of Latin and Greek, so far as it depends on their being inflected languages, and on their giving an introduction to a new world of thought.

The knowledge of Anglo-Saxon is also valuable in itself; it is a record of mind in which all men have an interest. To special students of English history and of modern civilization it may be of special service in original investigations. In the old charters and records is locked up much valuable material for making out the rise of the English constitution and the growth of English customs, and so the history of the Teutonic races. To original investigators in the science of languages it also offers a most inviting field, and much aid to labor in other fields.

It is mainly, however, in its relation to our modern English that the study of Anglo-Saxon is important. The names of the objects which we speak of most and most warmly, of the actions and thoughts which stir the blood, the words and idioms around which move the dearest associations, and on which the beauty of our poetry and the power of eloquence, wit, and humor depend, are mainly Anglo-Saxon. The power to speak well springs from familiarity with choice idioms and synonymes, and this is to be attained by studying them in connection with the history of their origin and meanings, and by becoming familiar with the writings in which they are used with simplicity.

Almost all our grammatical forms are Anglo-Saxon. The difficulties of our language, whether in spelling, in the irregular formation of modes and tenses, or of plurals or genders, or in the peculiar combinations of syntax, are almost all to be referred to Anglo-Saxon, and most of them are there easily understood; they are now difficult because they are relics of habits and forms which have passed away. *Took* is the past tense of *take, loved of love; took* is a contraction of a reduplicated perfect *ta-tak,* loved of an aorist compounded with *did* (*love-did*). *Sheep, deer, swine,* do not use the plural *s*; that was the regular way with all such neuters in Anglo-Saxon. *Men* is the plural of *man;* the change of *a* to *e* is a matter of euphony produced by a following *i*, which is now lost. *Methinks I see him* seems strange, but in Anglo-Saxon we learn that this *thinks* is a different verb from the common English *think,* and means *seem,* and governs a dative; *methinks* means *it seems to me. Be it so—be* is the old subjunctive used with the force of an imperative as in Latin, and having *it* for its subject. *He went a-hunting—a* is the old preposition *on.*

METHODS OF STUDY.

Languages are studied in many ways. French and German are often studied by repeating phrases, so as to learn to talk. French is often read in free translation, without knowing the modes and tenses or other grammatical forms, skipping the strange words and particles, and guessing at the general meaning of the sentences, very much as many of us read English. Latin and Greek are usually read more carefully. Students are expected to know the meanings of all the words, and observe the modes and tenses, cases, and the like. This is about all that is done in many colleges. But the best teachers attempt more. They try to master the author read. They dwell on the particles which show the connections of thought, the modes and tenses and synonyms, so as fully to get the thought, and they recreate the environment. This is called historical and esthetical study.

Then there is philological study. In a few of the best colleges, Latin and Greek are read with a careful scrutiny of every word in view of the modern science of language. The best students regularly look up the etymology of every word, and prepare for questions on its history and its relations to kindred words in other languages, the phonetic laws which govern the changes of form, the laws of thought which govern the changes of meaning, historical inferences to be drawn from it, and similar matters. They prepare for comparative syntax, to give the forms in other languages of expressing each relation of thought, and their history. This philological study may be turned more toward the past, to Greek and Sanskrit, or more toward the modern languages, to English, French, and German.

Nobody would study Anglo-Saxon to learn to speak it. The-off-hand manner of reading has, however, been much used. President Jefferson thought that the old books were written in a rude form of colloquial English disguised by bad spelling, and that the supposed case endings, and the like, were figments, "aberrations," he says, "into which our great Anglo-Saxon leader, Dr. Hickes, has been seduced by too much regard to the structure of the Greek and Latin languages." He thought that after getting used to the bad spelling we could read Anglo-Saxon as easily as

Burns's poems. He wished to have text books prepared with parallel columns, having the Anglo-Saxon in one and the words respelt into their modern English form in the other, with occasional notes explaining such words as have become wholly obsolete. With such an apparatus he thought a sufficient acquaintance with the language might be very easily and rapidly made. Wherever Anglo-Saxon study consists in putting a gospel in Anglo-Saxon into the hands of beginners, and reading it through in a few lessons, the method must be not unlike Mr. Jefferson's; and it is true that a good deal of very interesting and valuable knowledge of the language may be caught up in that way with little pains. It is, however, plainly desirable, if time can be spared, to use a more accurate and thorough method; and since the value of the study is greatest as the key to English grammar and the coloring for English style, it would seem that here more than with other languages it is desirable to use the philological method, and scrutinize word after word and phrase after phrase with minute attention, so that the relation of each to our modern English may be clearly understood. This thorough philological study also implies, for the full understanding of the Anglo-Saxon itself, a comparison with other languages, with Latin and Greek and Sanskrit, if the students know them, and with German, as its nearest of kin, if without the means of studying Gothic and Icelandic. Parallel paradigms of all these, and other languages, may, in fact, be found in a comparative grammar of the Anglo-Saxon, arranged for easy comparison and for careful examination where the history and meaning of Anglo-Saxon forms are doubtful.

THE TIME FOR THIS STUDY.

The best time to introduce Anglo-Saxon in the common classical course would seem to be after studying German, near the end of the hard work on Latin and Greek. This is, in most colleges, during the Junior year. The students will then be comparative grammarians of more or less skill in Latin and Greek, French and German, and will make rapid progress in Anglo-Saxon. Four recitations a week for a single term will then count as much as a whole Freshman year. It may be well introduced in connection with the study of an English classic, Shakespeare, for example, or Chancer, giving out a lesson in both for the same half day, under the same instructor, and making them mutually aid each other. The great difficulty in the way of valuable study of English is the fatal facility of extemporizing the recitations. The Anglo-Saxon, on the contrary, is hard to prepare, and needs the stimulus of interesting applications. In the earnest struggle for life now going on among the thick coming studies of our old classical courses, Anglo-Saxon can hope for little space.

Where there are scientific courses, so-called, from which Greek, or even Greek and Latin, are dropt to make way for modern languages, it would seem possible to secure time for the scientific study of our own tongue. And then it might be thought best to begin at the beginning, with Anglo-Saxon, and come down in the actual order of historic development, through the various stages of Old English. There would be obvious advantages in this method. There are other reasons for approaching it through the German. The class of students who take our scientific courses do so in large part because they dislike Greek and Latin, and do not see the use of studying them. They are likely to dislike Anglo-Saxon at first for similar reasons. The study is hard for them, and the interest to a great extent archæological. The thought is foreign, the environment strange. German is easier, is modern, has all sorts of uses and attractions. But German well taught is an introduction to Anglo-Saxon. It has retained the old Teutonic forms much better than English. Anglo-Saxon is much easier to a German than an Englishman. To an Englishman who has learned German it is very easy, and the philological study of it, which was so difficult, becomes simple and delightful. It is a truly practical as well as scientific procedure to have Anglo-Saxon taught by a professor of English and German literature, as it is at the Washington University at St. Louis. It is good to have some of it read, if there is plenty of time, in the early part of the course; but the real work should be put off, as in the classical course, till other languages have been studied.

Our universities which have a separate school of English language and literature, or a course of study in them running through three or four years, will naturally aim to give thorough philological training of the same kind and extent as that given in Latin or Greek.

NORMAL SCHOOLS.

No class of persons need to know Anglo-Saxon so much as teachers of English grammar. Teachers in our common schools, and much more in our high schools and academies, might use it with every lesson in grammar or language; and they are always in danger of being asked questions they cannot answer without knowing it. Pupils will ask whether *John's book* is a contraction of John his book; how comes *goose* to have *geese* for its plural, and *gander* for its masculine; how comes *lady* to be the feminine of *lord;* what does the *to* mean when you say *to err is human;* should we say *the sun sets* or *sits;* should we parse *I asked him a question* by supplying *to* before *him;* and so on without end. But such questions cannot be answered without knowing Anglo-Saxon. Ingenious teachers reason about them with infinite subtlety and no end, and demonstrate how they must be,—both ways; when a single look at an Anglo-Saxon sentence settles the matter. No teacher can safely decide such questions without knowing the old forms. No normal school ought to send out graduates from its grammar department wholly ignorant of Anglo-Saxon. A lesson a day during the last school term, skilfully directed to the examples in which this knowledge is oftenest called for, would perhaps answer the most pressing needs of the common school. A really good high school teacher ought to have had much more study.

ANGLO-SAXON IN AMERICA.

The history of this study in America has a little of the centennial interest. There was a revival of etymological study of English about a hundred years ago, when Dr. Johnson published his dictionary. He knew nothing of Anglo-Saxon, and his critics showed up his ignorance very fully. Horne Tooke, among others, was attracted to that field of study, and having original linguistic genius, and plenty of leisure in prison, prepared *The Diversions of Purley,* a book that proved an epoch-making work in this kind of study. He was a fierce opponent of the ministry who were making war in America, and had been imprisoned for saying that Americans were "*murdered*" by the king's troops at Lexington. He was regarded in this country as a martyr in the cause of our liberties, and his book was at once reprinted here, and read everywhere with peculiar interest. It bore fruit a hundredfold in the minds of Noah Webster and Thomas Jefferson. Jefferson sent to Europe for the old folios in which the knowledge of Anglo-Saxon was then buried, and read them, as he had time. He became strongly impressed with the thought that the language ought to be studied in our schools, and when he organized the University of Virginia he made it the duty of the professor of modern languages to given instruction in Anglo-Saxon. It has accordingly been one of the regular studies there since 1825. Prof. George Blattermann, Ph.D., gave the first course of lectures, and continued them till 1840. Prof. Charles Kraitsir, Ph.D., gave them from 1841 to 1844. Prof. M. Schele De Vere, Ph.D., LL.D., has since filled his chair. During the earlier period, the lectures had been given, in pursuance of what was understood to be Mr. Jefferson's plan, merely as a means of imparting a knowledge of English; but Prof. Schele De Vere has given lectures on the science of language and the history of the changes from Anglo-Saxon to English, and has used his "Studies in English" as a text book. Students elect their studies at this university. Four hundred and ninety-eight (498) students have been in the classes since 1845, and the number who have taken Anglo-Saxon from the first is computed to be over 600. Many of these have become teachers, several of them professors in southern colleges and universities, and they have exerted a considerable influence in favor of this study. Among them may be mentioned Prof. J. L. Johnson, who has championed the study with great success in the University of Mississippi. Mr. Jefferson's plans for his university attracted great attention through the whole country, and it was very likely on their suggestion that the founders of Lafayette College, which was chartered in 1826, made the study of Anglo-Saxon and English prominent in their proposed curriculum.

Noah Webster's *Dictionary* was the most notable product of his Anglo-Saxon studies. It is not known that he made any earnest effort to introduce the language into the college at Amherst, which he helped to found, but his influence was felt there through occasional addresses to the students and the teaching of his son-in-law, Professor Fowler (1838–1843), who was preparing books on the history of the English language and lectured on such topics to his classes. The attention of some of those who have been teachers of Anglo-Saxon elsewhere was there first drawn to it.

In 1850, Prof. John S. Hart, LL.D., introduced the study of Anglo-Saxon into the Philadelphia High School. The course run through the second, third, and fourth years of study, with five hours a week in the first two years, and four a week the last year. They read the Gospels and Klipstein's *Analecta*. Professor Hart gave a course of lectures on the history of the English language and English literature. About 250 students were engaged in the study each year. The course was dropped in 1854 "in consequence of the pressure of other studies and the prejudice excited against this."

Not far from the same date (1851), this study was introduced into Harvard College in the University at Cambridge, where it has been continued ever since. It is part of the instruction given by Prof. F. J. Child, Ph.D., whose title is Professor of Rhetoric and Oratory. At first, all the Sophomore class had lessons in the elements of Anglo-Saxon. Now it is elective for students of the three higher classes, and continues for two years. There are two recitations a week the first year and three the second. Sixteen to twenty are a good class for the first year, when they read March's *Reader*. The second year, when the text books are German, Heyne's *Beowulf* and Mätzner's *Altenglische Sprachproben,* five or six would be a good class, and it is apt to fail altogether.

In 1858, a professorship of the English language and comparative philology was created at Lafayette College. This was the formal establishment of a course of study which had been two years carried on in the college, and was supposed to be the first authoritative recognition of the English and Anglo-Saxon as a separate department of philological study coördinate with Greek and Latin, and the central object of comparative study. At Lafayette, four recitations a week in Anglo-Saxon during the two last terms of Junior year are taken by the whole class, and two recitations more a week are optional for one term. It is also used continually in the philological study of the later English authors. Post graduate studies are also carried on as far as students may wish. Text books have been published by which it is thought possible to give a portion of this language as thorough study as our college text books enable us to give the Latin and Greek. Many teachers and several professors of this study have graduated at Lafayette, and its course and text books have attracted attention in Europe. Prof. S. G. Barnes, of Iowa College, and Prof. R. H. Carothers, of Westminster College have aided in the preparation of text books.

In 1868, Prof. H. Corson, LL.D., began this study at St. John's College, where he was professor of rhetoric and English literature, and in 1871 he accepted a chair of Anglo-Saxon and English in Cornell University. The study has been continued at St. John's College with earnestness and efficiency by Prof. J. M. Garnett. Professor Corson soon after published a valuable *Handbook of Anglo-Saxon and Early English*, representing the language and literature from Ælfred to the end of the fourteenth century with glossary, grammar, and other apparatus. Students in the School of Literature at Cornell are required, and others may elect, to devote to the study of Anglo-Saxon and early English four recitations a week during two terms of the Freshman year and three a week during two terms of the Sophomore year. They read a large part of Professor Corson's handbook. The present class (1875) numbers thirty-two (32), of whom three elect the study from other schools, and ten (10) are "lady students." "The lady students," Professor Corson says, "do the best."

Other handbooks for beginners have been published by Professor Shute of Columbia College, and Professor Carpenter of the University of Wisconsin, and the interest in the study has been greatly increased within the last five years.

The answers to a circular of inquiry issued by the Bureau of Education to our principal colleges show that twenty-three of them study Anglo-Saxon, reading more or less of it. The study at Yale is in the Sheffield School and in one of its post graduate courses. Eight more claim to study it incidentally in their course of English literature. Almost all of them, except those before named, have begun it within the last four years; several have offered it this year for the first time. Haverford dates back to 1867. Of those who do not study it, nine couple the statement of that fact with some expression of regret or anticipation. The answer from the University of Michigan is: "Sorry to say that the study is not pursued at all"; so from Dartmouth. From Princeton we learn that it may be introduced hereafter; so from the Central University at Richmond, Kentucky, and Vanderbilt University, which is recently opened. The Chancellor of the University of Georgia says that "the study is more important than that of any modern language." Only sixteen of those returning answers are content with simply stating that they do not study Anglo-Saxon.

A CALL FOR ANGLO-SAXON SCHOLARS.

This is great progress for any linguistic study to make in these times when the natural sciences are crowding everywhere. The time is all full in the old colleges, and the supply of good teachers for the new study is very scant. The professors of rhetoric who are oftenest turned to are not often linguists; it is better to try the Latin or Greek professor, as is done at Haverford. But special attainments are needed. To the coming generation of scholars, Anglo-Saxon has prizes to offer as tempting as any. There are professorships, and then the eminence which waits on successful original work in a prominent field. There is nowhere in the world so much of this study as in America. Professor Child says, in his answer to the circular of the Bureau, that "Anglo-Saxon is *utterly* neglected in England—at present there is but one man in England that is known to know anything of it—and not *extensively* pursued anywhere in America." The Germans, he adds, "cannot do their best for want of properly edited texts. Two or three American scholars, devoted to Anglo-Saxon, would have a great field to distinguish themselves in, undisputed by Englishmen."

The Study of English

No language is so wel worthy of study by English-speaking men as the English language. Every one of them must use it with some intelligence to pass current, to do business, to develop and utter himself.

Erly thought is almost all stimulated, guided and supported by the mother tung, and few persons ever advance beyond the knowledge stored up for them in their nativ speech. The formal study of English begins in the infant scools, the kindergartens. Care should be here taken to teach accurate words for the objects and processes which the children lern. Unnamed objects and processes, however amusing or ingenious, enter litl into thought, educate litl. A leading purpose is, of course, to giv valuabl ideas; but teachers make a great mistake who oppose the study of words to the study of things, and condemn the study of words insted of carefully teaching them. Ideas of right and wrong, the amiabl, the becuming, should be taught. Children should be made familiar with beutiful objects, notice the qualities which giv them beuty, and lern the names of the objects and the qualities. They should be told anecdotes in which beutiful persons do beutiful acts, and the words expressiv of beuty should be spoken with tones and gestures which may giv them lively associations: good and bad qualities should be markt by such tones and manner as wil giv their names correct and powerful associations. Passages of verse or rhythmical prose in which beutiful thoughts ar happily exprest and of which the teacher is fond, should be repeated til they ar caught by the pupils. These may be great passages. They need not be wholly comprehended. They wil be like music, producing by vague intellectual processes, but quickening mightily the emotional side of esthetic culture. Beutiful and nobl words thus lernd by heart wil be molds in which the expanding intellect may flow and form. The means of expressing affection should be carefully taught. Formulas of permanent importance should be committed to memory, to be fully comprehended afterward – such as the multiplication tabl, catechisms of moral and religious truth, and authoritativ statements of civic rights and duties.

Lerning to read should begin erly. The monstrous spelling of English makes it necessary to begin betimes and desirabl to begin with books prepared with fonetic reading. Practice in writing is one of the best aids in

"The Study of English." *Independent* 44 (August 4, 1892): 1-2.

lerning to read and spel. Copying choice extracts is useful, and rewriting them from memory. In some way every one should, if possibl, be traind to read with ease and pleasure, and with speed. Teaching wil do much for this, if it make youth acquainted with books that interest them. Short stories of adventure interest the youngest, fable and parable and facts of natural science; the style must be simpl, the movement rapid. Lyrics and orations, tender or nobl, follow, then epic and romantic narrativ, then minute delineation of character, the drama, the modern novel, and then descriptions and criticism of works of art, scenery, nature. Special cultivation is needed if it is desired to produce a strong liking in yung readers for ornate language, figures of speech, and other arts of style. The teacher may hav select passages red in class, read them or hav them red with care and expression, to bring out their thought and feeling. A pupil who is a good reader wil often stimulate a hole class wonderfully. Comment and criticism should be used mainly for pointing out beuties and exciting admiration; passages may be committed to memory.

In this way fondness for reading and for good books may be induced. This may be stimulated further by having writn accounts handed in of books or parts of books to be red out of scool. This is plezant study of English literature and the English language, and it lays a foundation for further historical, filosofical, filological study. Perhaps no study in our scools has made greater advances in the last ten years than this. A large number of English classics hav been publisht for scool reading, and very many scools use sum of them. The editors of them generally ad notes and apparatus of research of sum kind, sumtimes biografical, or bibliografical, or archeological or esthetic; but sum of them, and a few of the best of them, Hudson, for exampl, protest against all old-fashiond study of grammar, etymology, rhetoric and the like, in connection with the reading. These, he says, divert the attention from the thought. He never requires his classes to even read over the text in advance, and his exercises consist of "nothing more than reading the author under his direction, correction and explanation; a joint communing of teacher and pupils with the author for the time being; just that and nothing more." "It is litl less than downright sacrilege to be using Shakespeare as the raw material of filological exercitations." Abbott's *Shakespearian Grammar* is doutless a monster from which he would warn off susceptibl youth. "The work of education is necessarily secret and unconscious just in proportion as it is deep and generativ." To teach yung minds, in scool and college to analyze and discriminate and name, is a very bad mistake, he thinks. We all know how delightful it is to read Mr. Hudson's lectures and Shakespearian notes. He does not stint his own analysis or discrimination, or spare his commodity of good words, or any filology which he knows or thinks he knows. Perhaps he is too timid about letting college boys analyze and define. It might not hurt them as much as he fears. We must lern to speak and write English; then we must study it in the seats of its power, in the great English authors. Erly rapid reading givs us words without definition. We get the denotations of names of common material objects and acts somewhere near right, but without knowing their meaning, their connotation. Abstract terms and names of complex conceptions and idioms float vaguely thru the mind. There is no more delightful disciplin than that of clearing up these vague notions, defining them and nailing them down with their words, so as to make the scolar confident master of his thought. This is the preparation for all progress in advanced thinking or for original writing. It is because students of Latin and Greek ar more thuroly trained in this disciplin than others that they so often show superior command of thought and style to others.

The thought of the Latin and Greek books which ar red in our scools is not exhilarating or imposing, nor ar their forms of statement good for imitation in English; but translating into English, exact and idiomatic English, trains the translators to clear analysis and exact knowledge of the meaning of English words and their idiomatic sequences; it givs a habit of thinking what one says and saying it wel. In reading English the habit is to take up the words without thought til a sentence is complete, and then make up in thought a general result, neglecting words at plezure, just as girls used to read French. But the masters make the boys render every Greek particl. The same habits may be acquired by study of English words in English literature, just as the Greeks acquired their Greek by the study of Greek. Demosthenes studied Thucydides. Johnson tels the student of English style to spend his days and nights upon Addison. Franklin formd his admirabl style in that way, reading good passages in the *Spectator*, then after a time writing out the thoughts as wel as he coud, and comparing his work with Addison's, word by word, and studying all. John Bright formd his powerful oratory by English studies. Thousands of lesser lights hav trimd their lamps, such as Nature has furnisht them, in the same fashion. No study can create a great style without genius.

On the other hand, no adequate study of English can be carried on, no mastery of it for use in one's own speech, or thuro appreciation of the English classics, without grammatical knowledge. It is a mistake to suppose that if one never herd bad English he would use no bad English. Every one generalizes instinctively in his use of the mother tung. The child makes all his plurals in a says mouses for mice, mans for men; he makes his preterits in d, says buyed for bought, and the like. Every speaker goes on in this way until accurate generalizations, i.e. grammatical knowledge, ar substituted for instinctiv generalization. The subject usually precedes its verb, and so the instinctiv talker uses who for whom before a verb. The object usually follows a verb; instinctiv generalization suggests It is me for It is I. In educated households the yung folks ar continually corrected, til they lern the most common words and frases pretty thuroly; but in the great books, whre abridged constructions, tropical expressions, and relics of obsolescent forms occur continually, no one can move with accuracy without much grammatical study, and traind habits of analysis.

Richard Grant White is familiar to many readers as one who calld English the "grammar'ess tongue." Sum, no dout, yet remember his *Shakespeare Scholar* with its prefatory letter to George William Curtis proclaiming that it is folly to suppose that the writings of Shakespeare "need notes and comments to enabl readers of ordinary intelligence to apprehend their ful meaning," and belaboring the commentators for their stumbling-blocks and foolishness. He was going to point out plain meanings for passages overlaid and obscured by stupid and superfluous opposition. Many persons doutless red all this with plezure. I did for one. I had never lookt at commentators, not having any of their work in my Shakespeare, and never having wanted any. I turnd to read the common sense expositions with great expectations. One of the first is of the passage in *The Tempest*, where Ferdinand, dreaming of Miranda as he carries his logs, says:

> "But these sweet thoughts, doe even refresh my labours,
> Most busie lest, when I doe it."

The common sense reading is announced to be "most busyless"; and of all conjectural emendations "most busiest" is declared to be perhaps the most awkward, "nothing could be more graceless and inappropriate." Now I had always red "most busiest." A mental bouleversement followd. It became plain that ther ought to be higher authority than grammarless commentators.

Mr. Furness in one of his delightful excursions, this time in the preface of *As You Like It*, opens this matter, "Hours there ar," he says, "when we want no voice, charm it never so wisely, to break in upon Shakespeare's own words." "But this idl, receptiv mood does not last forever. The time comes when we would fain catch every ray of light flashing from these immortal plays, and pluck the heart out of every mystery there." Then we welcome every aid which notes can supply, not only those of antiquarian research or archeological knowledge, but those which require only keenness of intellect with clearness of thought and expression. Perhaps no thinker in this field difers from Mr. Furness. We have excellent editions of our English classics prepared for use in scools and colleges, with liberal notes of every useful kind. Those of the Clarendon Press and the American books prepared by Professor Lounsbury, Professor Cook, Professor Schelling and others ar of similar type and equal merit with text-books of the Greek and Latin classics. Our greatest literary works, the "Ballads," "Chaucer" and "Shakespeare," cum to us in such texts.

Difference of opinion as to English studies is concernd mainly with the time of life at which literary study, or grammatical, or filological study, should be taken up, or with the length of time which should be givn to each, or with the kind of persons who shoud take such studies, or the authors and books suited to each kind of study. Shoud filological study, for exampl, be begun in the high scool, or deferd to collegiate or graduate life? Shoud the study of English classics run thru the hole college course, or have only a term or two? Shoud long courses of English literature be taken mainly by editors, authors, and women? Shoud the same method be taken in studying Bacon, Milton, Shakespeare, as in studying Walter Scott, Goldsmith, Thackeray? To the last question answer may be made in the words of Bacon; "Some books are to be tasted, others to be swallowed, and some few to be chewed and digested." Pretty free tasting and swallowing shoud be allowd to youth; but happy ar those who erly find their proper food, and happy the teacher who can introduce them to it, who can carv at that repeat. One lingers long at that tabl, and returns always.

Bacon's essays, for exampl, never ar stale. "After the twentieth perusal." Says Dugald Stewart, "one seldom fails to remark sumthing overlookt before." They last from youth to age. They open out from gems of thought into revealers of character, fruits of Bacon's life, illuminators of the age of Elizabeth and of modern filosofy, masterpieces of style. It is a matter of course, that thuro grammatical and filological study should be givn to such a work if one finds it congenial. "The Scripture cannot be understood theologically," says Melancthon, "unless it be first understood grammatically." Men of one book, men who giv much of their time to chewing and digesting sum favorit volumes, hav always been markt men. Genius broods over. Luther calld Galatians his wife. What apparatus of grammars, dictionaries, concordances, cyclopedias, hav those who luv the Bible made for the study of it, what commentaries of every kind, what long continued studies of supreme passages. What mastery of Bible English is obtained by this study, and what luv of it! And this is a type of the highest kind of filological study. In this way Homer has been made near and dear to thousands, and Socrates, and Dante, and Shakespeare. There must be a great character behind the words of great literature. Then for profound and worthy admiration we must hav profound study long and continued and often repeated. Filological study used as a means of clearing up, enriching and impressing our apprehension of the thought and style makes the student rejoice in them and remember them forever. The English masters ought to be studied in the same way as the great ancients.

English at Lafayette College[1]

It is thought to be somewhat of a specialty in the Lafayette teaching of English, that the professors in all departments take part in it. The theory is that the main cause of mistakes in speaking and writing English is ignorance of the meaning of words. Our grammar is simple, but we catch up our words without thought, and utter them again in the same way. On the athletic field we do not know *walking* from *running,* nor at the banquet *pie* from *pudding.* When we undertake to talk about any scientific subject, the expert detects us instantly; we call whales fishes, mix up *sewage* and *sewerage,* and use *force, energy,* and *power* as if they were all the same.

An earnest attempt is made at Lafayette to train the students in each department to write on subjects connected with it in the words and phrases current among experts. The professors in each department are, of course, authorities. Every student is required to hand in two papers a term; there are three terms in the college year. The professors give out subjects which demand research and description in their own departments, and much time is spent by many of them in inculcating not only clear-cut meaning, but also the etymology of scientific terms. They find the sesquipedalia of the sciences cannot be held in memory with precision unless their elements are distinctly perceived. This leads to some knowledge of scientific philology, and of accurate spelling. The students in the chemical laboratory under Professor Hart, the president of the Chemical Section of the American Association for the Advancement of Science, use the rules of the Association for spelling and pronunciation; they know when to write the termination *–in*, and when *-ine*; they are not

---

"English at Lafayette College." *The Dial* 16 (May 16, 1894): 294-96; rept. as "The Teaching of English: Lafayette College," in *English in American Universities*. Ed. William Morton Payne. Boston: Heath, 1895, pp. 74-82.

[1]This article is the eighth of an extended series on the Teaching of English at American Colleges and Universities, of which the following have already appeared in *The Dial*: English at Yale University, by Professor Albert S. Cook (Feb. 1); English at Columbia College, by Professor Brander Matthews (Feb. 16); English at Harvard University, by Professor Barrett Wendell (March 1); English at Stanford University, by Professor Melville B. Anderson (March 16); English at Cornell University, by Professor Hiram Corson (April 1); English at the University of Virginia, by Professor Charles W. Kent (April 16); and English at the University of Illinois, by Professor D. K. Dodge (May 1).—[Ed. *Dial.*]

to be caught blundering with *chlorin* or *quinin, hydrid* or *oxid*, or *sulfur*. The amended spellings recommended by the joint action of the English and American Philological Societies and given in the *Century Dictionary* are accepted as correct in college papers, as well as the common spellings in *Webster* and *Worcester*.

Over and above all this is the study of English in literature. We find the statement in the histories of Lafayette that the college had "European recognition" for its study of English before the present historical and literary courses were known at other colleges. The Lafayette courses were established with the maxim that "English should be studied like Greek." A special professorship was established coördinate with the Greek and Latin professorships, with the arrangement emphasized that the professor was not to have the rhetoric, and general theme-writing, and other the like duties, but was to handle English classic authors with his classes, study Chaucer, Shakespeare, and Milton, after the same methods as Homer and Demosthenes. This was a pretty precise description fifty years ago. Now there are many ways of studying Greek, and all of them often scamped in our universities. It meant then thorough work. Teachers were fond of repeating after Dr. Arnold of Rugby, "What a treat it would be to teach Shakespeare to a good class of young Greeks in regenerate Athens; to dwell upon him line by line and word by word, and so to get all his pictures and thoughts leisurely into one's mind, till I verily think one would, after a time, almost give out light in the dark, after having been steeped, as it were, in such an atmosphere of brilliance."

The Lafayette courses are still constant to this central idea. They are primarily devoted to the study of language as it is found in masterpieces of literature, the immediate aim being the interpretation of these masterpieces, the rethinking of the thoughts of master minds, and storing the memory with their words. Four hours a week during two terms, Junior year, are spent with a professor in recitations; two additional hours are allotted to the preparation for each recitation. Three of the recitation hours each week are occupied in the Arnold fashion, dwelling line by line and word by word upon worthy passages. In a play of Shakespeare, for example,—and one term is regularly devoted to a play of Shakespeare,—a scene, a short scene, may be given out for a morning's study. A considerable part of it will be read rapidly, or the gist of it given in a few words, and most of the hour will be devoted to a few lines selected as worthy of thorough study. Any obsolete words or phrases, or singular constructions, will be explained; but the secret of Shakespeare's power is not to be found in these. The words which are bearers of special meaning or feeling are usually familiar words. In searching for their power and charm, the student will trace them through all the places where Shakespeare uses them, using the *Concordance* to bring them all together. He will use the *Historical Dictionary* to learn what associations had gathered around them in the earlier ages, beginning sometimes in *Beowulf*, and accumulating as they pass to Alfred, to Chaucer, to Tyndale, to Spenser, and are used by each with some happy turn or in some musical rhythm. He will often find that the peculiar meaning in Shakespeare begins with him, and then it will be pleasant to trace it in later authors, repeated in quotation or allusion until it becomes perhaps the most familiar meaning. All the resources of philology, the comparative study of languages and literatures, rhetoric and oratory, prosody and rhythmic art, psychology, and biography, may be drawn upon, and all available pedagogical arts used to lead the student livelily to rethink the thought and perceive and feel and remember the beauty of the language. In this way students come to rejoice in these noble passages, and remember them forever. They are thus provided with the very words to guide their higher thought, and with forms of graceful speech which prompt them to easy utterances of courtesy and affection and devotion.

Three of the four hours a week with the professor are used in this way; the fourth is given to a kind of symposium or seminar. Some topic of research belonging to the subject is given out for an essay, which all the class are required to hand in. The hour is spent in the reading of essays and criticism of them, and further discussion of the topic carried on by the class under the prompting and guidance of the professor. One such hour may be given to the life and environment of the author; another to the plot of the play, if one of Shakespeare's plays is to be studied; others to critical discussion of particular scenes as wholes and as proper parts of the play; others to notable characters in the play. There may be philological papers on the language of the play and of the poet; papers on the originality of the work, how much of it is Shakespeare; reports of the criticism of particular great critics; outlines of other related works. We used to have lively work of research, frequent peering into all corners of the library, and rejoicing in exploiting fresh mines of fact; but bibliographic indexing is now so copious,—Poole's *Indexes* in the van,—and the librarians are so at the service of everybody, and omniscient, that research begins and ends too often with asking the librarian to hand over everything there is on the topic, and point out the pages. And the essays are apt to show plainly enough that they were written with the books open before the writers, as Shakespeare had North's *Plutarch* when he wrote *Julius Cæsar*. The essays can hardly claim the credit of research, but often have merits which students rank higher than research, and make good material for collisions of memory and wit combats at the symposia.

All this is required work. For Shakespeare there is also a prize examination open to all who have finished the required work. This is general, covering his life, character, all his works, from any points of view which the examiners may choose at the examination. The professor is content with questions which call for direct knowledge of the works and reflection upon them; such as naming plays and asking for a description of them, and asking which is the best and why; when were written and the evidence for the dates; naming persons and asking for their characters and action; giving quotations and asking where they are found, and the like simplicities; but examining committees are apt to confront the student with the profoundest questions in psychology and history which the Germans have evolved. The winning of this prize is esteemed one of the highest college honors.

There are two divisions of the students who do not take courses in Greek and Latin. These take courses of English, German, and French, which are so taught as to supply similar linguistic training to that obtained from the Latin and Greek. They study term by term some English classic just as the others do their Latin classic, giving it four recitation hours a week. Authors commonly selected are Bunyan, Spenser, Chaucer, Bacon. With a general method such as has been spoken of in connection with Shakespeare, philological topics are taken up in progressive order, term after term, such as to prepare these students to unite with students of Latin and Greek in the second term of the Junior year, and go on with the philological study of English. Four lessons a week in Anglo-Saxon for two terms are required of all students except technicals. They are given near the end of the linguistic courses required in college when the students have studied their German, French, Latin, Greek, nearly to their completion. The West Saxon as it appears in the principal literary works is presented as a classical language, and the whole time is devoted to it as to a sister speech of classical Latin. It is studied, we say, like Greek. The class begin to read at once extracts from the Gospels. They also learn the grammar, the rules for pronunciation, and practice reading the text aloud. They learn the paradigms, and rules of syntax, so as to parse rapidly, declining and inflecting freely. They learn the rules of letter change, a selected set of them. They already know from their other language studies Grimm's law and the like. They learn for continual use the paradigms and syntax, and the common phonetic changes within the West Saxon, and from West Saxon to English. The examination at the end of the first term of Anglo-Saxon is almost wholly devoted to these matters, and it is known from the first that they must be learned in order to pass without conditions.

In the second term Anglo-Saxon prosody is added to the grammar work, but the time is given mainly to reading Anglo-Saxon authors as we read modern English authors in this course, and to throwing light upon modern English words and idioms by connecting them with their ancient forms. Besides the class examinations, a prize is offered to those who complete the courses for the best general examination in English before Chaucer; and an additional optional course is given to prepare for examination questions upon the deduction of the Anglo-Saxon forms from originals in the Parent Speech and other comparative grammar, and for additional reading, and literary and biographic and bibliographic study in connection with it.

The chief use of study of English before Chaucer to the American college graduate, the person who used to be known as the gentleman and scholar, is to help him to better understanding and mastery of English in Chaucer, and since Chaucer. The literary charm and power of the works which have survived from the earlier period is slight in comparison with that of the old masters of Greece and Rome, and of the still greater modern authors in our own language and other modern languages, who mold the thoughts of modern men. It would seem best, therefore, to devote that moderate portion of time which ought to be given to this study in college to a few typical specimens of Anglo-Saxon, and to the comparative study of their idioms in relation to modern English, so as to fix in memory illustrative originals to guide and strengthen our speech. No one but an incipient professor of languages can well afford to spend his days and nights for long periods of his crowded college life in studying books of specimens of all the various early dialects of those groping centuries.

This series of required studies for the whole class is continued during the second term of Senior year by two exercises a week, with weekly written papers from each student arranged for the general study of some author, and the writing of an elaborate article, as if for a quarterly review, which must contain a discussion of the language of the author. With the work of this term goes another prize. The best work is done when the author selected is an American. Students find their own life and thought depicted in the American authors. The language is their own. They are specially drawn to them. In the college reading-room the American periodicals are worn to tatters, while the English publications, which were the main reading of students of the last generation, lie in fair covers, looking fresh from the binder. Bryant, Irving, Longfellow, Lowell, Mrs.

Stowe, Whittier, Holmes, have been handled with most hearty and sympathetic admiration and intelligence. One of the traditional high-days of Lafayette is that on which Mr. Bryant made the public presentation of this prize for the best study of his own works to J. W. Bright, of '77, now Professor of English Philology in Johns Hopkins University, his torch still burning as he runs in the front.

During the same term a rapid general survey of English literature is given with a compendium, class discussions, and conversations, two hours a week. And four hours a week of the last term of the Senior year are given to a review and summary of the linguistic side of the college studies in connection with Professor Whitney's *Language and the Study of Language*, a required study.

Lafayette is a college of some three hundred students, and does not advertise University courses. It receives, however, graduate students, and there are always some such pursuing English studies. A few continue them, as major courses, far enough to earn a Ph.D. It might be said, therefore, that we have all the courses in English, the description of which fills so many pages of the great University catalogues. There are two professors: F. A. March, Professor of English and of Comparative Philology; and F. A. March, Jr., Professor of English Literature.

Method of Philological Study of English in Lafayette College, Easton, Penn.

Lafayette College claims to have been the first College in the country to establish a separate professorship for the philological study of English, and to elevate it to its proper rank by associating it with Comparative Philology, and making it the center of the study of languages.

The Lafayette course has an organization of all the languages taught, so that each shall be used as a means of progress in every other; but especially so that each may be made a means of special culture in English. The rendering of Latin into English, for example, is really just as much a study of English as of Latin, and may be made, and is made in this course, emphatically and deliberately so.

Fertile study proceeds by comparison. For the best study of language more than one tongue should be studied. For the best of English, Latin and Anglo-Saxon are needed; but French and German may be used in their places.

In view of these truths it is thought best that after parsing and analysis of English have been thoroughly learned, other languages should be studied up to about the Sophomore year. The following extract from the Catalogue will give a pretty good notion of the methods used when the English classics are taken up:—

> The English Language is studied in the same way as the Latin and the Greek. An English classic, Milton's *Paradise Lost*, for example, is studied just as the most skillful Professors of Greek teach the *Iliad* of Homer. The text is minutely analyzed, the idioms explored, and synonyms weighed; the mythology, biography, history, metaphysics, theology, geography, are all looked up; and whatever else is necessary, that every allusion may be comprehended.
>
> The character of the author, and his life and times are also studied, since these are necessary to a comprehension of his work and his speech; and

---

"Method of Philological Study of English in Lafayette College, Easton, Penn." *American Journal of Education* 16 (1866): 559-61.

comparison is continually made with the language of other great English authors, and of the English Bible; so that the relation of each author to English literature and the English race may be carefully examined.

The rhetorical laws of English Composition, and the principles of Epic and Dramatic art are applied to Milton, Shakspeare, and other English Classics, line by line; and an attempt is made to comprehend the particular beauties and apprehend the general plan of the great representative works of English literature.

The text is also made the foundation of more general study of language; the origin and history of recurring words, the laws by which words grow up from their roots in our language; the laws by which changes from one language to another are governed, are stamped on the mind by continual iteration; and an attempt is made to ground all these facts and laws in laws of mind, and of the organs of speech.

For this best discipline and learning which modern philology enables us to draw from the study of language, no language affords a better field than our own English; and it is believed that the culture in this department will be to a considerable extent a substitute in the Scientific course, for that derived from the study of Greek and Latin, as it is usually pursued in our colleges.

Anglo-Saxon, German, and French, are studied in the same way, and all the languages of the course are systematically compared in the light of modern philology, so as to illustrate each other and language in general.

Possibly a more minute description of the common RECITATION DRILL with beginners may be of some interest.

A grammar lesson is first heard. The other lesson is, say ten lines in Milton. A name is drawn, the student rises, and is told to read. He reads in their natural order those words which belong to the first clause. If there are words understood to complete the syntax, those are read too in their proper places. Then the analysis of the clause is completed more or less minutely, as it is more or less difficult or interesting. The relations of the clauses to each other are asked about. Corresponding forms of syntax in Latin, Greek, and other languages which have been studied, are called for, and more or less attempt made to ground syntactical rules in the laws of thought. If there are proper names, allusions, passages imitated from other authors, peculiar opinions, famous phrases, etc., those are asked about, and explained if information about them is not accessible.

Then we go into the discussion of words and phrases, asking first for the corresponding words and laws of change (Grimm's law and the like) in all the other languages they have studied; the root; radical idea; kindred words; meaning by derivation; original meaning in actual use; changes of meaning and explanation of the connection of thought; every thing in Trench's line,—indications of history, character, moral suggestions, etc., being specially noted; then the precise meanings in present use; synonyms; analysis and history of idioms. The rhetorical figures are also called for. This is the staple of drill. At first we get over only five or six lines a day, as every word is called for; but soon the recurring words become familiar, and the class gets on faster,—thirty, forty, fifty lines a day. The topics embraced in the drill change, of course, as the classes advance. Those who are interested in the matter may find more minute details in *March's Method of Philological Study of the English Language*.

WRITING.—The use of writing can not be overrated as a means of compelling study and reading. Handing in a written analysis makes sure that the student does not extemporize his analysis. Written derivation papers make sure that the words are really looked out in the dictionary. Synonym papers have a similar use. So in respect to reading; to require papers giving the views of certain authors who should be read, compels the reading of them. A paper treating a subject according to an outline of topics given beforehand, will require the investigation of each of the topics indicated. In the Lafayette course daily short papers of analysis, etymology, or translation into a foreign language are required, and weekly essays on given subjects connected with the study of the author. A play of Shakspeare can be handled pretty well in one term with five recitations a week, a class made to study as hard as on Latin or Greek, and read the most famous Shakspearian commentators. The Professor should see to it that they have the books to be read, by actually putting them in their hands. This writing should be distinctly understood to be a simple recording of thought, and not one of the grand rhetorical performances which students must write for great occasions.

CONVERSATION is encouraged at all times when the class is not under drill; but on the essay day it is made a part of the regular business in this way. Those who are to read are drawn one by one, and as soon as each has finished, criticism, remark, discussion, is invited under the direction and aid of the Professor. It is intended that this talking shall make sure that what has been written about is understood. Questions are asked particular persons as to their views of this and that, and their reasons for them when there is backwardness.

LECTURES.—Very little reliance is placed on formal lectures. On most of those topics on which they are usually given, an outline of heads of thought and references to books are given, and students are required to write their own lectures.

DECLAMATION.—Weekly declamations in class are had. The class studying any author in which suitable passages occur, are required to declaim such passages, and their delivery specially criticised as to whether it brings out the precise shades of meaning which have been noticed in the critical study. An important end is to have these passages learned by heart.

HISTORY OF LITERATURE.—The only good way to master a literature is by picking out representative authors of representative eras; then representative works of these authors; and lastly representative passages from the works. The representative passages should be studied with all possible thoroughness, and their representative character grasped; the works also as æsthetic wholes should be carefully handled, and understood in their relations to their author, their age, the whole literature. Such study is kept up through the whole course. A summary of the whole is reserved for the Senior year, when a compendium of English Literature is gone over.

DIFFICULTIES.—To a teacher who can teach any language the only difficulty of importance in teaching English is that of getting the students to work up the lesson beforehand—the fatal facility of extemporizing English. In order to understand, and master, and love an author, we must dwell on him word by word and line by line. The main formal helps to conquer this difficulty are thorough drill in etymology, translating into a foreign tongue, and abundant use of writing; but a thorough conquest must doubtless come from the enthusiasm and vigor of the teacher.

Finally, it is to be noticed that this Lafayette course of philological study is not intended as a substitute for the usual study of rhetoric and oratory, the writing of themes as an art, vocal culture, and the like. All these are also studied at Lafayette as at other colleges. It is to be classed with the study of the Latin and Greek classics. It is also interesting for the classical scholar to notice (we use the language of the inaugural address of that most judicious and learned supporter of this new department, President McPhail) that "such a study of English is also a study of Greek and Latin; a study of exactly that part of them which it is most important for us to know, namely, that which enters into our own language; and a study of them exactly in that way which will make what we learn of them most useful, available, and thoroughly known, namely, in connection with those English words and phrases to which they have given rise."

"We do not then substitute English for Latin and Greek; but rather pursue the mutual and coördinate study of all three for the better understanding and acquisition of the whole. We expect more knowledge of Latin and Greek from our ten terms of ancient languages plus two of English, than from twelve of ancient." . . .

Study of English Classics for Admission to College

The practical purport of this paper may be stated as follows:

1. It is desirable that an examination upon the language of two or three English Classics should be required for admission to college.

2. That these books should be of moderate size, not larger than those prescribed for the examinations in Greek or Latin.

3. That the same books should be adopted by all colleges, and continue permanently, so that, for example, "Two books of *Paradise Lost* and Franklin's *Autobiography*" might be on the same footing in the high schools as "Two books of he *Iliad* and the *Anabasis*."

Resolved: That a committee be appointed by the College Association of the Middle States and Maryland to report two or three English Classics as permanent texts for entrance examinations in the English language.

First Remark. The study of classic authors here aimed at is not all the study of English which should be required in the high school. The mother tongue has very peculiar relations and functions. It is the scholar's true foster mother. There are four principal uses in studying it: 1, to understand what is said in it; 2, to speak it well; 3, to write it well; 4, to master English literature; and there are three remoter ends: 1, scientific mastery of the language; 2, knowledge of language in general; 3, general culture.

The high school teacher should carefully teach good conversational habits, should be a model and censor at once. He should give attention to common errors of speech. Translations from foreign languages are good, recitation by topics is good, so is learning pieces for declamation. There should be much practice in writing, in the kinds of writing students are likely to need—business letters, descriptions of meetings, persons, places, written examinations in school studies, and the like. The study of the masterpieces of literature is more than all this. The language of such masterpieces is not common speech. It is shaped to peculiar forms by men of genius. The main object in the study of it is to rethink the thoughts of those men of genius. This is the richest birthright of a cultivated race. The youth who, if they had no classic speech, could do

---

"Study of English Classics for Admission to College." *Proceedings of the Annual Convention of the College Association of the Middle States and Maryland*, November 1890, pp. 16-18.

nothing better than tend machines, or watch birds and bugs to snare and kill them, can, by means of speech, rise almost in childhood to the highest thoughts of all the ages before them. It is the best birthright of an American to think the thoughts of Washington, Franklin, Webster, Newton, Milton, Shakespeare, Chaucer, and the Bible.

This study, the study of literature, is the study which this paper proposes. And it urges a particular kind of literature.

Second Remark. One way of studying the great masterpieces is by rapid sympathetic reading. A teacher who feels the beauties of a passage will read it with expression, will direct attention to beautiful thoughts, figures and idioms, quote similar passages, perhaps, from other authors, tell anecdotes of admiration, and repeat admiring criticism, have choice passages committed to memory, and repeated with feeling. Such appreciative reading, comment and memorizing may be made a delightful introduction to literature, and to some biographical and bibliographical knowledge of authors and books.

I suppose such is the purpose of those colleges which publish lists of novels, poems, literary essays and the like, changing each year, upon which they require examinations. They mean to promote the reading of good books in the schools above board instead of under the desks, as they used to be read. This is all good. It is certainly good as listening to music is good; it makes me feel good. But it is only preliminary to the thorough study intended in this paper, which is aimed at in the provision, that the books for examination shall be of moderate size and few in number. The purpose is to have the books studied word by word, clause by clause, sentence by sentence, as the Greek and Latin text-books are studied in good schools—each word studied etymologically and in its connection so as to comprehend its meaning, each clause and sentence studied in its connection so as to repeat the train of thought of the author. Knowledge of English consists mainly of knowledge of the precise meaning of words, in distinction from knowledge of grammatical forms. The grammatical forms are few in number and their uses simple. Mistakes in speaking or writing English are usually mistakes in the meaning of words; either in their general meaning or in the denotation, the particular objects to which they may be idiomatically applied.

Few persons except teachers of English in colleges have any adequate notion of the rareness of accurate knowledge of the meaning of English words. I heard for years the same class, college juniors, in the same term, in a play of Shakespeare and a Greek classic, and I found they made more mistakes about the exact meaning in English than in Greek. And, after all, that is what one might expect, because they never had been taught the meaning of the English words. We pick up English from the first. Nobody defines words to us. We gradually get the denotation of names of common material objects and acts somewhere near right, but often we cannot define them. I have seen persons at a Thanksgiving dinner unable to discriminate pie and pudding, and learned persons often criticise athletic contests who do not know the difference between walking and running. Mere abstract terms and names of complex conceptions and idioms float vaguely in most minds, having such notions attached to them as the words with which they are usually connected suggest.

Our habit is to hear and remember the words of a sentence without thought till the sentence is complete, and then perhaps make up in the thought a very general result, which neglects half the words.

There is no more delightful discipline than that of clearing up these vague notions, defining them and nailing them down with their words, so as to make the scholar confident master of his thought. This is the work of a Socrates. It is the preparation for all progress in advanced thinking, or for original writing. There is much talk about reading Latin and Greek as we do English. There ought to be more about learning to read English as we do Greek.

It is sometimes objected to verbal study of classics that it destroys our love of them; and there is teaching to which the objection applies. But it is certain that for profound and worthy love and admiration, minute and profound study, long continued and often repeated, is the great need. Philological study, used as means of clearing up, enriching and impressing the thought and the merits of the style, instead of making students hate the authors studied, makes them rejoice in them and remember them forever. "What a treat it would be to teach Shakespeare to a good class of young Greeks in regenerate Athens," said Dr. Arnold; "to dwell upon him, line by line and word by word; and so to get all his pictures and thoughts leisurely into one's mind, till I verily think one would, after a time, almost give out light in the dark, after having been steeped, as it were, in such an atmosphere of brilliance."

Third Remark. It is suggested that the same books be used year after year. Many bright young teachers object to this. They like a fresh book every year. Perhaps this is a good way to tell which schoolmasters like teaching and which like reading new books. To go over and over the same author is very desirable, if the teacher is a true teacher, loving and studying the mode of imparting, of making scholars think the thoughts of the author. He will accumulate illustrations, see new beauties, see what to emphasize, what difficulties to remove, gain prompt and vivid expression, just as an orator or lecturer does, or a teller of good stories. The teacher has a fresh audience in each new class. Again, if the books are permanent, the best books will be likely to be chosen. Excellent editions will be prepared by eminent teachers, with the best notes and other apparatus. There is said to be dense ignorance of good methods of teaching English. Teachers, like other persons, are imitative. When definite permanent courses are established, great teachers will propagate themselves, and excellent modes of teaching will become traditional in English just as they are in Latin and Greek.

On the Civil War

One of March's most important and intriguing writings is one of the most unfamiliar today since it dealt not with academic or intellectual matters but with the major political cataclysm facing the United States in the mid-nineteenth century: the Civil War.

March's lengthy essay in the January 12, 1861, issue of the *Supplement to the New-York Times* (early predecessor to the newspaper's subsequent *Magazine* and *Book Review* supplements) reflected the sometimes ponderous prose style of the period, but its "pacification" message was clear: a compromise between the interests of the slave-holding South and the federal North was not only possible but necessary and could be best achieved through a proposed amendment to the U.S. Constitution. March addressed his message as a letter to the Hon. Henry J. Raymond (1820-69), American journalist, politician, and (most relevant to the occasion) owner and first editor of the *New York Times*, who had corresponded with William Lowndes Yancey (1814-63), militant Southern politician who for many years had strongly advocated the South's secession from the Union.

March, who sided with the North on the question of whether slaves were "persons," had a broader perspective than many other northerners, for he had roots in both regions: he had lived in Virginia and his wife was from that state, though from an anti-slavery family from the "southern aristocracy." His proposal, which would transfer power from the federal government to the individual states, thus served as an open letter to advocates of both North and South and was received respectfully, despite the tensions of the occasion, by both sides. The Virginia legislature endorsed the proposal, and the distinguished statesman Sen. Charles Sumner (1811-74) took it before the U.S. Congress, where it died without action being taken.

The essay remains an interesting though problematic footnote to the history of the Civil War. One wonders what the history of the country would have been had March's proposal been accepted.

An Appeal for Calmness, Reason and Concession: The Evil and the Remedy.

Suggestions as to the Nature of the Political Crisis, and the Means of Meeting It

Hon. Henry J. Raymond—Dear Sir: Your able letters to Mr. [William Lowndes] Yancey have given me great satisfaction, and the patriotic spirit which is shown in them, encourages me to hope that you may not wholly disagree with a somewhat different train of thought which I wish to present to you, and, with your leave, to the readers of the *New-York Times*.

It is a startling fact to us country folks, that while we are drifting into a civil war, the papers of the great Metropolis devote themselves so exclusively to proving that the South is wholly wrong and that we are wholly right; to stirring the blood and stiffening the back bone of the North, and say so little of measures of peace. I must say, Sir, that we do not need stimulus here just new. This President of ours [Lincoln] is driving us all mad. We are trying to keep cool. We are trying, some of us, to feel as we remember we always used to think that wise men feel,—steady for right, earnest for peace. However absorbing the war spirit may now be, there must come a time when we shall be tired of fighting, and ready to adopt measures of peace. A discussion of the principles on which we can make peace can never be out of season.

I take it for granted that the fifteen Southern States may be considered one nation, armed for resistance to the use of the powers of the Federal Government against domestic Slavery. You have shown that there is ample precedent for such a use of those powers, and you infer that resistance is wrong. But it is no satisfaction to the wise statesman to put a great body of the people ruinously in the wrong; his effort is to keep them right. It is easy to put people in the wrong. We have only to go wrong ourselves against them, and they are sure to spring to the opposite wrong.

"An Appeal for Calmness, Reason and Concession: The Evil and the Remedy. Suggestions as to the Nature of the Political Crisis, and the Means of Meeting It." *Supplement to the New York Times*, January 12, 1861, pp. 1-2.

In such a crisis as this the true question is not what is constitutional or right in the sense of the lawyer or politician—not what is there precedent for; but what are the real dangers of the present; what are the interests and opinions now in conflict; what are the maladies of the body politic; and, then, what guidance in the present circumstances can be drawn from those fundamental principles of our Government which are still unshaken, and have been approved by the hearty assent of the people; what cure is there for our maladies; what would our fathers do in our case.

THE ISSUES OF THE PRESENT.

The main issue has been well brought out in your letters. The South claims that slaves are guaranteed as *property* by the Constitution. The North claims that they are recognized as "*persons,*" and that they are "held in service" only by the local law of the States. The South claims a constitutional right to carry slaves into all the Territories, and have them "protected" by the whole powers of the Government. The North claims that Slavery can be legal nowhere until it is established by local law, and that the Territories are and shall be free. The South claims that the Constitution recognizes Slavery as an institution to be protected and cherished. The North claims that it refuses to recognize chattel Slavery at all, and that the powers of the General Government shall be used against its extension, and to aid in its extinction. As subordinate points may be mentioned the Fugitive Slave law and the Slave-trade. The South also fears the abolition of Slavery in the States by an amendment to the Constitution.

DANGERS.

The first danger, which I shall mention, will sound paradoxical. It is the disposition on both sides to regard the present Constitution as a finality, as covering the whole ground, and as being the very best compromise that can be made. This is a danger, because both North and South insist that their own views are embodied in the present Constitution, that the subject is already disposed of, and that the other party is maintaining unconstitutional and revolutionary views. While such is the belief, there is no hope of measures of peace. Attachment to the old is in ordinary times a sentiment which all influential men among us ought to foster. We need it most, and have it least of any great nation. But when great interests change—their aspect, and the opinions of great geographical divisions of our people change, and diverge so as to form two nations, the attempt of each to construe history and the Constitution, solely to support their own views, leads to many evils—this chief one, that both nations claiming to hold a position already formally decided, will not yield or meet.

It has been often said that no impartial history of England ever has been or could be written by an English statesman, because it is a vital necessity for him to justify the present by representing the past as full of precedents for his own policy. A similar cause produces similar effects here. Permit me to say, Sir, that your statements do not seem to be wholly free from this fault. You truly state that the Fathers who framed the Constitution were harmonious in viewing Slavery as an evil, and that, as members of Congress, after the Constitution was formed, they were agreed to use the powers of the General Government to restrict it and to prepare the way for its extinction; but do you not ignore what is just as plain as fact, that this action, except in relation to the foreign Slave-trade, was not in pursuance of a definite agreement or compromise deliberately discussed and distinctly embodied in the Constitution; but was harmonious action under vague and general powers, if any, and undisputed only because unexamined?

In every system of government or philosophy parts which their framers left undecided and unconsidered gradually rise into new prominence, and become vital points in the system. Such are the relations of domestic Slavery to our Government. There was no fundamental difference of opinion about it when the Constitution was formed. But the pecuniary relations of Slavery in the Southern States changed. Slaves became the most valuable property of the South. The action of the South changed. They supported it at first as a necessity. Then political writers arose who put forward new theories of the State and of social ethics, and believe themselves to have demonstrated that Slavery is a fundamental element of every stable social organization; and now the preachers prove it a Divine institution. Truth is great and will prevail some time in the eternal years of God; but meantime no organized interest, having great pecuniary power, ever was or ever will be without able defenders to show how it is legitimately based in admitted first principles.

The North, on the other hand, has day by day grown more clear in its perception of the social, political, moral and religious evils of Slavery, and more and more determined not to be responsible for its existence, and not to take part in any Government which supports chattel Slavery. It also claims that the early action of Congress is good precedent for restricting it. But it cannot fairly be claimed that precedents on points of this kind stand on the same footing as provisions thoroughly discussed and explicitly adopted. They are indeed precedents in times of peace, but they cannot be expected to bind the consciences or honor of men when conflicting interests of vital importance organize revolution. Whatever may have been the fact when you took up your pen, there can be doubt now that revolution is organized; that the passions of the Southern people are roused; that feeling runs ahead even of the extremest demand for rights, and that the time has come of which Hamilton speaks:

"As to those mortal feuds, which, in certain conjunctures, spread a conflagration through a whole nation, or through a very large portion of it, proceeding either from weighty causes of discontent given by the Government, or from the contagion of some violent popular paroxysm, they do not fall within any ordinary rules of calculation. When they happen, they commonly amount to revolutions and dismemberments of empire. No form of government can always either avoid or control them."—*Federalist,* No. XVI.

COERCION.

I have the more insisted on this difference, as to binding authority, between incidental precedents and deliberately considered and definitely adopted ordinances, because the difference is so vital in regard to the moral right of coercion. It is of no use to deny the fact that secession is a very different thing from nullification. Nullification is an illegal attempt to resist some action of a government to which the resisting party admits that it owes allegiance. Secession is a total casting off of allegiance; is a revolutionary declaration of independence; an attempt forcibly to destroy a government. Our Constitution recognizes no such action, either as one to be done, or to be remedied or punished. It is an act, however, that can be done and as the Constitution prescribes no course of action in such a case, the whole powers of the nation are to be used with large discretion to preserve itself unharmed. What it is right to do in the view of the public law of civilized nations and the bar of conscience must be very different in different cases. If Cuba, just bought for $200,000,000, with the assent of its inhabitants, were to secede to open the Slave-trade, she might justly be considered to have abdicated her right as a coequal State, and to have reverted to the position of a territory to be governed at all hazards. A similar course, though involving war, would be justifiable to retain the mouth of the Mississippi. If New-Jersey were to secede to open free ports, to pilfer the commerce of New-York and Philadelphia, she might justly be blockaded, and hugged fast in the peaceable embrace of the Union till she should cease to struggle. But if a sovereign State, especially if a whole geographical empire, secedes, because by the unanimous voice of its citizens it will not submit to the exercise of certain powers by the General Government, we could not justify ourselves in the eyes of the civilized world enforcing these powers by arms, unless they have been deliberately and explicitly given in the Constitution. The fact that such powers have been exercised before would not justify it. In such a crisis we must adopt new measures of peace, or become two nations; and even it we become two nations, we must still adopt measures of peace—we cannot fight forever. Shall we try to conquer a peace on our own terms?

CONSOLIDATION UNCONSTITUTIONAL.

If there is any radical principle in our institutions, it is that government lives in the assent of the governed. Our Government is a union of the people of separate States, of separate, co-equal States. It would change it into a consolidated despotism to carry into effect a course of measures affecting the domestic policy of a whole geographical section, in opposition to their armed protest. Standing armies, mutual hatred and insecurity, and all the evils of despotism, would be the necessary attendants of such a course; while *revolutionary tribunals must permanently displace in the resisting States, the Republican form of government which the Constitution guarantees to every State in the Union* (Art. 4, Sect. 4). We cannot do this thing. We cannot conquer a peace in the Union. Peace, after such a war, is always a peace between two nations.

MEASURES OF PEACE.

Must we, then, become two nations? In that case the North would give up all power over domestic Slavery. Can we not, as a measure of peace, give up all power over it, without becoming two nations? We may declare it, by an amendment of the Constitution, to be a subject reserved to the States, over which Congress has no power whatever. The Northern States will then be relieved of responsibility for its existence, and the Slaveholding States be let alone. Such an amendment would be exactly in the spirit of the Constitution. Our whole system of government is built upon the thought that different interests of the community may be intrusted to different hands; that communities the most unlike have yet some interests in common; and that, whatever may be the *conflict* as to other interests, they can unite in a Government whose powers are limited to the common interests. There are certain very general interests common to the whole nation. These are intrusted to a General Government of the nation, and those alone are intrusted to it. Other less general interests are intrusted to the Government of the States; less general still to the Government of the county, town, the district; and some rights remain to be enforced by the family and even the individual. The Congress of early times seem to have supposed certain relations of Slavery to be among those general interests upon which the whole were agreed. We now find that it is not so. It has grown to be a subject of uncompromising differences.

In the spirit of our Government it is for us to declare it distinctly to be reserved to the States. We believe such an amendment would be adopted by the requisite number of States. All parties have again and again united in declaring that they meant to banish the question utterly from the Halls of Congress. The people have again and again acquiesced in the most distasteful compromises because they were told that now we should have peace and an end of the Slavery question. A large body of Northern people have no moral convictions on the subject of Slavery. The great body of those who have, would be glad to be relieved of responsibility for it; would be glad if they had no more to do with it than they have with Slavery in Africa. They feel it their duty while they have the power, to exercise it everywhere against Slavery, but they would be very glad if the power had never been bequeathed them. Let me have a vote then on the following AMENDMENT:

Article XIII.—CONGRESS SHALL MAKE NO LAW RESPECTING DOMESTIC SLAVERY.

Let us also banish the fugitive-slave clause from the halls of Congress, and leave it to the Courts and the lawyers.

Article XIV.—Judicial officers of the United States shall have process to carry the last clause of section second, article fourth of the Constitution, (the fugitive-slave clause,) into effect according to the rules of the Supreme Court of the United States. No person resident one year in any State shall be delivered up on such process without trial by jury. In case of failure to deliver up any person taken on such process, and proved to owe service or labor, judgment of compensation in damages shall be entered, which may be paid by the United States, and be recovered against the county in which a rescue may have taken place.

THE TERRITORIES.

A final settlement of the Territorial question is a difficult one, chiefly because of the manifest destiny of our Republic to absorb the Continent. And yet this very sentiment of "manifest destiny" assures us that there is a solution of the question, because it indicates that our people are much more settled on annexation than on any exclusive doctrine of free-soil. If Cuba should throw off the yoke of Spain, and ask to-morrow to be annexed to the United States, it can hardly be doubted that an overwhelming majority of our people, both North and South, would vote for her, not withstanding her Slavery. Can we not agree upon the principle that new Territory shall be divided between the North and South? Can we not regard ourselves as two nations united for the purchase of Territory, which we are to pay for together, and divide between us? Do you say such was not the policy of our fathers, that they devoted all the Territories to freedom? The answer is plain.

The South did not demand her share. It was done by common consent, in execution of the trust of Virginia. That common consent cannot now be obtained. The South demands her share. Do you say Slavery is wrong, and that we cannot compromise with Slave States? That is not the doctrine of the fathers. It is not more certain that they held Slavery to be an evil, than it is that they did *not* hold it to be a sin with which there can be no compromise. Even that "sum of all villainies," the African Slave-trade, was continued and guaranteed by a compromise of the Constitution.

It is worth remembering, also, that while the Union lasts every citizen has access to the whole territory of the Republic; but should we become two nations, the Southern nation would exclude the Northern laborer by stringent prohibitions. Under the Union, Slavery is but a temporary occupation of the soil, just scratching the surface and leaving it almost as good as new for free labor. We are spreading already faster than refinement and religion can keep pace. Many good ends may be achieved by holding territory always ready for the surplus of our population. But if we become two nations, there is little hope that the Mexican territories will ever be opened to free labor without war. A conquering tropical Empire is the dream of the young South, and the philosopher well knows that a proud nation of masters with their slaves, though weak against invasion, is strong for conquest.

Now if the principle of division can be adopted, surely it is possible to agree on some mode of division. A line across the Continent has been suggested,—the Missouri line; but that is exposed to many objections. We have repealed it once, and our people never go backward. There is much land South of it on the Continent, fitted only for free labor, and mineral wealth waiting the brain and hand of the Anglo-Saxon craftsman.

We have tried leaving the division to actual settlers; but they fight for it, and neither the States, nor the Executive of the United States, can keep their hands off—and the North takes the lion's share.

Cannot an amendment pass which shall provide for arbitration out of Congress.

Article XV.—Whenever any treaty shall be made by which Territory shall be acquired by the United States, a copy of the same shall be sent by the President to the Governor of each State, who shall within ____ months thereafter nominate to the President a Commissioner to divide such Territory, the two persons having most nominations shall be commissioned by the President, and shall designate in what portion, if any, of the Territory persons of African descent may be held to involuntary service of labor by the fundamental law of the same; and if they shall be unable to agree, they shall select an umpire whose decision shall be final. And Territories shall be organized by Congress in accordance therewith. Whenever any portion of the Territory of the United States having a sufficient number of inhabitants to entitle them to a Representative in Congress, shall apply for admission into the Union as a State, it shall be admitted by Congress with or without domestic Slavery, as its inhabitants shall have provided in its Constitution.

Article XVI.—No amendment shall be made to the Constitution (except by assent of all the States) which shall abolish or interfere with the institutions of any State by which persons are held to service or labor therein.

These amendments are an attempt at a final adjustment of the relations of Slavery to the General Government. They recognize throughout that slaves are persons, and that Slavery is the creature of local law, and yet they give the South every security she ought to ask. I believe they would be accepted by the South if the North would offer them now. After the South shall have organized in Convention or otherwise, to demand her rights, the *ultimatum* will be different. It is for the dominant party to propose measures of peace. If there is any teaching of history plain, it is that incipient revolution for great interests must be stayed by prompt and cordial concessions, if they can be made without sacrifice of principle. Historians have united to commend Elizabeth of England for her sagacity of concession. It was the source and the security of her greatness. They contrast her course with that of Charles I., who always yielded too late, and of James II., who would not yield at all.

The history of our own Colonies comes nearer home to us. We were driven into revolution and independence by the inexorable stupidity of ministers and a monarch who knew not when to yield. Does any one suppose that Slavery will disappear the sooner if we compel the founding of an independent empire of slaveholding States? The contrary seems certain. The progress of free labor southward is the only hope of freedom. It is now going steadily on. Pennsylvania, every year, flows somewhat further down into Virginia. Free soil is worth more than slave territory. It will continue while the Union continues. It will cease when the Union shall be dissolved. Is it suggested that after slave empire is formed, the slaves will win their own freedom by insurrection, or the masters fall into anarchy? That would be the strongest of reasons for preserving the Union, even against the wishes of the South itself. Can any Christian man bring before his mind the picture of this "insurrection," this "anarchy," and thru coolly upon his heel, or go on rejoicing because "it serves them right?"

THE HEAT OF THE MALADY.

We cannot always tell from the pain where the seat of disease is. A man with a diseased liver may feel a pain in his shoulder. So it is with the body politic. I believe the Presidential patronage is the real seat of our malady. Two armies of the ablest and most corrupt men in the country are in a perpetual struggle for the spoils of office. The whole fortunes and character of numbers of them are staked on the Presidential election. It is these desperate men who are leaders for disunion. It is they who hang around the post-office and the tavern in every village and inflame the minds of the weak and passionate. They cut off all sources of correct information, and transform the honest prejudices of political preference into hate and violence. The President, and not the people, is the fountain of power for these men. They care for the people only as popularity may be a source of personal weight in their party cabals. It is no wonder that a disunion sentiment follows our Presidential elections. Our corruption is a perpetual source of danger and disgrace. *An amendment which should give the election of post-masters to the town in which they serve, and the election of collectors, etc., to the United States District in which they act,* would do more than all other measures to insure our permanent prosperity and peace. The President can insure responsibility and activity in such officers as long as he commissions them, removes them at pleasure, stating his reasons in writing, and fills vacancies.

Other Writings by Francis A. March

Editors' Note: Any listing of Francis A. March's extensive writings must necessarily begin with the anonymous bibliography that appeared in *Addresses Delivered at a Celebration in Honor of Prof. Francis A. March, LL.D., L.H.D.* (Easton: Lafayette Press, 1895), pp. 107-17. Unfortunately, that bibliography, with 195 items, contains so many errors that we did not feel it would be helpful to reproduce it here. Rather, we have used the work of the anonymous bibliographer as a starting point to compile a fresh bibliography, which we have divided into sections roughly corresponding to the contents of this volume. From the 1895 listing, we have included only those items that we could corroborate, either through an examination of the original source (often difficult to obtain) or through an item's inclusion in a reliable secondary source. If we could not determine with certainty that an item was, indeed, written by March and published, we omitted it from our list, with this decision complicated by the fact that most of March's periodical writings, in common with the practice of the time, were published anonymously. In addition, when it was possible, we have updated the earlier bibliography, which covered March's career only through 1895. (Bracketed titles were created for the bibliography.)

ON PHILOLOGY

"Comparative Grammar" (reviews of *Deutsche Grammatik*, by Jacob Grimm; *Grammatik der Romanische Sprachen*, by Frederick Diez; *The English Language, Past and Present*, by Richard Chenevix Trench; and *The English Language in Its Elements and Forms*, by William C. Fowler). *American Theological Review* 4 (July 1862): 414-28.

Method of Philological Study of the English Language. New York: Harper & Brothers, 1865.

A Parser and Analyzer for Beginners, with Diagrams and Suggestive Pictures. New York: Harper & Brothers, 1869, 1873.

A Comparative Grammar of the Anglo-Saxon Language, in Which its Forms Are Illustrated, by those of the Sanskrit, Greek, Latin, Gothic, Old Saxon, Old Friesic, Old Norse, and Old High German. New York: Harper & Brothers, 1870.

Introduction to Anglo-Saxon: An Anglo-Saxon Reader, with Philological Notes, Vocabulary, and A Brief Grammar. New York: Harper & Brothers, 1870.
"Anglo-Saxon Language and Literature." *Johnson's New Universal Cyclopædia.* New York: A. J. Johnson, 1873, pp. 154-59.
Review of *English of the XIVth Century*, by Stephen H. Carpenter. *Nation* 15 (March 20, 1873): 202-03.
"Anglo-Saxon and Early English Pronunciation." *Transactions and Proceedings of the American Philological Association* 2 (1871): 108-13; *Englische Studien* 1 (1877): 312-17.
"The Origin of Language." *Proceedings of the American Philological Association* 2 (1871): 18.
"Some Irregular Verbs in Anglo-Saxon." *Transactions of the American Philological Association* 4 (1872): 110-12.
Review of *English Etymology*, by Hensleigh Wedgwood. *Nation* 15 (August 15, 1872): 108.
Review of *Historical Outlines of English Accidence*, by Richard Morris. *Nation* 15 (September 5, 1872): 154-55.
"A German Critic on American Philologists." *Nation* 15 (September 26, 1872): 204-05.
"Anglo-Saxon and Old English." *Nation* 15 (October 17, 1872): 249-50.
"Some Irregular Verbs in Anglo-Saxon." *Transactions of the American Philological Association* 4 (1872): 110-12.
Review of *Grimm's Law*, by T. L. Douse. *North American Review* 125 (1872): 177-82.
Review of *Oriental and Linguistic Studies*, by William Dwight Whitney. *Nation* 16 (February 6, 1873): 96-97.
"Recent Discussions of Grimm's Law." *Transactions of the American Philological Association* 4 (1873): 80-102.
"The Study of Comparative Grammar in College." *Transactions and Proceedings of the American Philological Association* 4 (1873): 18-19.
Review of *Talk and Travel*, by "Biceps." *Nation* 16 (February 13, 1873): 119.
Review of *An English Grammar and Reading Book*, by O. W. Tancock. *Nation* 16 (March 20, 1873): 203.
Review of *Über das Wesen und die Geschichte der Sprache*, by W. Rösch. *Nation* 17 (October 16, 1873): 262.
Review of *A School Manual of English Etymology*, by Epes Sargent. *Nation* 17 (November 6, 1873): 310.
Review of *Essays, Philological and Critical*, by James Hadley. *Nation* 17 (December 11, 1873): 388.

Address at the Sixth Annual Session of the American Philological Association at Hartford, July 14, 1874 (Hartford: Hawley, Goodrich, 1874); reprinted from the *Hartford Daily Courant*, July 15, 1874.

Review of *Modern English*, by Fitzedward Hall. *Nation* 18 (March 5, 1874): 158-59.

Review of *The Sources of Standard English*, by T. L. Kington Oliphant. *Nation* 18 (April 23, 1874): 269-70.

Review of *The History of the English Language*, by Harry E. Shepherd. *Nation* 19 (December 3, 1874): 366-67.

["The Future of Philology. A President's Address."] *Proceedings of the American Philological Association* 5 (1874); 6-7; *Princeton Review* 3 (1874): 698-714.

Review of *Oriental and Linguistic Studies, second series: American Phonology*, by W. D. Whitney. *Nation* 20 (April 29, 1875): 296-97.

"Dissimilated Gemination." *Proceedings of the American Philological Association* 6 (1875): 21-22.

"Remarks on No. CCCXXVIII of Codex Diplomaticus Anglo-Saxonum." *Proceedings of the American Philological Association* 7 (1876): 42.

"What acts are to be attributed to the Faculty of Speech and how far are they instructive?" *Proceedings of the American Philological Association* 7 (1876): 43-45.

"Anglo Saxon." *Cyclopædia of Education*, ed. Henry Kiddle and Alexander Schem. New York: Steiger 1877, pp. 29-31.

Review of *An Anglo-Saxon Reader*, by Henry Sweet. *Nation* 24 (May 31, 1877): 326.

"On Dissimilated Gemination." *Transactions of the American Philological Association* 8 (1877): 145-62.

"Anglo-Saxon." *Yearbook of Education*, ed. Henry Kiddle and Alexander J. Schem. New York: Steiger, 1878, pp. 2-4.

Review of *Origin, Progress and Destiny of the English Language and Literature*, by John A. Weisse. *Nation* 28 (February 28, 1879): 153-54.

"Recent Philological Works." *North American Review* 132 (1881): 99-106.

Review of *Principles of Comparative Philology*, by A. H. Sayce. *American Church Review* 34 (April 1881): 127-33.

Review of *Anglo-Saxon Metaphor*, by Francis B. Gummer. *Nation* 32 (April 14, 1881): 261.

Review of *Aryo-Semitic Speech*, by J. F. McCurdy. *American Church Review* 39 (July 1882): 289-91.

"The Locutions *two first* and *first two*." *Proceedings of the American Philological Association* 12 (1882): xxx-xxxiii.

"Surds and Sonnants." *Proceedings of the American Philological Association* 12 (1882): 33-34.

Review of *Contested Etymologies in The Dictionary of the Rev. W. W. Skeat*, by HensleighWedgwood. *Nation* 36 (March 29, 1883): 283-84.

Review of *Specimens of Early English: An Anglo-Saxon Primer*, by Richard Morris, and *An Anglo-Saxon Primer*, by Henry Sweet. *Nation* 36 (May 10, 1883): 409-10.

"The Influence of Written English and of the Linguistic Authorities upon Spoken English." *Proceedings of The American Philological Association* 15 (1884): xxv-xxxvi.

Review of *Folk Etymology: A Dictionary of Verbal Corruptions*, by A. Smythe Palmer. *Nation* 40 (January 8, 1885): 39-40.

"The Neogrammarians." *Proceedings of the American Philological Association* 16 (1885): 19-20.

"On Consonant Notation and Vowel Definition." *Proceedings of the American Philological Association* 17 (1886): xxx-xxxi.

["Phonetic Change, the Inviolability of Phonetic Law."] *Proceedings of the American Philological Association* 17 (1886): xxxvi.

Review of *The New English*, by T. L. Kington Oliphant. *Nation* 44 (March 17, 1887): 236-37.

Review of *Elemente der Phonetik und Orthoepie des Deutschen, Englischen und Franzosischen*, by Wilhelm Vietor. *Nation* 44 (March 31, 1887): 274.

"Standard English." *Proceedings of the American Philological Association* 18 (1887): x.

Review of *Life and Letters*, Vol. 1, by George Perkins Marsh. *Nation* 47 (September 13, 1888): 213-14.

"Volapük and the Law of Least Effort." *Transactions of the American Philological Association* 19 (1888): xxxviii.

"Preface," *A Comparative Glossary of the Gothic Language with Especial Reference to English and German*, by G. H. Balg. Mayville, WI: G. H. Balg, 1889, pp. v-viii.

"Some Points in Anglo-Saxon Phonology." *Proceedings of the American Philological Association* 11 (1890): 6.

"Sweet's System of Phonetics." *Sunday School Times* 33.14 (April 4, 1891): 219-20.

Review of *Principles of English Etymology*, by Walter W. Skeat. *Nation* 52 (April 16, 1891): 325-26.

"Laws of Language, with a Word on Verner's Law." *Proceedings of the American Philological Association* 22 (1891): ll.

"The Pronunciation of Scientific Terms in English." *Proceedings of the American Philological Association* 23 (1892), lxi.

"The Influence of the Greeks on the English Language." *Chautauquan* 17 (January 1893): 660-66; 17 (February 1893): 20-23.

"Time and Space in Word Concepts." *Proceedings of the American Philological Association* 25 (1894): liii-liv.

"The Eye and Ear in Learning to Read." *Proceedings of the American Philological Association* 25 (1894): liv.

"Phonetic Spelling: Diagraphs for Elementary Sounds." *Languages* [London] 3.2 (February 15, 1895): 32.

ON LEXICOGRAPHY

Review of *A Dictionary of The Derivations of the English Language*, by G. P. Putnam. *Nation* 16 (June 12, 1873): 405.

Review of *Chambers's Etymological Dictionary of the English Language*, ed. James Donald. *Nation* 24 (March 1, 1877): 137.

"The Historical Dictionary of the English Language of the Philological Society, London." *Nation* 29 (September 4, 1879): 158.

"On The English Dictionary of the Philological Society." *Proceedings of the American Philological Association* 10 (1879): 23-24.

Review of *The New Historical English Dictionary of the Philological Society, London. Proceedings of the American Philological Association* 11 (1880): 26.

Review of *A Dictionary of the English Language*, by Joseph E. Worcester. *The American* 2.28 (April 1881): 26.

Review of *Etymological Dictionary of the English Language*, by W. W. Skeat. *Independent* 35 (July 27, 1882): 11.

Review of *Anglo-Saxon Dictionary*, by Northcote Toller and Joseph Bosworth. *Nation* 36 (April 5, 1883): 305.

Review of *The Imperial Dictionary*, by John Ogilvie. *Independent* 37 (April 17, 1884): 11.

Review of *A Dictionary of the English Language*, by James Stormonth. *American Church Review* 45 (April 1885): 540-48; *Independent* 37 (April 9, 1885): 10.

Review of *A Handy Anglo-Saxon Dictionary*, by James A. Harrison & W. M. Baskerville. *Nation* 41 (December 17, 1885): 515.

Review of *A New English Dictionary on Historical Principles*, Part 3. *Nation* 45 (August 18, 1887): 137-38; 45 (August 25, 1887): 155-56.

Review of *A New English Dictionary on Historical Princples*, Parts 2 & 3. *Independent* 39 (October 13, 1887): 32-33.

Review of *The Century Dictionary*, Vol. 1. Section 5. *Nation* 48 (May 30, 1889): 450-51; *Independent* 41 (August 29, 1889): 17-18.

Review of *A New English Dictionary on Historical Principles*, Part 5. *Presbyterian and Reformed Review* 2 (1891): 171-72; *Nation* 50 (June 5, 1890): 453-54; *Independent* 42 (June 19, 1890): 17.

"Dictionaries, New." *Appletons' Annual Cyclopædia and Register of Important Events of the Year 1891*. New York: Appleton, 1892, pp. 249-51.

Review of *A New English Dictionary on Historical Principles*, Vol. 2, Part 6. *Independent* 44 (April 14, 1892): 20-21; *Presbyterian and Reformed Review* 3 (1892): 788-91.

"Whitney's Influence on the Study of Modern Languages and on Lexicography. An Address at a Memorial Meeting of the Linguistic and Archaeological Societies of America in Honor of William Dwight Whitney," Philadelphia, December 28, 1894 [n.p., n.d.].

A Standard Dictionary, the pronunciation, etc. New York: Funk & Wagnalls Co., 1894.

(with Francis A. March, Jr.). *A Thesaurus Dictionary of the English Language, Designed to Suggest Immediately any Desired Word Needed to Express Exactly a Given Idea: a Dictionary, Synonyms, Antonyms, Idioms, Foreign Phrases, Pronunciations, A Copious Correlation of Words*. Philadelphia: Historical Publishing Co., 1902, 1906, 1925.

ON ORTHOGRAPHY

"Spelling." *Appletons' New American Cyclopædia*. New York: Appleton, 1873.

"Orthography." *Cyclopædia of Education*, ed. Henry Kiddle and Alexander Schem. New York: Steiger, 1877, pp. 672-74.

"Orthography." *The Year-Book of Education*, ed. Henry Kiddle and Alexander Schem. New York: Steiger, 1878, pp. 154-56.

"The Reform of English Spelling." *Buletinz of the Spelling Reform Asoshiashun* 5 (April 1878): 4-13.

"The Present Condition of the Spelling Reform." *Annual Meeting of The American Institute of Instruction: Proceedings, Constitution, List of Active Members, and Addresses*, 1878, 136-61.

"Orthography in High Schools and Colleges" and "The Present State of the Speling Reform in America." *Addresses and Journal of Proceedings of the National Educational Association* 14 (1879): 249-60, 109-11; *Bulletin of the Spelling Reform Association* 14 (1879): 1-21; *Independent* 31 (August 14, 1879): 6-8.

"New Types and the *New York Observer*." *Independent* 31 (October 16, 1879): 1.

An A-B-C Book. Boston: Ginn and Heath, 1880.

"Dhi Speling Reform Accomplisht." *Buletin of dhi Speling Reform Asochieshun* 16 (1880): 1-7.

"Spelling Reform, Etymological and Philological View." *Princeton Review* 56 (January 1880): 125-46.

"Spelling Reform, Progress of." *Addresses and Journal of the Proceedings of The National Educational Association*, 1880, 146-51.

"The Relation of Educators to Spelling Reform." *Addresses and Journal of the Proceedings of the National Educational Association*, 1880, 257-61.

"Report of the American Committee on the Reform of English Spelling." *Transactions of the American Philological Association* 12 (1881): 69-70.

The Spelling Reform, U. S. Bureau of Education. Circular No. 7. Washington: U. S. Government Printing Office, 1881. Rev., and enlarged as Bureau of Education Circular No. 8. Washington: U. S. Government Printing Office, 1893.

"The New Spellings of the Philological Society, London." *Transactions of the American Philological Association* 12 (1881): 52-68; *Proceedings of the American Philological Association* 15 (1884): xli-xlii.

"The Influence of Written English and of the Linguistic Authorities on Spoken English." *Proceedings of the American Philological Association* 15 (1884): xxxvi.

"List of Amended Spellings, Recommended by the Philological Society of London and the American Philological Association." *Transactions of the American Philological Association* 17 (1886): 127-49.

["English's Monstrous Spelling."] *Spelling: A Magazine Devoted to the Simplification of English Orthography* 1.1 (May 1887): 8-9.

"Spelling Reform." *The Chautauquan* 7 (1887): 546-49.

["Amending English Spelling."] *Spelling: A Magazine Devoted to the Simplification of English Orthography* 1.2 (July 1887): 93-95.

["Outline of the Action of the American Philological Association on Spelling Reform."] *Proceedings of the American Philological Association* 24 (1893): xxxv-xxxvi.

"Is Simplified Spelling Feasible as Proposed by the English and American Philological Societies? The Opening Address of a Symposium of the Anthropological Society of Washington, D. C., December 20, 1892." *The American Anthropologist* 6 (April 1893): 137-48; (with Edwin Orlando Valle, Max Müller, William D. Whitney, and others). *Our Accursed Spelling: What to Do with It*. Chicago: E. O. Valle, 1901.

"A Scientific Alphabet for Giving Pronunciation." *Journal of Education* 42.5 (July 25, 1895): 99.

ON LITERATURE

Review of *La Mort d'Arthure*, ed. Thomas Wright. *American Theological Review* 3 (August 1859): 466-82.

Review of *The English of Shakespeare*, by G. L. Craik. *North American Review* 105 (1867): 302-08.

Review of *Specimens of English Literature*, by W. W. Skeat. *Nation* 14 (June 6, 1872): 379.

Review of *Love Is Enough*, by William Morris. *Independent* 26 (January 8, 1874): 9-10.

Latin Hymns, with English Notes. Douglass Series of Christian, Greek, and Latin Classics for Use in Schools and Colleges, Vol. 1. New York: Harper & Brothers, 1874.

Ecclesiastical History of Eusebius. Douglass Series of Christian, Greek, and Latin Classics for Use in Schools and Colleges, Vol. 2. New York: Harper & Brothers, 1874.

Review of *Shakespeare Diversions*, by Francis Jacox. *Nation* 21 (October 7, 1875): 234.

"The Immaturity of Shakespeare as Shown in *Hamlet*." *Proceedings of the American Philological Association* 6 (1875): 28-29; *A New Variorum Edition of Hamlet*, ed. H. H. Furness, Vol. 2. Philadelphia: Lippincott, 1875, pp.185-86.

Select Works of Tertullian. Douglass Series of Christian, Greek, and Latin Classics for Use in Schools and Colleges, Vol. 3. New York: Harper & Brothers, 1876.

Athenagoras. Douglass Series of Christian, Greek, and Latin Classics for Use in Schools and Colleges, Vol. 4. New York: Harper & Brothers, 1876.

"Belles-Lettres." *Cyclopædia of Education*, ed. Henry Kiddle and Alexander J. Schem. New York: Steiger, 1877, pp. 78-80.

"Classics, Christian." *Cyclopædia of Education*, ed. Henry Kiddle and Alexander J. Schem. New York: Steiger, 1877, pp. 142-43.

Review of *Wit, Humor and Shakspeare: Twelve Essays*, by John Weiss. *Nation* 24 (April 12, 1877): 225-26.

"The Point of View in *King Lear*." *Proceedings of the American Philological Association* 11 (1880): 6-8.

Review of *The Englishman and the Scandinavian*, by Frederick Metcalfe. *Nation* 31 (November 4, 1880): 324.

Review of *Chaucer and Dante*, by A. Rambeau. *Nation* 31 (November 4, 1880): 324.

Review of *Ausgewählte Kleinere Dichtungen Chaucers*, by John Koch. *Nation* 31 (November 4, 1880): 324-25.

Review of *Faust, from the German of Chamisso*, by Henry Phillips, Jr. *Nation* 32 (March 10, 1881): 167-68.

Review of *Syllabus of Anglo-Saxon Literature*, by J. M. Hart, adapted from Bernhard Ten Brink. *Independent* 32 (March 17, 1881): 11.

Review of *Altenglische Legenden*, by C. Horstmann. *Nation* 32 (April 7, 1881): 242.

"The Harmonies of Verse." *Proceedings of the American Philological Association* 14 (1883): xi-xii.

"The Personal Element in Dactylic Hexameters." *Proceedings of the American Philological Association* 14 (1883): xxvi-xxix.

"Remarks" on "Hamlet's 'Dram of Eal,'" by C. P. G. Scott. *Proceedings of the American Philological Association* 14 (1883): xxiv.

Review of *Caedmon's Exodus and Daniel*, ed. Theodore W. Hunt. *Presbyterian Review* 5 (1884): 180-81.

Review of *William Tyndale's Five Books of Moses*, ed. J. I. Mombert. *Nation* 40 (April 9, 1885): 306-07.

"Remarks" on "Quantity in English Verse," by Thomas D. Goodell. *Proceedings of the American Philological Association* 16 (1885): viii-ix.

"On Once-used words in Shakespeare." *Proceedings of the American Philological Association* 17 (1886): xxx.

Review of *The Viking Age*, by Paul B. Du Chaillu. *Epoch* 3 (December 1889): 773-74.

"The Meter of Milton's *Paradise Lost*." *Proceedings of the American Philological Association* 20 (1889): xiii-xvii.

"Studies in the Vocabularies of the English Poets." *Proceedings of the American Philological Association* 21 (1890): xxx-xxxi.

Review of *The Ancient Classical Drama,* by Richard C. Moulton. *Independent* 42 (April 10, 1890): 16.

ON EDUCATION AND PHILOSOPHY

"The Relation of the Study of Jurisprudence to the Origin and Progress of the Baconian Philosophy. A Master's Oration at Amherst Commencement, 1848." *New Englander* 6 (1848): 543-48.

"Sir William Hamilton's Theory of Perception." *Princeton Review* 32 (1860): 273-307, and "Sir William Hamilton's Philosophy of the Conditioned." *Princeton Review* 32 (1860): 472-510; *British and Foreign Evangelical Review* 10.35 (January 1861): 1-33.

"Methods of Teaching English in the High School." *Addresses and Journal of Proceedings of the National Educational Association Session of the Year 1872*, 1873, pp. 240-44.

"The Educative Power of Manipulation. An Address before the Worcester Free Institute of Industrial Science at Commencement, July, 1876." Worcester, MA, 1876.

"English, The Study of." *Cyclopædia of Education*, ed. Henry Kiddle and Alexander J. Schem. New York: Steiger 1877, pp. 272-77.

"Lafayette College." *Cyclopædia of Education*, ed. Henry Kiddle and Alexander J. Schem. New York: Steiger, 1877, p. 506.

"Lafayette College." *The College Book*, ed. Charles F. Richardson and Henry A. Clark. Boston: Houghton, Osgood & Co., 1878, pp. 282-300.

"The Teachers of Leicester Academy. An Address at the Centennial Celebration." *The Centenary of Leicester Academy*. Worcester, MA: Hamilton, 1884, pp. 81-82.

"Greek Letters and Letters Literary. At the Semi-Centennial Celebration of Amherst Alpha Delta Phi." *Amherst Alpha Delta Phi 1837-1887, Memorial Volume*. New York: Fleming, Brewster & Alley, 1887, pp. 130-31.

"The Study of English in Preparation for College." *Proceedings of the American Philological Association* 20 (1889): xxxvi.

"The Needs of Lafayette. An Address before the Philadelphia Association of Alumni of Lafayette College, March 5, 1891."

"Recollections of Language Teaching." President's Address, Modern Language Association, December 29, 1892." *PMLA* 8 (1893): xix-xxii; *PMLA* 115 (2000): 1738-41.

"The Enlargement of the English Department." Transactions and Proceedings of the American Philological Association 28 (1897): 88-91.

ON HISTORY

Review of *The Norman Conquest*, by E. A. Freeman. *Independent* 26 (January 15, 1874): 9-10.